THE

POETICAL WORKS

OF

EDWARD YOUNG.

VOLUME II.

BOSTON:
LITTLE, BROWN AND COMPANY.
SHEPARD, CLARK AND BROWN.
M.DCCC.LIX.

CAMBRIDGE:
ALLEN AND FARNHAM, PRINTERS.

CONTENTS.

VOL. II.

THE LAST DAY.

IN THREE BOOKS.

Venit summa dies.—VIRG.

BOOK I.

Ipse pater, media nimborum in nocte, corusca
Fulmina molitur dextra. Quo maxima motu
Terra tremit: fugêre feræ! et mortalia corda
Per gentes humilis stravit pavor. VIRG.

WHILE others sing the fortune of the great;
Empire and arms, and all the pomp of state;
With Britain's hero* set their souls on fire,
And grow immortal as his deeds inspire;
I draw a deeper scene: a scene that yields
A louder trumpet, and more dreadful fields;
The world alarm'd, both earth and heaven o'erthrown,
And gasping nature's last tremendous groan;
Death's ancient sceptre broke, the teeming tomb,
The righteous Judge, and man's eternal doom.
'Twixt joy and pain I view the bold design,

* The Duke of Marlborough.

And ask my anxious heart, if it be mine.
Whatever great or dreadful has been done
Within the sight of conscious stars or sun,
Is far beneath my daring: I look down
On all the splendours of the British crown.
This globe is for my verse a narrow bound ;
Attend me, all the glorious worlds around !
O ! all ye angels, howsoe'er disjoin'd,
Of every various order, place, and kind,
Hear, and assist, a feeble mortal's lays ;
'Tis your Eternal King I strive to praise.
But chiefly thou, great Ruler ! Lord of all !
Before whose throne archangels prostrate fall;
If at thy nod, from discord, and from night,
Sprang beauty, and yon sparkling worlds of light,
Exalt e'en me ; all inward tumults quell ;
The clouds and darkness of my mind dispel;
To my great subject thou my breast inspire,
And raise my lab'ring soul with equal fire.
Man, bear thy brow aloft, view every grace
In God's great offspring, beauteous nature's face :
See spring's gay bloom ; see golden autumn's store;
See how earth smiles, and hear old ocean roar.
Leviathans but heave their cumbrous mail,
It makes a tide, and wind-bound navies sail.
Here, forests rise, the mountains awful pride ;
Here, rivers measure climes, and worlds divide ;
There, valleys fraught with gold's resplendent seeds,
Hold kings, and kingdoms' fortunes, in their beds :
There, to the skies, aspiring hills ascend,

And into distant lands their shades extend.
View cities, armies, fleets; of fleets the pride,
See Europe's law, in Albion's channel ride.
View the whole earth's vast landscape unconfin'd,
Or view in Britain all her glories join'd.
  Then let the firmament thy wonder raise;
'Twill raise thy wonder, but transcend thy praise.
How far from east to west? the lab'ring eye
Can scarce the distant azure bounds descry:
Wide theatre! where tempests play at large,
And God's right hand can all its wrath discharge.
Mark how those radiant lamps inflame the pole,
Call forth the seasons, and the year control:
They shine thro' time, with an unalter'd ray:
See this grand period rise, and that decay:
So vast, this world 's a grain; yet myriads grace,
With golden pomp, the throng'd ethereal space;
So bright, with such a wealth of glory stor'd,
'Twere sin in heathens not to have ador'd.
  How great, how firm, how sacred, all appears!
How worthy an immortal round of years!
Yet all must drop, as autumn's sickliest grain,
And earth and firmament be sought in vain:
The tract forgot where constellations shone,
Or where the Stuarts fill'd an awful throne:
Time shall be slain, all nature be destroy'd,
Nor leave an atom in the mighty void.
  Sooner, or later, in some future date,
(A dreadful secret in the book of fate!)
This hour, for aught all human wisdom knows,

Or when ten thousand harvests more have rose;
When scenes are chang'd on this revolving earth,
Old empires fall, and give new empires birth;
While other Bourbons rule in other lands,
And (if man's sin forbids not) other Annes;
While the still busy world is treading o'er
The paths they trod five thousand years before,
Thoughtless as those who now life's mazes run,
Of earth dissolv'd, or an extinguish'd sun;
(Ye sublunary worlds, awake, awake!
Ye rulers of the nation, hear, and shake!)
Thick clouds of darkness shall arise on day;
In sudden night all earth's dominions lay;
Impetuous winds the scatter'd forests rend;
Eternal mountains, like their cedars, bend:
The valleys yawn, the troubled ocean roar,
And break the bondage of his wonted shore;
A sanguine stain the silver moon o'erspread;
Darkness the circle of the sun invade;
From inmost heaven incessant thunders roll,
And the strong echo bound from pole to pole.

When, lo, a mighty trump, one half conceal'd
In clouds, one half to mortal eye reveal'd,
Shall pour a dreadful note; the piercing call
Shall rattle in the centre of the ball;
Th' extended circuit of creation shake,
The living die with fear, the dead awake.

Oh powerful blast! to which no equal sound
Did e'er the frighted ear of nature wound,
Tho' rival clarions have been strain'd on high,

And kindled wars immortal thro' the sky,
Tho' God's whole enginery discharg'd, and all
The rebel angels bellow'd in their fall.
Have angels sinn'd? and shall not man beware?
How shall a son of earth decline the snare?
Not folded arms, and slackness of the mind,
Can promise for the safety of mankind:
None are supinely good: thro' care and pain
And various arts, the steep ascent we gain.
This is the scene of combat, not of rest,
Man's is laborious happiness at best;
On this side death his dangers never cease,
His joys are joys of conquest, not of peace.
If then, obsequious to the will of fate,
And bending to the terms of human state,
When guilty joys invite us to their arms,
When beauty smiles, or grandeur spreads her charms,
The conscious soul would this great scene display,
Call down th' immortal hosts in dread array,
The trumpet sound, the Christian banner spread,
And raise from silent graves the trembling dead;
Such deep impression would the picture make,
No power on earth her firm resolve could shake;
Engag'd with angels she would greatly stand,
And look regardless down on sea and land;
Not proffer'd worlds her ardour could restrain,
And death might shake his threat'ning lance in vain!
Her certain conquest would endear the sight,
And danger serve but to exalt delight.

Instructed thus to shun the fatal spring,
Whence flow the terrors of that day I sing;
More boldly we our labours may pursue,
And all the dreadful image set to view.
The sparkling eye, the sleek and painted breast,
The burnish'd scale, curl'd train, and rising crest,
All that is lovely in the noxious snake,
Provokes our fear, and bids us flee the brake:
The sting once drawn, his guiltless beauties rise
In pleasing lustre, and detain our eyes;
We view with joy, what once did horror move,
And strong aversion softens into love.
Say then, my muse, whom dismal scenes delight,
Frequent at tombs, and in the realms of night;
Say, melancholy maid, if bold to dare
The last extremes of terror and despair;
Oh say, what change on earth, what heart in man,
This blackest moment since the world began.
Ah mournful turn! the blissful earth, who late
At leisure on her axle roll'd in state;
While thousand golden planets knew no rest,
Still onward in their circling journey prest;
A grateful change of seasons some to bring,
And sweet vicissitude of fall and spring:
Some thro' vast oceans to conduct the keel,
And some those watery worlds to sink, or swell:
Around her some their splendours to display,
And gild her globe with tributary day:
This world so great, of joy the bright abode,
Heaven's darling child, and fav'rite of her God,

Now looks an exile from her father's care,
Deliver'd o'er to darkness and despair.
No sun in radiant glory shines on high;
No light, but from the terrors of the sky:
Fall'n are her mountains, her fam'd rivers lost,
And all into a second chaos tost:
One universal ruin spreads abroad;
Nothing is safe beneath the throne of God.
Such, earth, thy fate: what then canst thou afford
To comfort and support thy guilty lord?
Man, haughty lord of all beneath the moon,
How must he bend his soul's ambition down
Prostrate, the reptile own, and disavow
His boasted stature, and assuming brow?
Claim kindred with the clay, and curse his form,
That speaks distinction from his sister worm?
What dreadful pangs the trembling heart invade?
Lord, why dost thou forsake whom thou hast made?
Who can sustain thy anger? who can stand
Beneath the terrors of thy lifted hand?
It flies the reach of thought; oh, save me, Power
Of powers supreme, in that tremendous hour!
Thou who beneath the frown of fate hast stood,
And in thy dreadful agony sweat blood;
Thou, who for me, thro' every throbbing vein,
Hast felt the keenest edge of mortal pain;
Whom death led captive thro' the realms below,
And taught those horrid mysteries of woe;
Defend me, O my God! Oh, save me, Power
Of powers supreme, in that tremendous hour!

From east to west they fly, from pole to line,
Imploring shelter from the wrath divine;
Beg flames to wrap, or whelming seas to sweep,
Or rocks to yawn, compassionately deep;
Seas cast the monster forth to meet his doom,
And rocks but prison up for wrath to come.
So fares a traitor to an earthly crown;
While death sits threat'ning in his prince's frown
His heart 's dismay'd; and now his fears command,
To change his native for a distant land:
Swift orders fly, the king's severe decree
Stands in the channel, and locks up the sea;
The port he seeks, obedient to her lord,
Hurls back the rebel to his lifted sword.
But why this idle toil to paint that day?
This time elaborately thrown away?
Words all in vain pant after the distress,
The height of eloquence would make it less;
Heavens! how the good man trembles! —
And is there a last day? and must there come
A sure, a fix'd, inexorable doom?
Ambition swell, and, thy proud sails to show,
Take all the winds that vanity can blow;
Wealth on a golden mountain blazing stand,
And reach an India forth in either hand;
Spread all thy purple clusters, tempting vine,
And thou, more dreaded foe, bright beauty, shine;
Shine all; in all your charms together rise;
That all, in all your charms, I may despise;

While I mount upward on a strong desire,
Borne, like Elijah, in a car of fire.
In hopes of glory to be quite involv'd!
To smile at death! to long to be dissolv'd!
From our decays a pleasure to receive!
And kindle into transport at a grave!
What equals this? And shall the victor now
Boast the proud laurels on his loaded brow?
Religion! Oh, thou cherub, heavenly bright!
Oh, joys unmix'd, and fathomless delight!
Thou, thou art all; nor find I in the whole
Creation aught, but God and my own soul.
For ever, then, my soul, thy God adore,
Nor let the brute creation praise him more.
Shall things inanimate my conduct blame,
And flush my conscious cheek with spreading shame?
They all for him pursue, or quit, their end
The mountain flames their burning power suspend;
In solid heaps th' unfrozen billows stand,
To rest and silence aw'd by his command:
Nay, the dire monsters that infest the flood,
By nature dreadful, and athirst for blood,
His will can calm, their savage tempers bind,
And turn to mild protectors of mankind.
Did not the prophet this great truth maintain
In the deep chambers of the gloomy main;
When darkness round him all her horrors spread,
And the loud ocean bellow'd o'er his head?
When now the thunder roars, the lightning flies,

And all the warring winds tumultuous rise;
When now the foaming surges, tost on high,
Disclose the sands beneath, and touch the sky;
When death draws near, the mariners aghast,
Look back with terror on their actions past;
Their courage sickens into deep dismay,
Their hearts, thro' fear and anguish, melt away;
Nor tears, nor prayers, the tempest can appease;
Now they devote their treasure to the seas;
Unload their shatter'd barque, tho' richly fraught,
And think the hopes of life are cheaply bought
With gems and gold; but oh, the storm so high!
Nor gems nor gold the hopes of life can buy.
  The trembling prophet then, themselves to save,
They headlong plunge into the briny wave;
Down he descends, and, booming o'er his head,
The billows close; he 's number'd with the dead.
(Hear, O ye just! attend, ye virtuous few!
And the bright paths of piety pursue)
Lo! the great Ruler of the world, from high,
Looks smiling down with a propitious eye,
Covers his servant with his gracious hand,
And bids tempestuous nature silent stand;
Commands the peaceful waters to give place,
Or kindly fold him in a soft embrace:
He bridles in the monsters of the deep:
The bridled monsters awful distance keep:
Forget their hunger, while they view their prey;
And guiltless gaze, and round the stranger play.
  But still arise new wonders; nature's Lord

Sends forth into the deep his powerful word,
And calls the great leviathan : the great
Leviathan attends in all his state ;
Exults for joy, and, with a mighty bound,
Makes the sea shake, and heaven and earth resound ;
Blackens the waters with the rising sand.
And drives vast billows to the distant land.
As yawns an earthquake, when imprison'd air
Struggles for vent, and lays the centre bare,
The whale expands his jaws' enormous size ;
The prophet views the cavern with surprise ;
Measures his monstrous teeth, afar descried,
And rolls his wond'ring eyes from side to side :
Then takes possession of the spacious seat,
And sails secure within the dark retreat.
Now is he pleas'd the northern blast to hear,
And hangs on liquid mountains, void of fear ;
Or falls immers'd into the depths below,
Where the dead silent waters never flow ;
To the foundation of the hills convey'd,
Dwells in the shelving mountain's dreadful shade :
Where plummet never reach'd, he draws his breath,
And glides serenely thro' the paths of death.
Two wondrous days and nights thro' coral groves,
Thro' labyrinths of rocks and sands, he roves :
When the third morning with its level rays
The mountains gilds, and on the billows plays,

It sees the king of waters rise and pour
His sacred guest uninjur'd on the shore:
A type of that great blessing, which the muse
In her next labour ardently pursues.

BOOK II.

——'Εκ γαίης ἐλπίζομεν ἐς φάος ἐλθεῖν.
Λείψαν ἀποιχομένων· ὀπίσω δὲ Θεοὶ τελέθονται.
PHOCYL.

——We hope that the departed will rise again from the dust: after which, like the gods, they will be immortal.

Now man awakes, and from his silent bed,
Where he has slept for ages, lifts his head;
Shakes off the slumber of ten thousand years,
And on the borders of new worlds appears.
Whate'er the bold, the rash, adventure cost,
In wide eternity I dare be lost.
The muse is wont in narrow bounds to sing,
To teach the swain, or celebrate the king.
I grasp the whole, no more to parts confin'd,
I lift my voice, and sing to humankind:
I sing to men and angels; angels join,
While such the theme, their sacred songs with mine.
Again the trumpet's intermitted sound
Rolls the wide circuit of creation round,
A universal concourse to prepare

Of all that ever breath'd the vital air:
In some wide field, which active whirlwinds sweep,
Drive cities, forests, mountains, to the deep,
To smooth and lengthen out th' unbounded space,
And spread an area for all human race.
  Now monuments prove faithful to their trust,
And render back their long committed dust.
Now charnels rattle; scatter'd limbs, and all
The various bones, obsequious to the call,
Self-mov'd, advance; the neck perhaps to meet
The distant head; the distant legs the feet.
Dreadful to view, see thro' the dusky sky
Fragments of bodies in confusion fly,
To distant regions journeying, there to claim
Deserted members, and complete the frame.
  When the world bow'd to Rome's almighty sword,
Rome bow'd to Pompey, and confess'd her lord.
Yet one day lost, this deity below
Became the scorn and pity of his foe.
His blood a traitor's sacrifice was made,
And smok'd indignant on a ruffian's blade.
No trumpet's sound, no gasping army's yell,
Bid, with due horror, his great soul farewell.
Obscure his fall! all welt'ring in his gore,
His trunk was cast to perish on the shore!
While Julius frown'd the bloody monster dead,
Who brought the world in his great rival's head.
This sever'd head and trunk shall join once more,
Tho' realms now rise between, and oceans roar.
The trumpet's sound each fragrant mote shall hear,

Or fix'd in earth, or if afloat in air,
Obey the signal wafted in the wind,
And not one sleeping atom lag behind.
So swarming bees, that on a summer's day
In airy rings, and wild meanders play,
Charm'd with the brazen sound, their wand'rings end,
And, gently circling, on a bough descend.
The body thus renew'd, the conscious soul,
Which has perhaps been flutt'ring near the pole,
Or midst the burning planets wond'ring stray'd,
Or hover'd o'er where her pale corpse was laid;
Or rather coasted on her final state,
And fear'd or wish'd for her appointed fate:
This soul, returning with a constant flame,
Now weds for ever her immortal frame.
Life, which ran down before, so high is wound,
The springs maintain an everlasting round.
Thus a frail model of the work design'd
First takes a copy of the builder's mind,
Before the structure firm with lasting oak,
And marble bowels of the solid rock,
Turns the strong arch, and bids the columns rise,
And bear the lofty palace to the skies;
The wrongs of time enabled to surpass,
With bars of adamant, and ribs of brass.
That ancient, sacred, and illustrious dome,*
Where soon or late fair Albion's heroes come,

* Westminster Abbey.

From camps, and courts, tho' great, or wise, or just,
To feed the worm, and moulder into dust;
That solemn mansion of the royal dead,
Where passing slaves o'er sleeping monarchs tread,
Now populous o'erflows: a num'rous race
Of rising kings fill all th' extended space:
A life well spent, not the victorious sword,
Awards the crown, and styles the greater lord.
Nor monuments alone, and burial-earth,
Labours with man to this his second birth;
But where gay palaces in pomp arise,
And gilded theatres invade the skies,
Nations shall wake, whose unrespected bones
Support the pride of their luxurious sons.
The most magnificent and costly dome
Is but an upper chamber to the tomb.
No spot on earth but has supplied a grave,
And human skulls the spacious ocean pave.
All 's full of man; and at this dreadful turn,
The swarm shall issue, and the hive shall burn.
Not all at once, nor in like manner, rise:
Some lift with pain their slow, unwilling eyes:
Shrink backward from the terror of the light,
And bless the grave, and call for lasting night.
Others, whose long-attempted virtue stood
Fix'd as a rock, and broke the rushing flood,
Whose firm resolve, nor beauty could melt down,
Nor raging tyrants from their posture frown;

Such, in this day of horrors, shall be seen
To face the thunders with a godlike mien;
The planets drop, their thoughts are fixt above;
The centre shakes, their hearts disdain to move:
An earth dissolving, and a heaven thrown wide,
A yawning gulf, and fiends on every side,
Serene they view, impatient of delay,
And bless the dawn of everlasting day.
Here, greatness prostrate falls; there, strength gives place;
Here, lazars smile; there, beauty hides her face.
Christians, and Jews, and Turks, and Pagans stand,
A blended throng, one undistinguish'd band.
Some who, perhaps, by mutual wounds expir'd,
With zeal for their distinct persuasions fir'd,
In mutual friendship their long slumber break,
And hand in hand their Saviour's love partake.
But none are flush'd with brighter joy, or, warm
With juster confidence, enjoy the storm,
Than those, whose pious bounties, unconfin'd,
Have made them public fathers of mankind.
In that illustrious rank, what shining light
With such distinguish'd glory fills my sight?
Bend down, my grateful muse, that homage show,
Which to such worthies thou art proud to owe.
Wickham! Fox! Chichley! hail, illustrious names,*
Who to far distant times dispense your beams;

* Founders of New College, Corpus Christi, and All Souls, in Oxford; of all which the author was a member.

Beneath your shades, and near your crystal springs,
I first presum'd to touch the trembling strings.
All hail, thrice honour'd! 'Twas your great renown
To bless a people, and oblige a crown.
And now you rise, eternally to shine,
Eternally to drink the rays divine.
  Indulgent God! Oh how shall mortal raise
His soul to due returns of grateful praise,
For bounty so profuse to humankind,
Thy wondrous gift of an eternal mind?
Shall I, who, some few years ago, was less
Than worm, or mite, or shadow can express,
Was nothing; shall I live, when every fire
And every star shall languish and expire?
When earth 's no more, shall I survive above,
And thro' the radiant files of angels move?
Or, as before the throne of God I stand,
See new worlds rolling from his spacious hand,
Where our adventures shall perhaps be taught,
As we now tell how Michael sung or fought?
All that has being in full concert join,
And celebrate the depths of love divine!
  But oh! before this blissful state, before
Th' aspiring soul this wondrous height can soar,
The Judge, descending, thunders from afar,
And all mankind is summon'd to the bar.
  This mighty scene I next presume to draw:
Attend, great Anna, with religious awe.
Expect not here the known successful arts
To win attention, and command our hearts:

Fiction, be far away; let no machine
Descending here, no fabled god, be seen;
Behold the God of gods indeed descend,
And worlds unnumber'd his approach attend!
  Lo! the wide theatre, whose ample space
Must entertain the whole of human race,
At heaven's all-powerful edict is prepar'd,
And fenc'd around with an immortal guard.
Tribes, provinces, dominions, worlds, o'erflow
The mighty plain, and deluge all below:
And every age, and nation, pours along,
Nimrod and Bourbon mingle in the throng:
Adam salutes his youngest son; no sign,
Of all those ages, which their births disjoin.
  How empty learning, and how vain is art,
But as it mends the life, and guides the heart!
What volumes have been swell'd, what time been spent,
To fix a hero's birth-day, or descent!
What joy must it now yield, what rapture raise,
To see the glorious race of ancient days!
To greet those worthies who perhaps have stood
Illustrious on record before the flood!
Alas! a nearer care your soul demands,
Cæsar unnoted in your presence stands.
  How vast the concourse! not in number more
The waves that break on the resounding shore,
The leaves that tremble in the shady grove,
The lamps that gild the spangled vaults above:
Those overwhelming armies, whose command

Said to one empire, fall; another, stand:
Whose rear lay wrapt in night, while breaking dawn
Rous'd the broad front, and call'd the battle on:
Great Xerxes' world in arms, proud Cannæ's field,
Where Carthage taught victorious Rome to yield,
(Another blow had broke the fates' decree,
And earth had wanted her fourth monarchy,)
Immortal Blenheim, fam'd Ramillia's host,
They all are here, and here they all are lost:
Their millions swell to be discern'd in vain,
Lost as a billow in th' unbounded main.
This echoing voice now rends the yielding air,
For judgment, judgment, sons of men, prepare!
Earth shakes anew; I hear her groans profound;
And hell through all her trembling realms resound.
Whoe'er thou art, thou greatest power of earth,
Blest with most equal planets at thy birth;
Whose valour drew the most successful sword,
Most realms united in one common lord;
Who, on the day of triumph, saidst, Be thine
The skies, Jehovah, all this world is mine:
Dare not to lift thine eye — Alas! my muse,
How art thou lost! what numbers canst thou choose?
A sudden blush inflames the waving sky,
And now the crimson curtains open fly;
Lo! far within, and far above all height,

Where heaven's great Sov'reign reigns in worlds of light,
Whence nature he informs, and with one ray
Shot from his eye, does all her works survey,
Creates, supports, confounds! Where time, and place,
Matter, and form, and fortune, life, and grace,
Wait humbly at the footstool of their God,
And move obedient at his awful nod;
Whence he beholds us vagrant emmets crawl
At random on this air-suspended ball
(Speck of creation): if he pour one breath,
The bubble breaks, and 'tis eternal death.
Thence issuing I behold (but mortal sight
Sustains not such a rushing sea of light!)
I see, on an empyreal flying throne
Sublimely rais'd, heaven's everlasting Son;
Crown'd with that majesty which form'd the world,
And the grand rebel flaming downward hurl'd.
Virtue, dominion, praise, omnipotence,
Support the train of their triumphant prince.
A zone, beyond the thought of angels bright,
Around him, like the zodiac, winds its light.
Night shades the solemn arches of his brows,
And in his cheek the purple morning glows.
Where'er serene, he turns propitious eyes,
Or we expect, or find, a paradise:
But if resentment reddens their mild beams,
The Eden kindles, and the world 's in flames.

On one hand, knowledge shines in purest light;
On one, the sword of justice fiercely bright.
Now bend the knee in sport, present the reed;
Now tell the scourg'd impostor he shall bleed!
Thus glorious thro' the courts of heav'n, the source
Of life and death eternal bends his course;
Loud thunders round him roll, and lightnings play;
Th' angelic host is rang'd in bright array:
Some touch the string, some strike the sounding shell,
And mingling voices in rich concert swell;
Voices seraphic; blest with such a strain,
Could Satan hear, he were a god again.
Triumphant King of Glory! Soul of bliss!
What a stupendous turn of fate is this!
O! whither art thou rais'd above the scorn
And indigence of him in Bethlem born;
A needless, helpless, unaccounted guest,
And but a second to the fodder'd beast!
How chang'd from him, who, meekly prostrate laid,
Vouchsaf'd to wash the feet himself had made!
From him who was betray'd, forsook, denied,
Wept, languish'd, pray'd, bled, thirsted, groan'd, and died;
Hung pierc'd and bare, insulted by the foe,
All heaven in tears above, earth unconcern'd below!
And was 't enough to bid the sun retire?
Why did not nature at thy groan expire?

I see, I hear, I feel, the pangs divine;
The world is vanish'd, — I am wholly thine.
  Mistaken Caiaphas! Ah! which blasphem'd;
Thou, or thy pris'ner? which shall be condemn'd?
Well might'st thou rend thy garments, well exclaim;
Deep are the horrors of eternal flame!
But God is good! 'Tis wondrous all! Ev'n he
Thou gav'st to death, shame, torture, died for thee.
  Now the descending triumph stops its flight
From earth full twice a planetary height.
There all the clouds condens'd, two columns raise
Distinct with orient veins, and golden blaze.
One fix'd on earth, and one in sea, and round
Its ample foot the swelling billows sound.
These an immeasurable arch support,
The grand tribunal of this awful court.
Sheets of bright azure, from the purest sky,
Stream from the crystal arch, and round the columns fly.
Death, wrapt in chains, low at the basis lies,
And on the point of his own arrow dies.
  Here high enthron'd th' eternal Judge is plac'd,
With all the grandeur of his godhead grac'd;
Stars on his robes in beauteous order meet,
And the sun burns beneath his awful feet.
  Now an archangel eminently bright,
From off his silver staff of wondrous height,
Unfurls the Christian flag, which waving flies,
And shuts and opens more than half the skies:

The cross so strong a red, it sheds a stain,
Where'er it floats, on earth, and air, and main;
Flushes the hill, and sets on fire the wood,
And turns the deep-dy'd ocean into blood.
Oh formidable glory! dreadful bright!
Refulgent torture to the guilty sight.
Ah turn, unwary muse, nor dare reveal
What horrid thoughts with the polluted dwell.
Say not, (to make the sun shrink in his beam,)
Dare not affirm, they wish it all a dream;
Wish, or their souls may with their limbs decay,
Or God be spoil'd of his eternal sway.
But rather, if thou know'st the means, unfold
How they with transport might the scene behold.
Ah how! but by repentance, by a mind
Quick, and severe its own offence to find?
By tears, and groans, and never-ceasing care,
And all the pious violence of prayer?
Thus then, with fervency till now unknown,
I cast my heart before th' eternal throne,
In this great temple, which the skies surround,
For homage to its lord, a narrow bound.
"O thou! whose balance does the mountains weigh,
Whose will the wild tumultuous seas obey,
Whose breath can turn these watery worlds to flame,
That flame to tempest, and that tempest tame;
Earth's meanest son, all trembling, prostrate falls,
And on the boundless of thy goodness calls.
"Oh! give the winds all past offence to sweep,

To scatter wide, or bury in the deep:
Thy power, my weakness, may I ever see,
And wholly dedicate my soul to thee:
Reign o'er my will; my passions ebb and flow
At thy command, nor human motive know!
If anger boil, let anger be my praise,
And sin the graceful indignation raise.
My love be warm to succour the distress'd,
And lift the burden from the soul oppress'd.
Oh may my understanding ever read
This glorious volume, which thy wisdom made!
Who decks the maiden spring with flow'ry pride?
Who calls forth summer, like a sparkling bride?
Who joys the mother autumn's bed to crown?
And bids old winter lay her honours down?
Not the great Ottoman, or greater Czar,
Not Europe's arbitress of peace and war.
May sea and land, and earth and heaven be join'd
To bring th' eternal author to my mind!
When oceans roar, or awful thunders roll,
May thoughts of thy dread vengeance shake my soul!
When earth 's in bloom, or planets proudly shine,
Adore, my heart, the majesty divine!

" Thro' every scene of life, or peace, or war,
Plenty, or want, thy glory be my care!
Shine we in arms? or sing beneath our vine?
Thine is the vintage, and the conquest thine:
Thy pleasure points the shaft, and bends the bow;
The cluster blasts, or bids it brightly glow:

'Tis thou that lead'st our powerful armies forth,
And giv'st great Anne thy sceptre o'er the north.
" Grant I may ever, at the morning ray,
Open with prayer the consecrated day;
Tune thy great praise, and bid my soul arise,
And with the mounting sun ascend the skies:
As that advances, let my zeal improve,
And glow with ardour of consummate love;
Nor cease at eve, but with the setting sun
My endless worship shall be still begun.
" And, oh! permit the gloom of solemn night
To sacred thought may forcibly invite.
When this world 's shut, and awful planets rise,
Call on our minds, and raise them to the skies;
Compose our souls with a less dazzling sight,
And show all nature in a milder light;
How every boisterous thought in calm subsides!
How the smooth'd spirit into goodness glides!
O how divine! to tread the milky way,
To the bright palace of the lord of day;
His court admire, or for his favour sue,
Or leagues of friendship with his saints renew;
Pleas'd to look down, and see the world asleep,
While I long vigils to its founder keep!
" Canst thou not shake the centre? Oh! control,
Subdue by force, the rebel in my soul:
Thou, who canst still the raging of the flood,
Restrain the various tumults of my blood;
Teach me, with equal firmness, to sustain
Alluring pleasure, and assaulting pain.

O may I pant for thee in each desire!
And with strong faith foment the holy fire!
Stretch out my soul in hope, and grasp the prize,
Which in eternity's deep bosom lies!
At the great day of recompense behold,
Devoid of fear, the fatal book unfold!
Then wafted upward to the blissful seat,
From age to age, my grateful song repeat;
My light, my life, my God, my Saviour see,
And rival angels in the praise of thee."

BOOK III.

> Esse quoque in fatis reminiscitur, affore tempus,
> Quo mare, quo tellus, correptaque regia cæli
> Ardeat; et mundi moles operosa laboret. — Ovid. Met.

The book unfolding; the resplendent seat
Of saints and angels; the tremendous fate
Of guilty souls; the gloomy realms of woe;
And all the horrors of the world below;
I next presume to sing: what yet remains
Demands my last, but most exalted strains.
And let the muse or now affect the sky,
Or in inglorious shades for ever lie.
She kindles, she 's inflam'd so near the goal;
She mounts, she gains upon the starry pole;
The world grows less as she pursues her flight,
And the sun darkens to her distant sight.

Heaven op'ning, all its sacred pomp displays,
And overwhelms her with the rushing blaze!
The triumph rings! archangels shout around!
And echoing nature lengthens out the sound!
Ten thousand trumpets now at once advance;
Now deepest silence lulls the vast expanse:
So deep the silence, and so strong the blast,
As nature died, when she had groan'd her last.
Nor man, nor angel, moves; the Judge on high
Looks round, and with his glory fills the sky:
Then on the fatal book his hand he lays,
Which high to view supporting seraphs raise;
In solemn form the rituals are prepar'd,
The seal is broken, and a groan is heard.
And thou, my soul, (oh fall to sudden pray'r,
And let the thought sink deep!) shalt thou be there?
See on the left (for by the great command
The throng divided falls on either hand);
How weak, how pale, how haggard, how obscene,
What more than death in ev'ry face and mien!
With what distress, and glarings of affright.
They shock the heart, and turn away the sight!
In gloomy orbs their trembling eye-balls roll,
And tell the horrid secrets of the soul.
Each gesture mourns, each look is black with care,
And ev'ry groan is loaden with despair.
Reader, if guilty, spare the muse, and find
A truer image pictur'd in thy mind.
Shouldst thou behold thy brother, father, wife,
And all the soft companions of thy life,

Whose blended int'rests levell'd at one aim,
Whose mix'd desires sent up one common flame,
Divided far; thy wretched self alone
Cast on the left, of all whom thou hast known;
How would it wound! what millions wouldst thou give
For one more trial, one more day to live!
Flung back in time an hour, a moment's space,
To grasp with eagerness the means of grace;
Contend for mercy with a pious rage,
And in that moment to redeem an age?
Drive back the tide, suspend a storm in air,
Arrest the sun! — but still of this despair.
Mark, on the right, how amiable a grace!
Their Maker's image fresh in ev'ry face!
What purple bloom my ravish'd soul admires!
And their eyes sparkling with immortal fires!
Triumphant beauty! charms that rise above
This world, and in blest angels kindle love!
To the great Judge with holy pride they turn,
And dare behold th' Almighty's anger burn;
Its flash sustain, against its terror rise,
And on the dread tribunal fix their eyes.
Are these the forms that moulder'd in the dust?
Oh the transcendent glory of the just!
Yet still some thin remains of fear and doubt,
Th' infected brightness of their joy pollute.
Thus the chaste bridegroom, when the priest draws nigh,
Beholds his blessing with a trembling eye,

Feels doubtful passions throb in every vein,
And in his cheeks are mingled joy and pain,
Lest still some intervening chance should rise,
Leap forth at once, and snatch the golden prize;
Inflame his woe, by bringing it so late,
And stab him in the crisis of his fate.
Since Adam's family, from first to last,
Now into one distinct survey is cast;
Look round, vainglorious muse, and you whoe'er
Devote yourselves to fame, and think her fair;
Look round, and seek the lights of human race,
Whose shining acts time's brightest annals grace;
Who founded sects; crowns conquer'd, or resign'd;
Gave names to nations: or fam'd empires join'd;
Who raised the vale, and laid the mountain low;
And taught obedient rivers where to flow;
Who with vast fleets, as with a mighty chain,
Could bind the madness of the roaring main:
All lost? all undistinguish'd? nowhere found?
How will this truth in Bourbon's palace sound?
That hour, on which the Almighty King on high
From all eternity has fix'd his eye,
Whether his right hand favour'd, or annoy'd,
Continu'd, alter'd, threaten'd, or destroy'd;
Southern or eastern sceptre downward hurl'd,
Gave north or west dominion o'er the world;
The point of time, for which the world was built,
For which the blood of God himself was spilt,
That dreadful moment is arriv'd.
Aloft, the seats of bliss their pomp display

Brighter than brightness, this distinguish'd day;
Less glorious, when of old th' eternal Son
From realms of night return'd with trophies won:
Thro' heaven's high gates, when he triumphant rode,
And shouting angels hail'd the victor God.
Horrors, beneath, darkness in darkness, hell
Of hell, where torments behind torments dwell;
A furnace formidable, deep, and wide,
O'erboiling with a mad sulphureous tide,
Expands its jaws, most dreadful to survey,
And roars outrageous for the destin'd prey.
The sons of light scarce unappall'd look down,
And nearer press heaven's everlasting throne.
Such is the scene; and one short moment's space
Concludes the hopes and fears of human race.
Proceed who dares! — I tremble as I write,
The whole creation swims before my sight:
I see, I see, the Judge's frowning brow;
Say not, 'tis distant; I behold it now;
I faint, my tardy blood forgets to flow,
My soul recoils at the stupendous woe;
That woe, those pangs, which from the guilty breast,
In these, or words like these, shall be exprest.
"Who burst the barriers of my peaceful grave?
Ah! cruel death, that would no longer save,
But grudg'd me e'en that narrow dark abode,
And cast me out into the wrath of God;
Where shrieks, the roaring flame, the rattling chain,

And all the dreadful eloquence of pain,
Our only song; black fire's malignant light,
The sole refreshment of the blasted sight.
Must all those pow'rs, heaven gave me to supply
My soul with pleasure, and bring in my joy,
Rise up in arms against me, join the foe,
Sense, reason, memory, increase my woe?
And shall my voice, ordain'd on hymns to dwell,
Corrupt to groans, and blow the fires of hell?
Oh! must I look with terror on my gain,
And with existence only measure pain?
What! no reprieve, no least indulgence given,
No beam of hope, from any point of heaven!
Ah mercy! mercy! art thou dead above?
Is love extinguish'd in the source of love?
"Bold that I am, did heaven stoop down to hell?
Th' expiring Lord of life my ransom seal?
Have I not been industrious to provoke?
From his embraces obstinately broke?
Pursu'd and panted for his mortal hate,
Earn'd my destruction, labour'd out my fate?
And dare I on extinguish'd love exclaim?
Take, take full vengeance, rouse the slack'ning flame;
Just is my lot — but oh! must it transcend
The reach of time, despair a distant end?
With dreadful growth shoot forward, and arise,
Where thought can't follow, and bold fancy dies?
"Never! where falls the soul at that dread sound?

Down an abyss how dark, and how profound?
Down, down, (I still am falling, horrid pain!)
Ten thousand thousand fathoms still remain;
My plunge but still begun — And this for sin?
Could I offend, if I had never been,
But still increas'd the senseless happy mass,
Flow'd in the stream, or shiver'd in the grass?
"Father of mercies! why from silent earth
Didst thou awake, and curse me into birth?
Tear me from quiet, ravish me from night,
And make a thankless present of thy light?
Push into being a reverse of thee,
And animate a clod with misery?
"The beasts are happy; they come forth, and keep
Short watch on earth, and then lie down to sleep.
Pain is for man; and oh! how vast a pain
For crimes, which made the Godhead bleed in vain!
Annull'd his groans, as far as in them lay,
And flung his agonies, and death, away!
As our dire punishment for ever strong,
Our constitution too for ever young,
Curs'd with returns of vigour, still the same,
Powerful to bear, and satisfy the flame:
Still to be caught, and still to be pursu'd!
To perish still, and still to be renew'd!
"And this, my help! my God! at thy decree?
Nature is chang'd, and hell should succour me.
And canst thou then look down from perfect bliss,
And see me plunging in the dark abyss?

Calling thee Father, in a sea of fire?
Or pouring blasphemies at thy desire?
With mortals' anguish wilt thou raise thy name,
And by my pangs omnipotence proclaim?
"Thou, who canst toss the planets to and fro,
Contract not thy great vengeance to my woe;
Crush worlds; in hotter flames fall'n angels lay;
On me Almighty wrath is cast away.
Call back thy thunders, Lord, hold in thy rage,
Nor with a speck of wretchedness engage:
Forget me quite, nor stoop a worm to blame;
But lose me in the greatness of thy name.
Thou art all love, all mercy, all divine,
And shall I make these glories cease to shine?
Shall sinful man grow great by his offence,
And from its course turn back Omnipotence?
"Forbid it! and oh! grant, great God, at least
This one, this slender, almost no request;
When I have wept a thousand lives away,
When torment is grown weary of its prey,
When I have rav'd ten thousand years in fire,
Ten thousand thousand, let me then expire."
Deep anguish! but too late; the hopeless soul,
Bound to the bottom of the burning pool,
Though loth, and ever loud blaspheming, owns
He's justly doom'd to pour eternal groans;
Enclos'd with horrors, and transfix'd with pain,
Rolling in vengeance, struggling with his chain:
To talk to fiery tempests; to implore
The raging flame to give its burnings o'er;

To toss, to writhe, to pant beneath his load,
And bear the weight of an offended God.
The favour'd of their Judge, in triumph move
To take possession of their thrones above;
Satan's accurs'd desertion to supply,
And fill the vacant stations of the sky;
Again to kindle long-extinguish'd rays,
And with new lights dilate the heavenly blaze;
To crop the roses of immortal youth,
And drink the fountain-head of sacred truth
To swim in seas of bliss, to strike the string,
And lift the voice to their Almighty King;
To lose eternity in grateful lays,
And fill heaven's wide circumference with praise.
But I attempt the wondrous height in vain,
And leave unfinish'd the too lofty strain:
What boldly I begin, let others end;
My strength exhausted, fainting I descend,
And choose a less, but no ignoble, theme,
Dissolving elements, and worlds, in flame.
The fatal period, the great hour, is come,
And nature shrinks at her approaching doom;
Loud peals of thunder give the sign, and all
Heaven's terrors in array surround the ball;
Sharp lightnings with the meteor's blaze conspire,
And, darted downward, set the world on fire;
Black rising clouds the thicken'd ether choke,
And spiry flames dart through the rolling smoke,
With keen vibrations cut the sullen night,
And strike the darken'd sky with dreadful light;

From heaven's four regions, with immortal force,
Angels drive on the wind's impetuous course,
T' enrage the flame: It spreads, it soars on high,
Swells in the storm, and billows through the sky:
Here winding pyramids of fire ascend,
Cities and deserts in one ruin blend;
Here blazing volumes wafted, overwhelm
The spacious face of a far distant realm;
There, undermin'd, down rush eternal hills,
The neighb'ring vales the vast destruction fills.
Hear'st thou that dreadful crack? that sound which broke
Like peals of thunder, and the centre shook?
What wonders must that groan of nature tell?
Olympus there, and mightier Atlas, fell;
Which seem'd above the reach of fate to stand,
A tow'ring monument of God's right hand;
Now dust and smoke, whose brow, so lately, spread
O'er shelter'd countries its diffusive shade.
Show me that celebrated spot, where all
The various rulers of the sever'd ball
Have humbly sought wealth, honour, and redress,
That land which heaven seem'd diligent to bless,
Once call'd Britannia: can her glories end?
And can't surrounding seas her realms defend?
Alas! in flames behold surrounding seas!
Like oil, their waters but augment the blaze.
Some angel say, where ran proud Asia's bound?
Or where with fruits was fair Europa crown'd?
Where stretch'd waste Lybia? Where did India's shore

Sparkle in diamonds, and her golden ore?
Each lost in each, their mingling kingdoms glow,
And all dissolv'd, one fiery deluge flow:
Thus earth's contending monarchies are join'd,
And a full period of ambition find.
And now whate'er or swims, or walks, or flies,
Inhabitants of sea, or earth, or skies;
All on whom Adam's wisdom fix'd a name,
All plunge, and perish in the conquering flame.
This globe alone would but defraud the fire,
Starve its devouring rage: the flakes aspire,
And catch the clouds, and make the heavens their
prey;
The sun, the moon, the stars, all melt away;
All, all is lost; no monument, no sign,
Where once so proudly blaz'd the gay machine.
So bubbles on the foaming stream expire,
So sparks that scatter from the kindling fire;
The devastations of one dreadful hour
The great Creator's six days' work devour.
A mighty, mighty ruin! yet one soul
Has more to boast, and far outweighs the whole
Exalted in superior excellence,
Casts down to nothing, such a vast expense.
Have you not seen th' eternal mountains nod,
An earth dissolving, a descending God?
What strange surprises through all nature ran?
For whom these revolutions, but for man?
For him, Omnipotence new measures takes,
For him, through all eternity, awakes;

Pours on him gifts sufficient to supply
Heaven's loss, and with fresh glories fill the sky.
  Think deeply then, O man, how great thou art;
Pay thyself homage with a trembling heart;
What angels guard, no longer dare neglect,
Slighting thyself, affront not God's respect.
Enter the sacred temple of thy breast,
And gaze, and wander there, a ravish'd guest;
Gaze on those hidden treasures thou shalt find,
Wander through all the glories of thy mind.
Of perfect knowledge, see, the dawning light
Foretells a noon most exquisitely bright!
Here, springs of endless joy are breaking forth!
There, buds the promise of celestial worth!
Worth, which must ripen in a happier clime,
And brighter sun, beyond the bounds of time.
Thou, minor, canst not guess thy vast estate,
What stores, on foreign coasts, thy landing wait:
Lose not thy claim, let virtue's path be trod;
Thus glad all heaven, and please that bounteous God,
Who, to light thee to pleasures, hung on high
Yon radiant orb, proud regent of the sky:
That service done, its beams shall fade away,
And God shine forth in one eternal day.

THE FORCE OF RELIGION; OR, VANQUISHED LOVE.

Gratior et pulchro veniens in corpore virtus. — VIRG.

BOOK I.

——— Ad cœlum ardentia lumina tollens,
Lumina; nam teneras arcebant vincula palmas.
VIRG.

FROM lofty themes, from thoughts that soar'd on high,
And open'd wondrous scenes above the sky,
My muse descend: indulge my fond desire;
With softer thoughts my melting soul inspire,
And smooth my numbers to a female's praise:
A partial world will listen to my lays,
While Anna reigns, and sets a female name
Unrival'd in the glorious lists of fame.
Hear, ye fair daughters of this happy land,
Whose radiant eyes the vanquish'd world command,
Virtue is beauty: but when charms of mind
With elegance of outward form are join'd;
When youth makes such bright objects still more bright,
And fortune sets them in the strongest light;
'Tis all of heaven that we below may view,
And all, but adoration, is your due.

Fam'd female virtue did this isle adorn,
Ere Ormond, or her glorious queen, was born:
When now Maria's powerful arms prevail'd,
And haughty Dudley's bold ambition fail'd,
The beauteous daughter of great Suffolk's race,
In blooming youth adorn'd with every grace;
Who gain'd a crown by treason not her own,
And innocently fill'd another's throne;
Hurl'd from the summit of imperial state,
With equal mind sustain'd the stroke of fate.
But how will Guilford, her far dearer part,
With manly reason fortify his heart?
At once she longs, and is afraid, to know:
Now swift she moves, and now advances slow,
To find her lord; and, finding, passes by,
Silent with fear, nor dares she meet his eye;
Lest that, unask'd, in speechless grief, disclose
The mournful secret of his inward woes.
Thus, after sickness, doubtful of her face,
The melancholy virgin shuns the glass.
At length, with troubled thought, but look serene,
And sorrow soften'd by her heavenly mien,
She clasps her lord, brave, beautiful, and young,
While tender accents melt upon her tongue;
Gentle, and sweet, as vernal zephyr blows,
Fanning the lily, or the blooming rose.
"Grieve not, my lord; a crown indeed is lost;
What far outshines a crown, we still may boast;
A mind compos'd; a mind that can disdain
A fruitless sorrow for a loss so vain.

Nothing is loss that virtue can improve
To wealth eternal; and return above;
Above, where no distinction shall be known
'Twixt him whom storms have shaken from a
throne,
And him, who, basking in the smiles of fate,
Shone forth in all the splendour of the great:
Nor can I find the diff'rence here below;
I lately was a queen; I still am so,
While Guilford's wife: thee rather I obey,
Than o'er mankind extend imperial sway.
When we lie down in some obscure retreat,
Incens'd Maria may her rage forget;
And I to death my duty will improve,
And what you miss in empire, add in love —
Your godlike soul is open'd in your look,
And I have faintly your great meaning spoke,
For this alone I'm pleas'd I wore the crown,
To find with what content we lay it down.
Heroes may win, but 't is a heavenly race
Can quit a throne with a becoming grace."

Thus spoke the fairest of her sex, and cheer'd
Her drooping lord; whose boding bosom fear'd
A darker cloud of ills would burst, and shed
Severer vengeance on her guiltless head:
Too just, alas, the terrors which he felt!
For, lo! a guard! — Forgive him, if he melt —
How sharp her pangs, when sever'd from his side,
The most sincerely lov'd, and loving bride,
In space confin'd, the muse forbears to tell;

Deep was her anguish, but she bore it well.
His pain was equal, but his virtue less;
He thought in grief there could be no excess.
Pensive he sat, o'ercast with gloomy care,
And often fondly clasp'd his absent fair;
Now, silent, wander'd thro' his rooms of state,
And sicken'd at the pomp, and tax'd his fate;
Which thus adorn'd, in all her shining store,
A splendid wretch, magnificently poor.
Now on the bridal-bed his eyes were cast,
And anguish fed on his enjoyments past;
Each recollected pleasure made him smart,
And every transport stabb'd him to the heart.
  That happy moon, which summon'd to delight,
That moon which shone on his dear nuptial night,
Which saw him fold her yet untasted charms
(Denied to princes) in his longing arms;
Now sees the transient blessing fleet away,
Empire and love! the vision of a day.
  Thus, in the British clime, a summer-storm
Will oft the smiling face of heaven deform;
The winds with violence at once descend,
Sweep flowers and fruits, and make the forest bend;
A sudden winter, while the sun is near,
O'ercomes the season, and inverts the year.
  But whither is the captive borne away,
The beauteous captive, from the cheerful day?
The scene is chang'd indeed; before her eyes
Ill boding looks and unknown horrors rise:
For pomp and splendour, for her guard and crown,

A gloomy dungeon, and a keeper's frown:
Black thoughts, each morn, invade the lover's
breast,
Each night, a ruffian locks the queen to rest.
Ah mournful change, if judg'd by vulgar minds!
But Suffolk's daughter its advantage finds.
Religion's force divine is best display'd
In deep desertion of all human aid:
To succour in extremes, is her delight,
And cheer the heart, when terror strikes the sight.
We, disbelieving our own senses, gaze,
And wonder what a mortal's heart can raise
To triumph o'er misfortunes, smile in grief,
And comfort those who come to bring relief:
We gaze; and as we gaze, wealth, fame, decay,
And all the world's vain glories fade away.
Against her cares she rais'd a dauntless mind,
And with an ardent heart, but most resign'd,
Deep in the dreadful gloom, with pious heat,
Amid the silence of her dark retreat,
Address'd her God, — "Almighty power divine!
'Tis thine to raise, and to depress, is thine;
With honour to light up the name unknown,
Or to put out the lustre of a throne.
In my short span both fortunes I have prov'd,
And though with ill frail nature will be mov'd,
I 'll bear it well: (O strengthen me to bear!)
And if my piety may claim thy care;
If I remember'd, in youth's giddy heat,
And tumult of a court, a future state;

O favour, when thy mercy I implore
For one who never guilty sceptre bore!
'Twas I receiv'd the crown; my lord is free;
If it must fall, let vengeance fall on me.
Let him survive, his country's name to raise,
And in a guilty land to speak thy praise!
O may th' indulgence of a father's love,
Pour'd forth on me, be doubled from above!
If these are safe, I 'll think my prayers succeed,
And bless thy tender mercies, whilst I bleed."
'Twas now the mournful eve before that day
In which the queen to her full wrath gave way;
Thro' rigid justice, rush'd into offence,
And drank in zeal the blood of innocence:
The sun went down in clouds, and seem'd to mourn
The sad necessity of his return;
The hollow wind, and melancholy rain,
Or did, or was imagin'd to, complain:
The tapers cast an inauspicious light;
Stars there were none, and doubly dark the night
Sweet innocence in chains can take her rest;
Soft slumber gently creeping through her breast,
She sinks; and in her sleep is reinthron'd,
Mock'd by a gaudy dream, and vainly crown'd.
She views her fleets and armies, seas and land,
And stretches wide her shadow of command:
With royal purple is her vision hung;
By phantom hosts are shouts of conquest rung;
Low at her feet the suppliant rival lies;
Our prisoner mourns her fate, and bids her rise.

Now level beams upon the waters play'd,
Glanc'd on the hills, and westward cast the shade;
The busy trades in city had began
To sound, and speak the painful life of man.
In tyrants' breasts the thoughts of vengeance rouse,
And the fond bridegroom turns him to his spouse.
At this first birth of light, while morning breaks,
Our spouseless bride, our widow'd wife, awakes;
Awakes, and smiles; nor night's imposture blames;
Her rèal pomps were little more than dreams;
A short-liv'd blaze, a lightning quickly o'er,
That died in birth, that shone, and were no more:
She turns her side, and soon resumes a state
Of mind, well suited to her alter'd fate,
Serene, though serious; when dread tidings come
(Ah wretched Guilford!) of her instant doom.
Sun, hide thy beams; in clouds as black as night
Thy face involve; be guiltless of the sight;
Or haste more swiftly to the western main;
Nor let her blood the conscious daylight stain!
Oh! how severe! to fall so new a bride,
Yet blushing from the priest, in youthful pride;
When time had just matur'd each perfect grace,
And open'd all the wonders of her face!
To leave her Guilford dead to all relief,
Fond of his woe, and obstinate in grief.
Unhappy fair! whatever fancy drew,
(Vain promis'd blessings,) vanish from her view;
No train of cheerful days, endearing nights,
No sweet domestic joys, and chaste delights;

Pleasures that blossom e'en from doubts and fears;
And bliss and rapture rising out of cares:
No little Guilford, with paternal grace,
Lull'd on her knee, or smiling in her face;
Who, when her dearest father shall return,
From pouring tears on her untimely urn,
Might comfort to his silver hairs impart,
And fill her place in his indulgent heart:
As where fruits fall, quick rising blossoms smile,
And the bless'd Indian of his care beguile,
  In vain these various reasons jointly press,
To blacken death, and heighten her distress;
She, thro' th' encircling terrors darts her sight
To the bless'd regions of eternal light,
And fills her soul with peace: to weeping friends
Her father, and her lord, she recommends;
Unmov'd herself: her foes her air survey,
And rage to see their malice thrown away.
She soars; now nought on earth detains her care ——
But Guilford; who still struggles for his share.
Still will his form importunately rise,
Clog and retard her transport to the skies;
As trembling flames now take a feeble flight,
Now catch the brand with a returning light,
Thus her soul onward from the seats above
Falls fondly back, and kindles into love:
At length she conquers in the doubtful field;
That heaven she seeks will be her Guilford's shield.
Now death is welcome; his approach is slow;
'Tis tedious longer to expect the blow.

Oh! mortals, short of sight, who think the past
O'erblown misfortune still shall prove the last:
Alas! misfortunes travel in a train,
And oft in life form one perpetual chain;
Fear buries fear, and ills on ills attend,
Till life and sorrow meet one common end.
She thinks that she has nought but death to fear,
And death is conquer'd. Worse than death is near.
Her rigid trials are not yet complete;
The news arrives of her great father's fate.
She sees his hoary head, all white with age,
A victim to th' offended monarch's rage.
How great the mercy, had she breath'd her last,
Ere the dire sentence on her father past!
A fonder parent nature never knew;
And as his age increas'd, his fondness grew.
A parent's love ne'er better was bestow'd;
The pious daughter in her heart o'erflow'd.
And can she from all weakness still refrain?
And still the firmness of her soul maintain?
Impossible! a sigh will force its way;
One patient tear her mortal birth betray;
She sighs and weeps! but so she weeps and sighs,
As silent dews descend, and vapours rise.
Celestial patience! how dost thou defeat
The foe's proud menace, and elude his hate!
While passion takes his part, betrays our peace;
To death and torture swells each slight disgrace;
By not opposing, thou dost ills destroy,
And wear thy conquer'd sorrows into joy.

Now she revolves within her anxious mind,
What woe still lingers in reserve behind.
Griefs rise on griefs, and she can see no bound,
While nature lasts, and can receive a wound.
The sword is drawn; the queen to rage inclin'd,
By mercy, nor by piety, confin'd.
What mercy can the zealot's heart assuage,
Whose piety itself converts to rage?
She thought, and sigh'd. And now the blood began
To leave her beauteous cheek all cold and wan.
New sorrow dimm'd the lustre of her eye,
And on her cheek the fading roses die.
Alas! should Guilford too — when now she 's brought
To that dire view, that precipice of thought,
While there she trembling stands, nor dares look down,
Nor can recede, till heaven's decrees are known;
Cure of all ills, till now, her lord appears —
But not to cheer her heart, and dry her tears!
Not now, as usual, like the rising day,
To chase the shadows, and the damps away:
But, like a gloomy storm, at once to sweep
And plunge her to the bottom of the deep.
Black were his robes, dejected was his air,
His voice was frozen by his cold despair;
Slow, like a ghost, he mov'd with solemn pace;
A dying paleness sat upon his face.
Back she recoil'd, she smote her lovely breast,
Her eyes the anguish of her heart confess'd;

Struck to the soul, she stagger'd with the wound,
And sunk, a breathless image, to the ground.
 Thus the fair lily, when the sky 's o'ercast,
At first but shudders in the feeble blast;
But when the winds and weighty rains descend,
The fair and upright stem is forc'd to bend;
Till broke at length, its snowy leaves are shed,
And strew with dying sweets their native bed.

BOOK II.

Hic pietatis honos? sic nos in sceptra reponis! — VIRG.

HER Guilford clasps her, beautiful in death,
And with a kiss recalls her fleeting breath,
To tapers thus, which by a blast expire,
A lighted taper, touch'd, restores the fire:
She rear'd her swimming eye, and saw the light,
And Guilford too, or she had loath'd the sight:
Her father's death she bore, despis'd her own,
But now she must, she will, have leave to groan:
Ah! Guilford, she began, and would have spoke;
But sobs rush'd in, and ev'ry accent broke:
Reason itself, as gusts of passion blew,
Was ruffled in the tempest, and withdrew.
 So the youth lost his image in the well,
When tears upon the yielding surface fell.
The scatter'd features slid into decay,
And spreading circles drove his face away.

To touch the soft affections, and control
The manly temper of the bravest soul,
What with afflicted beauty can compare,
And drops of love distilling from the fair?
It melts us down; our pains delight bestow;
And we with fondness languish o'er our woe.
This Guilford prov'd; and, with excess of pain,
And pleasure too, did to his bosom strain
The weeping fair: sunk deep in soft desire,
Indulg'd his love, and nurs'd the raging fire:
Then tore himself away; and, standing wide,
As fearing a relapse of fondness, cried,
With ill-dissembled grief; "My life, forbear!
You wound your Guilford with each cruel tear:
Did you not chide my grief? repress your own;
Nor want compassion for yourself alone:
Have you beheld, how, from the distant main,
The thronging waves roll on, a num'rous train,
And foam, and bellow, till they reach the shore;
There burst their noisy pride, and are no more?
Thus the successive flows of human race,
Chas'd by the coming, the preceding, chase;
They sound, and swell, their haughty heads they rear;
Then fall, and flatten, break, and disappear.
Life is a forfeit we must shortly pay;
And where 's the mighty lucre of a day?
Why should you mourn my fate? 'tis most unkind;
Your own you bore with an unshaken mind:
And which, can you imagine, was the dart

That drank most blood, sunk deepest in my heart?
I cannot live without you; and my doom
I meet with joy, to share one common tomb.—
And are again your tears profusely spilt!
Oh! then, my kindness blackens to my guilt;
It foils itself, if it recall your pain;—
Life of my life, I beg you to refrain!
The load which fate imposes, you increase;
And help Maria to destroy my peace."
But, oh! against himself his labour turn'd;
The more he comforted, the more she mourn'd:
Compassion swells our grief; words soft and kind
But soothe our weakness, and dissolve the mind:
Her sorrow flow'd in streams; nor hers alone,
While that he blam'd, he yielded to his own.
Where are the smiles she wore, when she, so late,
Hail'd him great partner of the regal state;
When orient gems around her temples blaz'd,
And bending nations on the glory gaz'd?
'Tis now the queen's command, they both retreat,
To weep with dignity, and mourn in state:
She forms the decent misery with joy,
And loads with pomp the wretch she would destroy.
A spacious hall is hung with black; all light
Shut out, and noon-day darken'd into night.
From the mid-roof a lamp depends on high,
Like a dim crescent in a clouded sky:
It sheds a quiv'ring melancholy gloom,
Which only shows the darkness of the room.

A shining axe is on the table laid;
A dreadful sight! and glitters through the shade.
In this sad scene the lovers are confin'd;
A scene of terrors, to a guilty mind!
A scene, that would have damp'd with rising cares,
And quite extinguish'd every love but theirs.
What can they do? They fix their mournful eyes ——
Then Guilford, thus abruptly; "I despise
An empire lost; I fling away the crown;
Numbers have laid that bright delusion down;
But where's the Charles, or Dioclesian where,
Could quit the blooming, wedded, weeping fair?
Oh! to dwell ever on thy lip! to stand
In full possession of thy snowy hand!
And, thro' th' unclouded crystal of thine eye,
The heavenly treasures of thy mind to spy!
Till rapture reason happily destroys,
And my soul wanders through immortal joys!
Give me the world, and ask me, where 's my bliss?
I clasp thee to my breast, and answer, this.
And shall the grave" — He groans, and can no more;
But all her charms in silence traces o'er;
Her lip, her cheek, and eye, to wonder wrought;
And, wond'ring, sees, in sad presaging thought,
From that fair neck, that world of beauty fall,
And roll along the dust, a ghastly ball!
Oh! let those tremble, who are greatly bless'd!
For who, but Guilford, could be thus distress'd?

Come hither, all you happy, all you great,
From flowery meadows, and from rooms of state;
Nor think I call, your pleasures to destroy,
But to refine, and to exalt your joy:
Weep not; but, smiling, fix your ardent care
On nobler titles than the brave or fair.
   Was ever such a mournful, moving sight?
See, if you can, by that dull, trembling light:
Now they embrace; and, mix'd with bitter woe,
Like Isis and her Thames, one stream they flow:
Now they start wide; fix'd in benumbing care,
They stiffen into statues of despair:
Now, tenderly severe, and fiercely kind,
They rush at once; they fling their cares behind,
And clasp, as if to death; new vows repeat;
And, quite wrapp'd up in love, forget their fate.
A short delusion! for the raging pain
Returns; and their poor hearts must bleed again.
   Meantime, the queen new cruelty decreed;
But, ill content that they should only bleed,
A priest is sent; who, with insidious art,
Instills his poison into Suffolk's heart;
And Guilford drank it: hanging on the breast,
He from his childhood was with Rome possest.
When now the ministers of death draw nigh,
And in her dearest lord she first must die,
The subtle priest, who long had watch'd to find
The most unguarded passes of her mind,
Bespoke her thus: "Grieve not; 'tis in your power
Your lord to rescue from this fatal hour."

Her bosom pants; she draws her breath with pain;
A sudden horror thrills through every vein;
Life seems suspended, on his words intent;
And her soul trembles for the great event.
The priest proceeds: "Embrace the faith of Rome,
And ward your own, your lord's, and father's doom."
Ye blessed spirits! now your charge sustain;
The past was ease; now first she suffers pain.
Must she pronounce her father's death? must she
Bid Guilford bleed? — It must not, cannot, be.
It cannot be! But 'tis the Christian's praise,
Above impossibilities to raise
The weakness of our nature; and deride
Of vain philosophy the boasted pride.
What though our feeble sinews scarce impart
A moment's swiftness to the feather'd dart;
Though tainted air our vig'rous youth can break,
And a chill blast the hardy warrior shake,
Yet are we strong: hear the loud tempest roar
From east to west, and call us weak no more;
The lightning's unresisted force proclaims
Our might; and thunders raise our humble names;
'Tis our Jehovah fills the heavens; as long
As he shall reign Almighty, we are strong:
We, by devotion, borrow from his throne;
And almost make Omnipotence our own:
We force the gates of heaven, by fervent prayer;
And call forth triumph out of man's despair.
Our lovely mourner, kneeling, lifts her eyes

And bleeding heart, in silence, to the skies,
Devoutly sad — then, bright'ning, like the day,
When sudden winds sweep scatter'd clouds away,
Shining in majesty, till now unknown,
And breathing life and spirit scarce her own;
She, rising, speaks: "If these the terms ——— "
Here, Guilford, cruel Guilford, (barb'rous man!
Is this thy love?) as swift as lightning ran;
O'erwhelm'd her with tempestuous sorrow fraught,
And stifled, in its birth, the mighty thought;
Then bursting fresh into a flood of tears,
Fierce, resolute, delirious with his fears;
His fears for her alone: he beat his breast,
And thus the fervour of his soul exprest:
"Oh! let thy thought o'er our past converse rove,
And show one moment uninflam'd with love!
Oh! if thy kindness can no longer last,
In pity to thyself, forget the past!
Else wilt thou never, void of shame and fear,
Pronounce his doom, whom thou hast held so dear:
Thou who hast took me to thy arms, and swore
Empires were vile, and fate could give no more;
That to continue, was its utmost power,
And make the future like the present hour.
Now call a ruffian; bid his cruel sword
Lay wide the bosom of thy worthless lord;
Transfix his heart (since you its love disclaim),
And stain his honour with a traitor's name.
This might perhaps be borne without remorse;
But sure a father's pangs will have their force!

Shall his good age, so near its journey's end,
Through cruel torment to the grave descend?
His shallow blood all issue at a wound,
Wash a slave's feet, and smoke upon the ground?
But he to you has ever been severe;
Then take your vengeance" — Suffolk now drew near;
Bending beneath the burden of his care;
His robes neglected, and his head was bare;
Decrepid winter, in the yearly ring,
Thus slowly creeps, to meet the blooming spring:
Downward he cast a melancholy look;
Thrice turn'd, to hide his grief; then faintly spoke·
"Now deep in years, and forward in decay,
That axe can only rob me of a day;
For thee, my soul's desire! I can't refrain;
And shall my tears, my last tears, flow in vain?
When you shall know a mother's tender name,
My heart's distress no longer will you blame."
At this, afar his bursting groans were heard;
The tears ran trickling down his silver beard:
He snatch'd her hand, which to his lips he prest,
And bid her plant a dagger in his breast;
Then, sinking, call'd her piety unjust,
And soil'd his hoary temples in the dust.

Hard-hearted men! will you no mercy know?
Has the queen brib'd you to distress her foe?
O weak deserters to misfortune's part,
By false affection thus to pierce her heart!
When she had soar'd, to let your arrows fly,

And fetch her bleeding from the middle sky!
And can her virtue, springing from the ground,
Her flight recover, and disdain the wound,
When cleaving love, and human interest, bind
The broken force of her aspiring mind;
As round the gen'rous eagle, which in vain
Exerts her strength, the serpent wreaths his train,
Her struggling wings entangles, curling plies
His pois'nous tail, and stings her as she flies!
While yet the blow's first dreadful weight she feels,
And with its force her resolution reels;
Large doors, unfolding with a mournful sound,
To view discover, welt'ring on the ground,
Three headless trunks, of those whose arms maintain'd,
And in her wars immortal glory gain'd:
The lifted axe assur'd her ready doom,
And silent mourners sadden'd all the room.
Shall I proceed; or here break off my tale;
Nor truths, to stagger human faith, reveal?
She met this utmost malice of her fate
With Christian dignity, and pious state:
The beating storm's propitious rage she blest,
And all the martyr triumph'd in her breast:
Her lord and father, for a moment's space,
She strictly folded in her soft embrace!
Then thus she spoke, while angels heard on high,
And sudden gladness smil'd along the sky:
"Your over fondness has not mov'd my hate;

I am well pleas'd you make my death so great;
I joy I cannot save you; and have giv'n
Two lives, much dearer than my own, to heaven,
If so the queen decrees:*— But I have cause
To hope my blood will satisfy the laws;
And there is mercy still, for you, in store:
With me the bitterness of death is o'er.
He shot his sting in that farewell embrace;
And all, that is to come, is joy and peace.
Then let mistaken sorrow be supprest,
Nor seem to envy my approaching rest."
Then, turning to the ministers of fate,
She, smiling, says, "My victory complete:
And tell your queen, I thank her for the blow,
And grieve my gratitude I cannot show:
A poor return I leave in England's crown,
For everlasting pleasure, and renown:
Her guilt alone allays this happy hour;
Her guilt,— the only vengeance in her power."
Not Rome, untouch'd with sorrow, heard her fate;
And fierce Maria pitied her too late.

* Here she embraces them.

LOVE OF FAME, THE UNIVERSAL PASSION.

IN SEVEN CHARACTERISTICAL SATIRES.

—— Fulgente trahit constrictos gloria curru.
Non minus ignotos generosis. — HOR.

PREFACE.

THESE satires have been favourably received at home and abroad. I am not conscious of the least malevolence to any particular person through all the characters; though some persons may be so selfish, as to engross a general application to themselves. A writer in polite letters should be content with reputation; the private amusement he finds in his compositions; the good influence they have on his severer studies; that admission they give him to his superiors; and the possible good effect they may have on the public; or else he should join to his politeness some more lucrative qualification.

But it is possible, that satire may not do much good: men may rise in their affections to their follies, as they do to their friends, when they are abused by others: it is much to be feared, that misconduct will never be chased out of the world by satire; all therefore that is to be said for it is, that misconduct will certainly be never chased out of the world by satire, if no satires are written: nor is that term unapplicable to graver compositions. Ethics, heathen and Christian, and the Scriptures themselves, are, in a great measure, a satire on the weakness and iniquity of men; and some part of that satire is in verse too: nay, in the first ages, philosophy and poetry were the same thing; wisdom wore no other dress: so that, I hope, these satires will be the more easily pardoned that misfortune by the severe. Nay, historians themselves may be considered as satirists, and satirists most severe; since such are most human actions, that to relate, is to expose them.

No man can converse much in the world, but, at what he meets with, he must either be insensible, or grieve, or be angry, or smile. Some passion (if we are not impassive) must be moved; for the general conduct of mankind is by no means a thing indifferent to a reasonable and virtuous man. Now to smile at it, and turn it into ridicule, I think most eligible; as it hurts ourselves least, and gives vice and folly the greatest offence: and that for this reason; because what men aim at by them, is, generally, public opinion and esteem; which truth is the subject of the following satire; and joins them together, as several branches from the same root: a unity of design, which has not, I think, in a set of satires, been attempted before.

Laughing at the misconduct of the world, will, in a great measure, ease us of any more disagreeable passion about it. One passion is more effectually driven out by another, than by reason; whatever some may teach: for to reason we owe our passions: had we not reason, we should not be offended at what we find amiss: and the cause seems not to be the natural cure of any effect.

Moreover, laughing satire bids the fairest for success: the world is too proud to be fond of a serious tutor; and when an author is in a passion, the laugh, generally, as in conversation, turns against him. This kind of satire only has any delicacy in it. Of this delicacy Horace is the best master: he appears in good humour while he censures; and therefore his censure has the more weight, as supposed to proceed from judgment, not from passion. Juvenal is ever in a passion; he has little valuable but his eloquence and morality: the last of which I have had in my eye: but rather for emulation, than imitation, through my whole work.

But though I comparatively condemn Juvenal, in part of the sixth satire (where the occasion most required it), I endeavoured to touch on his manner; but was forced to quit it soon, as disagreeable to the writer, and reader too. Boileau has joined both the Roman satirists with great success; but has too much of Juvenal in his very serious satire on woman, which should have been the gayest of all. An excellent critic of our own commends Boileau's closeness, or, as he calls it, pressness, particularly; whereas, it appears to me, that repetition is his fault, if any fault should be imputed to him.

There are some prose satirists of the greatest delicacy and wit; the last of which can never, or should never, succeed without the former. An author without it, betrays too great a contempt for mankind, and opinion of himself, which are bad advocates for reputation and success. What a difference is there between the merit, if not the wit, of Cervantes and Rabelais? The last has a particular art of throwing a great deal of genius and learning into frolic and jest; but the genius and the scholar is all you can admire; you want the gentleman to converse with in him: he is like a criminal who receives his life for some services; you commend, but you pardon too. Indecency offends our pride, as men; and our unaffected taste, as judges of composition: nature has wisely formed us with an aversion to it; and he that succeeds in spite of it, is, * aliena venia, quam sua providentia tutior.

Such wits, like false oracles of old (which were wits and cheats), should set up for reputation

* Val. Max.

among the weak, in some Bœotia, which was the land of oracles; for the wise will hold them in contempt. Some wits, too, like oracles, deal in ambiguities; but not with equal success: for though ambiguities are the first excellence of an impostor, they are the last of a wit.

Some satirical wits and humourists, like their father Lucian, laugh at every thing indiscriminately; which betrays such a poverty of wit, as cannot afford to part with any thing; and such a want of virtue, as to postpone it to a jest. Such writers encourage vice and folly, which they pretend to combat, by setting them on an equal foot with better things: and while they labour to bring every thing into contempt, how can they expect their own parts should escape? Some French writers, particularly, are guilty of this in matters of the last consequence; and some of our own. They that are for lessening the true dignity of mankind, are not sure of being successful, but with regard to one individual in it. It is this conduct that justly makes a wit a term of reproach.

Which puts me in mind of Plato's fable of the birth of love; one of the prettiest fables of all antiquity; which will hold likewise with regard to modern poetry. Love, says he, is the son of the goddess poverty, and the god of riches: he has from his father his daring genius; his elevation of thought; his building castles in the air; his prodigality; his neglect of things serious and useful; his vain opinion of his own merit; and his affectation of preference and distinction: from his mother he inherits his indigence, which makes him a constant beggar of favours; that importunity with which he begs; his flattery; his servility; his fear of being despised, which is inseparable from him. This addition may be made; viz. that poetry, like love, is a little subject to blindness, which makes her mistake her way to preferments and honours; that she has her satirical quiver; and, lastly, that she retains a dutiful admiration of her father's family; but divides her favours, and generally lives with her mother's relations.

However, this is not necessity, but choice: were wisdom her governess, she might have much more of the father than the mother; especially in such an age as this, which shows a due passion for her charms.

SATIRE I.

TO HIS GRACE THE DUKE OF DORSET.

——— Tanto major famæ sitis est, quam
Virtutis. JUV. SAT. X.

MY verse is satire; Dorset, lend your ear,
And patronize a muse you cannot fear.

To poets sacred is a Dorset's name:
Their wonted passport through the gates of fame:
It bribes the partial reader into praise,
And throws a glory round the shelter'd lays:
The dazzled judgment fewer faults can see,
And gives applause to Blackmore, or to me.
But you decline the mistress we pursue;
Others are fond of fame, but fame of you.
Instructive satire, true to virtue's cause!
Thou shining supplement of public laws!
When flatter'd crimes of a licentious age
Reproach our silence, and demand our rage;
When purchas'd follies, from each distant land,
Like arts, improve in Britain's skilful hand;
When the law shows her teeth, but dares not bite,
And south sea treasures are not brought to light;
When churchmen scripture for the classics quit,
Polite apostates from God's grace to wit;
When men grow great from their revenue spent,
And fly from bailiffs into parliament;
When dying sinners, to blot out their score,
Bequeath the church the leavings of a whore;
To chafe our spleen, when themes like these increase,
Shall panegyric reign, and censure cease?
Shall poesy, like law, turn wrong to right,
And dedications wash an Æthiop white,
Set up each senseless wretch for nature's boast,
On whom praise shines, as trophies on a post?
Shall fun'ral eloquence her colours spread,
And scatter roses on the wealthy dead?

Shall authors smile on such illustrious days,
And satirize with nothing — but their praise?
  Why slumbers Pope, who leads the tuneful train,
Nor hears that virtue, which he loves, complain?
Donne, Dorset, Dryden, Rochester, are dead,
And guilt's chief foe, in Addison, is fled;
Congreve, who, crown'd with laurels, fairly won,
Sits smiling at the goal, while others run,
He will not write; and (more provoking still!)
Ye gods! he will not write, and Mævius will.
  Doubly distrest, what author shall we find
Discreetly daring, and severely kind,
The courtly * Roman's shining path to tread,
And sharply smile prevailing folly dead?
Will no superior genius snatch the quill,
And save me, on the brink, from writing ill?
Tho' vain the strife, I 'll strive my voice to raise,
What will not men attempt for sacred praise?
  The love of praise, howe'er conceal'd by art,
Reigns, more or less, and glows, in ev'ry heart:
The proud, to gain it, toils on toils endure;
The modest shun it, but to make it sure.
O'er globes, and sceptres, now on thrones it swells;
Now, trims the midnight lamp in college cells:
'Tis tory, whig; it plots, prays, preaches, pleads,
Harangues in senates, squeaks in masquerades.
Here, to Steele's humour makes a bold pretence
There, bolder, aims at Pulteney's eloquence.

* Horace.

It aids the dancer's heel, the writer's head,
And heaps the plain with mountains of the dead;
Nor ends with life; but nods in sable plumes,
Adorns our hearse, and flatters on our tombs.
What is not proud? The pimp is proud to see
So many like himself in high degree:
The whore is proud her beauties are the dread
Of peevish virtue, and the marriage-bed;
And the brib'd cuckold, like crown'd victims born
To slaughter, glories in his gilded horn.
Some go to church, proud humbly to repent,
And come back much more guilty than they went:
One way they look, another way they steer,
Pray to the gods, but would have mortals hear;
And when their sins they set sincerely down,
They 'll find that their religion has been one.
Others with wishful eyes on glory look,
When they have got their picture tow'rds a book;
Or pompous title, like a gaudy sign,
Meant to betray dull sots to wretched wine.
If at his title T—— had dropt his quill,
T—— might have pass'd for a great genius still.
But T——, alas! (excuse him, if you can)
Is now a scribbler, who was once a man.
Imperious some a classic fame demand,
For heaping up, with a laborious hand,
A waggon-load of meanings for one word,
While A 's deposed, and B with pomp restor'd.
Some, for renown, on scraps of learning dote,
And think they grow immortal as they quote.

To patch-work learn'd quotations are allied;
Both strive to make our poverty our pride.
On glass how witty is a noble peer!
Did ever diamond cost a man so dear?
Polite diseases make some idiots vain,
Which, if unfortunately well, they feign.
Of folly, vice, disease, men proud we see;
And (stranger still!) of blockheads' flattery;
Whose praise defames; as if a fool should mean,
By spitting on your face, to make it clean.
Nor is 't enough all hearts are swoln with pride,
Her power is mighty, as her realm is wide.
What can she not perform? The love of fame
Made bold Alphonsus his Creator blame:
Empedocles hurl'd down the burning steep:
And (stronger still!) made Alexander weep.
Nay, it holds Delia from a second bed,
Tho' her lov'd lord has four half months been dead.
This passion with a pimple have I seen
Retard a cause, and give a judge the spleen.
By this inspir'd (O ne'er to be forgot!)
Some lords have learn'd to spell, and some to knot.
It makes Globose a speaker in the house;
He hems, and is deliver'd of his mouse.
It makes dear self on well-bred tongues prevail,
And I the little hero of each tale.
Sick with the love of fame, what throngs pour in,
Unpeople court, and leave the senate thin!
My glowing subject seems but just begun,
And, chariot-like, I kindle as I run.

Aid me, great Homer! with thy epic rules,
To take a catalogue of British fools.
Satire! had I thy Dorset's force divine,
A knave or fool should perish in each line;
Tho' for the first all Westminster should plead,
And for the last, all Gresham intercede.
Begin. Who first the catalogue shall grace?
To quality belongs the highest place.
My lord comes forward; forward let him come!
Ye vulgar! at your peril, give him room:
He stands for fame on his forefathers' feet,
By heraldry prov'd valiant or discreet.
With what a decent pride he throws his eyes
Above the man by three descents less wise!
If virtues at his noble hands you crave,
You bid him raise his fathers from the grave.
Men should press forward in fame's glorious chase;
Nobles look backward, and so lose the race.
Let high birth triumph! What can be more great?
Nothing — but merit in a low estate.
To virtue's humblest son let none prefer
Vice, though descended from the conqueror.
Shall men, like figures, pass for high, or base,
Slight, or important, only by their place?
Titles are marks of honest men, and wise;
The fool, or knave, that wears a title, lies.
They that on glorious ancestors enlarge,
Produce their debt, instead of their discharge.
Dorset, let those who proudly boast their line,
Like thee, in worth hereditary, shine.

Vain as false greatness is, the muse must own
We want not fools to buy that Bristol stone;
Mean sons of earth, who, on a south-sea tide
Of full success, swarm into wealth and pride;
Knock with a purse of gold at Anstis' gate,
And beg to be descended from the great.
When men of infamy to grandeur soar,
They light a torch to show their shame the more.
Those governments which curb not evils, cause!
And a rich knave 's a libel on our laws.
Belus with solid glory will be crown'd;
He buys no phantom, no vain empty sound;
But builds himself a name; and, to be great,
Sinks in a quarry an immense estate!
In cost and grandeur, Chandos he 'll outdo;
And Burlington, thy taste is not so true.
The pile is finish'd! ev'ry toil is past;
And full perfection is arriv'd at last;
When, lo! my lord to some small corner runs,
And leaves state-rooms to strangers and to duns.
The man who builds, and wants wherewith to pay,
Provides a home from which to run away.
In Britain, what is many a lordly seat,
But a discharge in full for an estate?
In smaller compass lies Pygmalion's fame;
Not domes, but antique statues, are his flame:
Not Fountaine's self more Parian charms has known,
Nor is good Pembroke more in love with stone.
The bailiffs come (rude men profanely bold!)

And bid him turn his Venus into gold.
" No, sirs," he cries; " I 'll sooner rot in jail;
Shall Grecian arts be truck'd for English bail?"
Such heads might make their very busto's laugh:
His daughter starves; but * Cleopatra's safe.
Men, overloaded with a large estate,
May spill their treasure in a nice conceit:
The rich may be polite; but, oh! 'tis sad
To say you 're curious, when we swear you 're mad.
By your revenue measure your expense;
And to your funds and acres join your sense.
No man is bless'd by accident or guess;
True wisdom is the price of happiness:
Yet few without long discipline are sage;
And our youth only lays up sighs for age.
But how, my muse, canst thou resist so long
The bright temptation of the courtly throng,
Thy most inviting theme? The court affords
Much food for satire; — it abounds in lords.
" What lords are those saluting with a grin?"
One is just out, and one as lately in.
" How comes it then to pass we see preside
On both their brows an equal share of pride?"
Pride, that impartial passion, reigns through all,
Attends our glory, nor deserts our fall.
As in its home it triumphs in high place,
And frowns a haughty exile in disgrace.
Some lords it bids admire their wands so white,

* A famous statue.

Which bloom, like Aaron's, to their ravish'd sight:
Some lords it bids resign ; and turn their wands,
Like Moses', into serpents in their hands.
These sink, as divers, for renown ; and boast,
With pride inverted, of their honours lost.
But against reason sure 'tis equal sin,
To boast of merely being out, or in.
What numbers here, through odd ambition, strive
To seem the most transported things alive !
As if by joy, desert was understood ;
And all the fortunate were wise and good.
Hence aching bosoms wear a visage gay,
And stifled groans frequent the ball and play.
Completely drest by * Monteuil, and grimace,
They take their birth-day suit, and public face:
Their smiles are only part of what they wear,
Put off at night, with Lady B——'s hair.
What bodily fatigue is half so bad ?
With anxious care they labour to be glad.
What numbers, here, would into fame advance,
Conscious of merit, in the coxcomb's dance ;
The tavern ! park ! assembly ! mask ! and play !
Those dear destroyers of the tedious day !
That wheel of fops ! that saunter of the town !
Call it diversion, and the pill goes down.
Fools grin on fools, and, stoic-like, support,
Without one sigh, the pleasures of a court.
Courts can give nothing, to the wise and good,

* A famous tailor.

But scorn of pomp, and love of solitude.
High stations tumult, but not bliss, create:
None think the great unhappy, but the great:
Fools gaze, and envy; envy darts a sting,
Which makes a swain as wretched as a king.
  I envy none their pageantry and show;
I envy none the gilding of their woe.
Give me, indulgent gods! with mind serene,
And guiltless heart, to range the sylvan scene;
No splendid poverty, no smiling care,
No well-bred hate, or servile grandeur, there:
There pleasing objects useful thought suggest;
The sense is ravish'd, and the soul is blest;
On every thorn delightful wisdom grows;
In every rill a sweet instruction flows.
But some, untaught, o'erhear the whisp'ring rill,
In spite of sacred leisure, blockheads still;
Nor shoots up folly to a nobler bloom
In her own native soil, the drawing-room.
  The squire is proud to see his coursers strain,
Or well-breath'd beagles sweep along the plain.
Say, dear Hippolitus, (whose drink is ale,
Whose erudition is a Christmas tale,
Whose mistress is saluted with a smack,
And friend receiv'd with thumps upon the back,)
When thy sleek gelding nimbly leaps the mound,
And Ringwood opens on the tainted ground,
Is that thy praise? Let Ringwood's fame alone;
Just Ringwood leaves each animal his own;
Nor envies, when a gipsy you commit,

And shake the clumsy bench with country wit;
When you the dullest of dull things have said,
And then ask pardon for the jest you made.
Here breathe, my muse! and then thy task renew:
Ten thousand fools unsung are still in view.
Fewer lay-atheists made by church debates;
Fewer great beggars fam'd for large estates;
Ladies, whose love is constant as the wind;
Cits, who prefer a guinea to mankind;
Fewer grave lords to Scrope discreetly bend;
And fewer shocks a statesman gives his friend.
Is there a man of an eternal vein,
Who lulls the town in winter with his strain,
At Bath, in summer, chants the reigning lass,
And sweetly whistles, as the waters pass?
Is there a tongue, like Delia's o'er her cup,
That runs for ages without winding up?
Is there, whom his tenth epic mounts to fame?
Such, and such only, might exhaust my theme:
Nor would these heroes of the task be glad;
For who can write so fast as men run mad?

SATIRE II.

My muse, proceed, and reach thy destin'd end;
Though toils and danger the bold task attend.

Heroes and gods make other poems fine;
Plain satire calls for sense in every line:
Then, to what swarms thy faults I dare expose!
All friends to vice and folly are thy foes.
When such the foe, a war eternal wage;
'Tis most ill-nature to repress thy rage:
And if these strains some nobler muse excite,
I'll glory in the verse I did not write.
So weak are human kind by nature made,
Or to such weakness by their vice betray'd,
Almighty vanity! to thee they owe
Their zest of pleasure, and their balm of woe.
Thou, like the sun, all colours dost contain,
Varying, like rays of light, on drops of rain.
For every soul finds reasons to be proud,
Tho' hiss'd and hooted by the pointing crowd.
Warm in pursuit of foxes, and renown,
*Hippolitus demands the sylvan crown;
But Florio's fame, the product of a shower,
Grows in his garden, an illustrious flower!
Why teems the earth? Why melt the vernal skies?
Why shines the sun? To make †Paul Diack rise.
From morn to night has Florio gazing stood,
And wonder'd how the gods could be so good;
What shape! what hue! was ever nymph so fair!
He dotes! he dies! he too is rooted there.

* This refers to the first satire.
† The name of a tulip.

O solid bliss! which nothing can destroy,
Except a cat, bird, snail, or idle boy.
In fame's full bloom lies Florio down at night,
And wakes next day a most inglorious wight;
The tulip 's dead! See thy fair sister's fate,
O C——! and be kind ere 'tis too late.
Nor are those enemies I mention'd, all;
Beware, O florist, thy ambition's fall.
A friend of mine indulg'd this noble flame;
A quaker serv'd him, Adam was his name;
To one lov'd tulip oft the master went,
Hung o'er it, and whole days in rapture spent;
But came, and miss'd it, one ill-fated hour:
He rag'd! he roar'd! "What demon cropt my flower?"
Serene, quoth Adam, "Lo! 'twas crusht by me;
Fall'n is the Baal to which thou bow'dst thy knee."
But all men want amusement; and what crime
In such a paradise to fool their time?
None: but why proud of this? to fame they soar;
We grant they 're idle, if they 'll ask no more.
We smile at florists, we despise their joy,
And think their hearts enamour'd of a toy:
But are those wiser whom we most admire,
Survey with envy, and pursue with fire?
What 's he who sighs for wealth, or fame, or power?
Another Florio doting on a flower;
A short liv'd flower; and which has often sprung
From sordid arts, as Florio's out of dung.

With what, O Codrus! is thy fancy smit?
The flower of learning, and the bloom of wit.
The gaudy shelves with crimson bindings glow,
And Epictetus is a perfect beau.
How fit for thee! bound up in crimson too,
Gilt, and, like them, devoted to the view!
Thy books are furniture. Methinks 'tis hard
That science should be purchas'd by the yard;
And Tonson, turn'd upholsterer, send home
The gilded leather to fit up thy room.
If not to some peculiar end design'd,
Study 's the specious trifling of the mind;
Or is at best a secondary aim,
A chase for sport alone, and not for game.
If so, sure they who the mere volume prize,
But love the thicket where the quarry lies.
On buying books Lorenzo long was bent,
But found at length that it reduc'd his rent;
His farms were flown; when, lo! a sale comes on,
A choice collection! what is to be done?
He sells his last; for he the whole will buy;
Sells ev'n his house; nay, wants whereon to lie:
So high the gen'rous ardour of the man
For Romans, Greeks, and Orientals ran.
When terms were drawn, and brought him by the clerk,
Lorenzo sign'd the bargain — with his mark.
Unlearned men of books assume the care,
As eunuchs are the guardians of the fair.
Not in his authors' liveries alone

Is Codrus' erudite ambition shown:
Editions various, at high prices bought,
Inform the world what Codrus would be thought;
And to his cost another must succeed
To pay a sage, who says that he can read;
Who titles knows, and indexes has seen;
But leaves to Chesterfield what lies between;
Of pompous books who shuns the proud expense,
And humbly is contented with their sense.
O Stanhope, whose accomplishments make good
The promise of a long illustrious blood,
In arts and manners eminently grac'd,
The strictest honour! and the finest taste!
Accept this verse; if satire can agree
With so consummate a humanity.
By your example would Hilario mend,
How would it grace the talents of my friend,
Who, with the charms of his own genius smit,
Conceives all virtues are compris'd in wit!
But time his fervent petulance may cool;
For though he is a wit, he is no fool.
In time he 'll learn to use, not waste, his sense;
Nor make a frailty of an excellence.
He spares nor friend, nor foe; but calls to mind,
Like doomsday, all the faults of all mankind.
What though wit tickles? tickling is unsafe,
If still 'tis painful while it makes us laugh.
Who, for the poor renown of being smart,
Would leave a sting within a brother's heart?
Parts may be prais'd, good-nature is ador'd;

Then draw your wit as seldom as your sword;
And never on the weak; or you 'll appear
As there no hero, no great genius here.
As in smooth oil the razor best is whet,
So wit is by politeness sharpest set:
Their want of edge from their offence is seen;
Both pain us least when exquisitely keen.
The fame men give is for the joy they find;
Dull is the jester, when the joke 's unkind.
Since Marcus, doubtless, thinks himself a wit,
To pay my compliment, what place so fit?
His most facetious *letters came to hand,
Which my first satire sweetly reprimand:
If that a just offence to Marcus gave,
Say, Marcus, which art thou, a fool, or knave?
For all but such with caution I forbore;
That thou wast either, I ne'er knew before:
I know thee now, both what thou art, and who;
No mask so good, but Marcus must shine through:
False names are vain, thy lines their author tell;
Thy best concealment had been writing well:
But thou a brave neglect of fame hast shown,
Of others' fame, great genius! and thy own.
Write on unheeded; and this maxim know,
The man who pardons, disappoints his foe.
In malice to proud wits, some proudly lull
Their peevish reason; vain of being dull;
When some home joke has stung their solemn souls,

* Letters sent to the author, signed Marcus.

In vengeance they determine to be fools;
Through spleen, that little nature gave, make less,
Quite zealous in the way of heaviness;
To lumps inanimate a fondness take;
And disinherit sons that are awake.
These, when their utmost venom they would spit,
Most barbarously tell you — "He 's a wit."
Poor negroes, thus, to show their burning spite
To cacodemons, say, they 're dev'lish white.
  Lampridius, from the bottom of his breast,
Sighs o'er one child; but triumphs in the rest.
How just his grief! one carries in his head
A less proportion of the father's lead;
And is in danger, without special grace,
To rise above a justice of the peace.
The dunghill breed of men a diamond scorn,
And feel a passion for a grain of corn;
Some stupid, plodding, monkey-loving wight,
Who wins their hearts by knowing black from white,
Who with much pains, exerting all his sense,
Can range aright his shillings, pounds, and pence.
  The booby father craves a booby son;
And by heaven's blessing thinks himself undone.
  Wants of all kinds are made to fame a plea;
One learns to lisp; another not to see:
Miss D——, tottering, catches at your hand:
Was ever thing so pretty born to stand?
Whilst these, what nature gave, disown, through pride,
Others affect what nature has denied;

What nature has denied, fools will pursue,
As apes are ever walking upon two.
  Crassus, a grateful sage, our awe and sport!
Supports grave forms; for forms the sage support.
He hems; and cries, with an important air,
"If yonder clouds withdraw it will be fair:"
Then quotes the Stagyrite, to prove it true;
And adds, "The learn'd delight in something new."
Is 't not enough the blockhead scarce can read,
But must he wisely look, and gravely plead?
As far a formalist from wisdom sits,
In judging eyes, as libertines from wits.
  These subtle wights (so blind are mortal men,
Though satire couch them with her keenest pen)
For ever will hang out a solemn face,
To put off nonsense with a better grace:
As pedlers with some hero's head make bold,
Illustrious mark! where pins are to be sold.
What 's the bent brow, or neck in thought reclin'd?
The body's wisdom to conceal the mind.
A man of sense can artifice disdain;
As men of wealth may venture to go plain;
And be this truth eternal ne'er forgot,
Solemnity 's a cover for a sot.
I find the fool, when I behold the screen;
For 'tis the wise man's interest to be seen.
  Hence, Chesterfield, that openness of heart,
And just disdain for that poor mimic art;
Hence (manly praise!) that manner nobly free,
Which all admire, and I commend, in thee.

With generous scorn how oft hast thou survey'd
Of court and town the noontide masquerade;
Where swarms of knaves the vizor quite disgrace,
And hide secure behind a naked face?
Where nature's end of language is declin'd,
And men talk only to conceal the mind;
Where gen'rous hearts the greatest hazard run,
And he who trusts a brother, is undone?
These all their care expend on outward show
For wealth and fame; for fame alone, the beau.
Of late at White's was young Florello seen!
How blank his look! how discompos'd his mien!
So hard it proves in grief sincere to feign!
Sunk were his spirits; for his coat was plain.
Next day his breast regain'd its wonted peace;
His health was mended with a silver lace.
A curious artist, long inur'd to toils
Of gentler sort, with combs, and fragrant oils,
Whether by chance, or by some god inspir'd,
So touch'd his curls, his mighty soul was fir'd.
The well swoln ties an equal homage claim,
And either shoulder has its share of fame;
His sumptuous watch-case, tho' conceal'd it lies,
Like a good conscience, solid joy supplies.
He only thinks himself (so far from vain!)
Stanhope in wit, in breeding Deloraine.
Whene'er, by seeming chance, he throws his eye
On mirrors that reflect his Tyrian dye,
With how sublime a transport leaps his heart!
But fate ordains that dearest friends must part.

In active measures, brought from France, he wheels,
And triumphs, conscious of his learned heels.
  So have I seen, on some bright summer's day,
A calf of genius, debonnair and gay,
Dance on the bank, as if inspir'd by fame,
Fond of the pretty fellow in the stream.
  Morose is sunk with shame, whene'er surpris'd
In linen clean, or peruke undisguis'd.
No sublunary chance his vestments fear;
Valu'd, like leopards, as their spots appear.
A fam'd surtout he wears, which once was blue,
And his foot swims in a capacious shoe;
One day his wife (for who can wives reclaim?)
Levell'd her barb'rous needle at his fame:
But open force was vain; by night she went,
And while he slept, surpris'd the darling rent:
Where yawn'd the frieze is now become a doubt;
And glory, at one entrance, quite shut out.*
  He scorns Florello, and Florello him;
This hates the filthy creature; that, the prim:
Thus, in each other, both these fools despise
Their own dear selves, with undiscerning eyes;
Their methods various, but alike their aim;
The sloven and the fopling are the same.
  Ye whigs and tories! thus it fares with you,
When party rage too warmly you pursue;
Then both club nonsense, and impetuous pride,
And folly joins whom sentiments divide.

* Milton.

You vent your spleen, as monkeys, when they pass,
Scratch at the mimic monkey in the glass;
While both are one: and henceforth be it known,
Fools of both sides shall stand for fools alone.
"But who art thou?" methinks Florello cries;
"Of all thy species art thou only wise?"
Since smallest things can give our sins a twitch,
As crossing straws retard a passing witch,
Florello, thou my monitor shalt be;
I'll conjure thus some profit out of thee.
O thou myself! abroad our counsels roam,
And, like ill husbands, take no care at home:
Thou too art wounded with the common dart,
And love of fame lies throbbing at thy heart;
And what wise means to gain it hast thou chose?
Know, fame and fortune both are made of prose.
Is thy ambition sweating for a rhyme,
Thou unambitious fool, at this late time?
While I a moment name, a moment's past;
I'm nearer death in this verse, than the last:
What then is to be done? Be wise with speed;
A fool at forty is a fool indeed.
And what so foolish as the chance of fame?
How vain the prize! how impotent our aim!
For what are men who grasp at praise sublime,
But bubbles on the rapid stream of time,
That rise, and fall, that swell, and are no more,
Born, and forgot, ten thousand in an hour?

SATIRE III.

TO THE RIGHT HONOURABLE MR. DODINGTON.

LONG, Dodington, in debt, I long have sought
To ease the burthen of my grateful thought;
And now a poet's gratitude you see;
Grant him two favours, and he 'll ask for three:
For whose the present glory, or the gain?
You give protection, I a worthless strain.
You love and feel the poet's sacred flame,
And know the basis of a solid fame;
Tho' prone to like, yet cautious to commend,
You read with all the malice of a friend;
Nor favour my attempts that way alone,
But, more to raise my verse, conceal your own.
An ill-tim'd modesty! turn ages o'er,
When wanted Britain bright examples more?
Her learning, and her genius too, decays,
And dark and cold are her declining days;
As if men now were of another cast,
They meanly live on alms of ages past.
Men still are men; and they who boldly dare,
Shall triumph o'er the sons of cold despair;
Or, if they fail, they justly still take place
Of such who run in debt for their disgrace;
Who borrow much, then fairly make it known,
And damn it with improvements of their own.
We bring some new materials, and what 's old
New cast with care, and in no borrow'd mould;

Late times the verse may read, if these refuse ;
And from sour critics vindicate the muse.
"Your work is long," the critics cry. 'Tis true,
And lengthens still, to take in fools like you:
Shorten my labour, if its length you blame ;
For, grow but wise, you rob me of my game ;
As hunted hags, who, while the dogs pursue,
Renounce their four legs, and start up on two.
Like the bold bird upon the banks of Nile,
That picks the teeth of the dire crocodile,
Will I enjoy, (dread feast !) the critic's rage,
And with the fell destroyer feed my page.
For what ambitious fools are more to blame,
Than those who thunder in the critic's name?
Good authors damn'd, have their revenge in this,
To see what wretches gain the praise they miss.
Balbutius, muffled in his sable cloak,
Like an old Druid from his hollow oak,
As ravens solemn, and as boding, cries,
"Ten thousand worlds for the three unities!"
Ye doctors sage, who thro' Parnassus teach,
Or quit the tub, or practise what you preach.
One judges as the weather dictates; right
The poem is at noon, and wrong at night:
Another judges by a surer gage,
An author's principles, or parentage ;
Since his great ancestors in Flanders fell,
The poem doubtless must be written well.
Another judges by the writer's look ;
Another judges, for he bought the book ;

Some judge, their knack of judging wrong to keep;
Some judge, because it is too soon to sleep.
  Thus all will judge, and with one single aim,
To gain themselves, not give the writer, fame.
The very best ambitiously advise,
Half to serve you, and half to pass for wise.
  Critics on verse, as squibs on triumphs wait,
Proclaim the glory, and augment the state;
Hot, envious, noisy, proud, the scribbling fry
Burn, hiss, and bounce, waste paper, stink, and die.
Rail on, my friends! what more my verse can crown
Than Compton's smile, and your obliging frown?
  Not all on books their criticism waste:
The genius of a dish some justly taste,
And eat their way to fame; with anxious thought
The salmon is refus'd, the turbot bought.
Impatient art rebukes the sun's delay,
And bids December yield the fruits of May;
Their various cares in one great point combine
The business of their lives, that is — to dine.
Half of their precious day they give the feast;
And to a kind digestion spare the rest.
Apicius, here, the taster of the town,
Feeds twice a week, to settle their renown.
  These worthies of the palate guard with care
The sacred annals of their bills of fare;
In those choice books their panegyrics read,
And scorn the creatures that for hunger feed.
If man by feeding well commences great,
Much more the worm to whom that man is meat.

To glory some advance a lying claim,
Thieves of renown, and pilferers of fame:
Their front supplies what their ambition lacks;
They know a thousand lords, behind their backs.
Cottil is apt to wink upon a peer,
When turn'd away, with a familiar leer;
And Harvey's eyes, unmercifully keen,
Have murder'd fops, by whom she ne'er was seen.
Niger adopts stray libels; wisely prone
To covet shame still greater than his own.
Bathyllus, in the winter of threescore,
Belies his innocence, and keeps a whore.
Absence of mind Brabantio turns to fame,
Learns to mistake, nor knows his brother's name;
Has words and thoughts in nice disorder set,
And takes a memorandum to forget.
Thus vain, not knowing what adorns, or blots,
Men forge the patents, that create them sots.
As love of pleasure into pain betrays,
So most grow infamous thro' love of praise.
But whence for praise can such an ardour rise,
When those, who bring that incense, we despise?
For such the vanity of great and small,
Contempt goes round, and all men laugh at all.
Nor can ev'n satire blame them; for, 'tis true,
They have most ample cause for what they do.
O fruitful Britain! doubtless thou wast meant
A nurse of fools, to stock the continent.
Tho' Phœbus and the Nine for ever mow,
Rank folly underneath the scythe will grow.

The plenteous harvest calls me forward still,
Till I surpass in length my lawyer's bill;
A Welsh descent, which well paid heralds damn;
Or, longer still, a Dutchman's epigram.
When, cloy'd, in fury I throw down my pen,
In comes a coxcomb, and I write again.
See Tityrus, with merriment possest,
Is burst with laughter, ere he hears the jest:
What need he stay? for when the joke is o'er,
His teeth will be no whiter than before.
Is there of these, ye fair! so great a dearth,
That you need purchase monkeys for your mirth?
Some, vain of paintings, bid the world admire;
Of houses some; nay, houses that they hire:
Some (perfect wisdom!) of a beauteous wife;
And boast, like Cordeliers, a scourge for life.
Sometimes, thro' pride, the sexes change their airs;
My lord has vapours, and my lady swears;
Then, stranger still! on turning of the wind,
My lord wears breeches, and my lady 's kind.
To show the strength, and infamy of pride,
By all 'tis follow'd, and by all denied.
What numbers are there, which at once pursue
Praise, and the glory to contemn it, too!
Vincenna knows self-praise betrays to shame,
And therefore lays a stratagem for fame;
Makes his approach in modesty's disguise,
To win applause; and takes it by surprise.
"To err," says he, "in small things, is my fate."

You know your answer, he 's exact in great.
" My style," says he, " is rude and full of faults."
But oh! what sense! what energy of thoughts!
That he wants algebra, he must confess;
But not a soul to give our arms success.
" Ah; that 's a hit indeed," Vincenna cries;
" But who in heat of blood was ever wise?
I own 'twas wrong, when thousands call'd me back,
To make that hopeless, ill-advis'd attack;
All say, 'twas madness; nor dare I deny;
Sure never fool so well deserv'd to die."
Could this deceive in others, to be free,
It ne'er, Vincenna, could deceive in thee;
Whose conduct is a comment to thy tongue,
So clear, the dullest cannot take thee wrong.
Thou on one sleeve wilt thy revenues wear;
And haunt the court, without a prospect there.
Are these expedients for renown? Confess
Thy little self, that I may scorn thee less.
Be wise, Vincenna, and the court forsake;
Our fortunes there, nor thou, nor I, shall make.
Ev'n men of merit, ere their point they gain,
In hardy service make a long campaign;
Most manfully besiege their patron's gate,
And oft repuls'd, as oft attack the great
With painful art, and application warm,
And take, at last, some little place by storm;
Enough to keep two shoes on Sunday clean,
And starve upon discreetly, in Sheer Lane.
Already this thy fortune can afford;

Then starve without the favour of my lord.
'Tis true, great fortunes some great men confer;
But often, ev'n in doing right, they err:
From caprice, not from choice, their favours come;
They give, but think it toil to know to whom:
The man that 's nearest, yawning, they advance:
'Tis inhumanity to bless by chance.
If merit sues, and greatness is so loth
To break its downy trance, I pity both.
I grant at court, Philander, at his need,
(Thanks to his lovely wife) finds friends indeed.
Of every charm and virtue she 's possest:
Philander! thou art exquisitely blest;
The public envy! Now then, 'tis allow'd,
The man is found, who may be justly proud:
But, see! how sickly is ambition's taste!
Ambition feeds on trash, and loaths a feast;
For, lo! Philander, of reproach afraid,
In secret loves his wife, but keeps her maid.
Some nymphs sell reputation; others buy;
And love a market where the rates run high:
Italian music 's sweet, because 'tis dear;
Their vanity is tickled, not their ear:
Their taste would lessen, if the prices fell,
And Shakespeare's wretched stuff do quite as well;
Away the disenchanted fair would throng,
And own that English is their mother tongue.
To show how much our northern tastes refine,
Imported nymphs our peeresses outshine;

While tradesmen starve, these Philomels are gay;
For generous lords had rather give than pay.
  Behold the masquerade's fantastic scene!
The legislature join'd with Drury Lane!
When Britain calls, th' embroider'd patriots run,
And serve their country — if the dance is done.
"Are we not then allow'd to be polite?"
Yes, doubtless; but first set your notions right.
Worth, of politeness, is the needful ground;
Where that is wanting, this can ne'er be found.
Triflers not e'en in trifles can excel;
'Tis solid bodies only polish well.
  Great, chosen prophet! For these latter days,
To turn a willing world from righteous ways!
Well, Heydegger, dost thou thy master serve;
Well has he seen his servant should not starve.
Thou to his name hast splendid temples rais'd;
In various forms of worship seen him prais'd,
Gaudy devotion, like a Roman, shown,
And sung sweet anthems in a tongue unknown.
Inferior off'rings to thy god of vice
Are duly paid, in fiddles, cards, and dice;
Thy sacrifice supreme, a hundred maids!
That solemn rite of midnight masquerades!
If maids the quite exhausted town denies,
A hundred heads of cuckolds may suffice.
Thou smil'st, well pleas'd with the converted land,
To see the fifty churches at a stand.
And that thy minister may never fail,
But what thy hand has planted still prevail,

Of minor prophets a succession sure
The propagation of thy zeal secure.
See commons, peers, and ministers of state,
In solemn council met, and deep debate!
What godlike enterprise is taking birth?
What wonder opens on th' expecting earth?
'Tis done! with loud applause the council rings!
Fix'd is the fate of whores and fiddle-strings!
Tho' bold these truths, thou, muse, with truths like these,
Wilt none offend, whom 'tis a praise to please:
Let others flatter to be flatter'd, thou,
Like just tribunals, bend an awful brow.
How terrible it were to common sense,
To write a satire, which gave none offence!
And, since from life I take the draughts you see,
If men dislike them, do they censure me?
The fool, and knave, 'tis glorious to offend,
And godlike an attempt the world to mend;
The world, where lucky throws to blockheads fall,
Knaves know the game, and honest men pay all.
How hard for real worth to gain its price!
A man shall make his fortune in a trice,
If blest with pliant, tho' but slender, sense,
Feign'd modesty, and real impudence:
A supple knee, smooth tongue, an easy grace,
A curse within, a smile upon his face;
A beauteous sister, or convenient wife,
Are prizes in the lottery of life;
Genius and virtue they will soon defeat,

And lodge you in the bosom of the great.
To merit, is but to provide a pain
For men's refusing what you ought to gain.
  May, Dodington, this maxim fail in you,
Whom my presaging thoughts already view
By Walpole's conduct fir'd, and friendship grac'd,
Still higher in your prince's favour plac'd;
And lending, here, those awful councils aid,
Which you, abroad, with such success obey'd:
Bear this from one, who holds your friendship dear;
What most we wish, with ease we fancy near.

SATIRE IV.

TO THE RIGHT HONOURABLE SIR SPENCER COMPTON.

ROUND some fair tree th' ambitious woodbine grows,
And breathes her sweets on the supporting boughs;
So sweet the verse, th' ambitious verse, should be,
(O! pardon mine) that hopes support from thee;
Thee, Compton, born o'er senates to preside,
Their dignity to raise, their councils guide;
Deep to discern, and widely to survey,
And kingdoms' fates, without ambition, weigh;
Of distant virtues nice extremes to blend,
The crown's asserter, and the people's friend:
Nor dost thou scorn, amid sublimer views,
To listen to the labours of the muse;
Thy smiles protect her, while thy talents fire,

And 'tis but half thy glory to inspire.
Vex'd at a public fame, so justly won,
The jealous Chremes is with spleen undone;
Chremes, for airy pensions of renown,
Devotes his service to the state and crown;
All schemes he knows, and, knowing, all improves,
Tho' Britain 's thankless, still this patriot loves:
But patriots differ; some may shed their blood,
He drinks his coffee, for the public good;
Consults the sacred steam, and there foresees
What storms, or sunshine, Providence decrees;
Knows, for each day, the weather of our fate;
A quid nunc is an almanack of state.
You smile, and think this statesman void of use:
Why may not time his secret worth produce?
Since apes can roast the choice Castanian nut,
Since steeds of genius are expert at put;
Since half the senate not content can say,
Geese nations save, and puppies plots betray.
What makes him model realms, and counsel kings?
An incapacity for smaller things:
Poor Chremes can't conduct his own estate,
And thence has undertaken Europe's fate.
Gehenno leaves the realm to Chremes' skill,
And boldly claims a province higher still:
To raise a name, th' ambitious boy has got,
At once, a Bible, and a shoulder-knot;
Deep in the secret, he looks thro' the whole,
And pities the dull rogue that saves his soul;

To talk with rev'rence you must take good heed,
Nor shock his tender reason with the creed:
Howe'er well bred, in public he complies,
Obliging friends alone with blasphemies.
Peerage is poison, good estates are bad
For this disease; poor rogues run seldom mad.
Have not attainders brought unhop'd relief,
And falling stocks quite cur'd an unbelief?
While the sun shines, Blunt talks with wondrous force;
But thunder mars small beer, and weak discourse.
Such useful instruments the weather show,
Just as their mercury is high or low:
Health chiefly keeps an atheist in the dark;
A fever argues better than a Clarke:
Let but the logic in his pulse decay,
The Grecian he'll renounce, and learn to pray;
While C—— mourns, with an unfeign'd zeal,
Th' apostate youth, who reason'd once so well.
C——, who makes so merry with the creed,
He almost thinks he disbelieves indeed;
But only thinks so; to give both their due,
Satan, and he, believe, and tremble too.
Of some for glory such the boundless rage,
That they're the blackest scandal of their age.
Narcissus the Tartarian club disclaims;
Nay, a free-mason, with some terror, names;
Omits no duty; nor can envy say,
He miss'd, these many years, the church, or play:
He makes no noise in parliament, 'tis true;

But pays his debts, and visit, when 'tis due;
His character and gloves are ever clean,
And then, he can out-bow the bowing dean;
A smile eternal on his lip he wears,
Which equally the wise and worthless shares.
In gay fatigues, this most undaunted chief,
Patient of idleness beyond belief,
Most charitably lends the town his face,
For ornament, in ev'ry public place;
As sure as cards, he to th' assembly comes,
And is the furniture of drawing-rooms:
When ombre calls, his hand and heart are free,
And, join'd to two, he fails not — to make three:
Narcissus is the glory of his race;
For who does nothing with a better grace?
To deck my list, by nature were design'd
Such shining expletives of human kind,
Who want, while thro' blank life they dream along,
Sense to be right, and passion to be wrong.
To counterpoise this hero of the mode,
Some for renown are singular and odd;
What other men dislike, is sure to please,
Of all mankind, these dear antipodes;
Thro' pride, not malice, they run counter still,
And birthdays are their days of dressing ill,
Arbuthnot is a fool, and F—— a sage,
S—ly will fright you, E—— engage;
By nature streams run backward, flame descends,
Stones mount, and Sussex is the worst of friends;
They take their rest by day, and wake by night,

And blush, if you surprise them in the right;
If they by chance blurt out, ere well aware,
A swan is white, or Queensberry is fair.
Nothing exceeds in ridicule, no doubt,
A fool in fashion, but a fool that 's out,
His passion for absurdity 's so strong.
He cannot bear a rival in the wrong;
Tho' wrong the mode, comply; more sense is shown
In wearing others' follies, than your own.
If what is out of fashion most you prize,
Methinks you should endeavour to be wise.
But what in oddness can be more sublime
Than Sloane, the foremost toyman of his time?
His nice ambition lies in curious fancies,
His daughter's portion a rich shell inhances,
And Ashmole's baby-house is, in his view,
Britannia's golden mine, a rich Peru!
How his eyes languish! how his thoughts adore
That painted coat, which Joseph never wore!
He shows, on holidays, a sacred pin,
That touch'd the ruff, that touch'd Queen Bess's chin.
"Since that great dearth our chronicles deplore,
Since that great plague that swept as many more,
Was ever year unblest as this?" he 'll cry,
"It has not brought us one new butterfly!"
In times that suffer such learn'd men as these,
Unhappy I——y! how came you to please?
Not gaudy butterflies are Lico's game;
But, in effect, his chase is much the same;

Warm in pursuit, he levees all the great,
Stanch to the foot of title and estate:
Where'er their lordships go, they never find
Or Lico, or their shadows, lag behind!
He sets them sure, where'er their lordships run,
Close at their elbows, as a morning dun;
As if their grandeur, by contagion, wrought,
And fame was, like a fever, to be caught:
But after seven years' dance, from place to place,
The *Dane is more familiar with his grace.
  Who 'd be a crutch to prop a rotten peer;
Or living pendant dangling at his ear,
For ever whisp'ring secrets, which were blown
For months before, by trumpets, thro' the town?
Who 'd be a glass, with flattering grimace,
Still to reflect the temper of his face;
Or happy pin to stick upon his sleeve,
When my lord 's gracious, and vouchsafes it leave;
Or cushion, when his heaviness shall please
To loll, or thump it, for his better ease;
Or a vile butt, for noon, or night, bespoke,
When the peer rashly swears he 'll club his joke?
Who 'd shake with laughter, tho' he could not find
His lordship's jest; or, if his nose broke wind,
For blessings to the gods profoundly bow,
That can cry, chimney sweep, or drive a plough?
With terms like these, how mean the tribe that close!
Scarce meaner they, who terms like these, impose.

*A Danish dog of the Duke of Argyle.

But what 's the tribe most likely to comply?
The men of ink, or ancient authors lie;
The writing tribe, who shameless auctions hold
Of praise, by inch of candle to be sold:
All men they flatter, but themselves the most,
With deathless fame, their everlasting boast:
For fame no cully makes so much her jest,
As her old constant spark, the bard profest.
" Boyle shines in council, Mordaunt in the fight,
Pelham 's magnificent; but I can write,
And what to my great soul like glory dear?"
Till some god whispers in his tingling ear,
That fame 's unwholesome taken without meat,
And life is best sustain'd by what is eat:
Grown lean, and wise, he curses what he writ,
And wishes all his wants were in his wit.
Ay! what avails it, when his dinner 's lost,
That his triumphant name adorns a post?
Or that his shining page (provoking fate!)
Defends sirloins, which sons of dulness eat?
What foe to verse without compassion hears,
What cruel prose-man can refrain from tears,
When the poor muse, for less than half a crown,
A prostitute on every bulk in town,
With other whores undone, tho' not in print,
Clubs credit for Geneva in the mint?
Ye bards! why will you sing, tho' uninspir'd?
Ye bards! why will you starve, to be admir'd?
Defunct by Phœbus' laws, beyond redress,
Why will your spectres haunt the frighted press?

Bad metre, that excrescence of the head,
Like hair, will sprout, altho' the poet 's dead.
All other trades demand, verse makers beg;
A dedication is a wooden leg;
A barren Labeo, the true mumper's fashion,
Exposes borrow'd brats to move compassion.
Tho' such myself, vile bards I discommend;
Nay more, tho' gentle Damon is my friend.
"Is 't then a crime to write?"—If talent rare
Proclaim the god, the crime is to forbear:
For some, tho' few, there are large-minded men,
Who watch unseen the labours of the pen;
Who know the muse's worth, and therefore court,
Their deeds her theme, their beauty her support;
Who serve, unask'd, the least pretence to wit;
My sole excuse, alas! for having writ.
Argyll true wit is studious to restore;
And Dorset smiles, if Phœbus smil'd before;
Pembroke in years the long-lov'd arts admires,
And Henrietta like a muse inspires.
But, ah! not inspiration can obtain
That fame, which poets languish for in vain.
How mad their aim, who thirst for glory, strive
To grasp, what no man can possess alive!
Fame 's a reversion in which men take place
(O late reversion!) at their own decease.
This truth sagacious Lintot knows so well,
He starves his authors, that their works may sell.
That fame is wealth, fantastic poets cry;
That wealth is fame, another clan reply;

Who know no guilt, no scandal, but in rags;
And swell in just proportion to their bags.
Nor only the low-born, deform'd and old,
Think glory nothing but the beams of gold;
The first young lord, which in the mall you meet,
Shall match the veriest hunchs in Lombard-street,
From rescu'd candles' ends, who rais'd a sum,
And starves to join a penny to a plumb.
A beardless miser! 'tis a guilt unknown
To former times, a scandal all our own.
  Of ardent lovers, the true modern band
Will mortgage Celia to redeem their land.
For love, young, noble, rich, Castalio dies:
Name but the fair, love swells into his eyes.
Divine Monimia, thy fond fears lay down;
No rival can prevail, — but half a crown.
  He glories to late times to be convey'd,
Not for the poor he has reliev'd, but made:
Not such ambition his great fathers fir'd,
When Harry conquer'd, and half France expir'd:
He'd be a slave, a pimp, a dog, for gain:
Nay, a dull sheriff, for his golden chain.
  "Who'd be a slave?" the gallant colonel cries,
While love of glory sparkles from his eyes:
To deathless fame he loudly pleads his right, —
Just is his title, — for he will not fight:
All soldiers valour, all divines have grace,
As maids of honour beauty, — by their place:
But, when indulging on the last campaign,
His lofty terms climb o'er the hills of slain;

He gives the foes he slew, at each vain word,
A sweet revenge, and half absolves his sword.
  Of boasting more than of a bomb afraid,
A soldier should be modest as a maid:
Fame is a bubble the reserv'd enjoy;
Who strive to grasp it, as they touch, destroy:
'T is the world's debt to deeds of high degree;
But if you pay yourself, the world is free.
  Were there no tongue to speak them but his own,
Augustus' deeds in arms had ne'er been known.
Augustus' deeds! if that ambiguous name
Confounds my reader, and misguides his aim,
Such is the prince's worth, of whom I speak,
The Roman would not blush at the mistake.

SATIRE V. ON WOMEN.

> O fairest of creation! last and best
> Of all God's works! Creature in whom excell'd
> Whatever can to sight, or thought, be form'd!
> Holy, divine, good, amiable, or sweet!
> How art thou lost! ——————   MILTON.

NOR reigns ambition in bold man alone;
Soft female hearts the rude invader own:
But there, indeed, it deals in nicer things,
Than routing armies, and dethroning kings:
Attend, and you discern it in the fair
Conduct a finger, or reclaim a hair;

Or roll the lucid orbit of an eye;
Or, in full joy, elaborate a sigh.
The sex we honour, tho' their faults we blame;
Nay, thank their faults for such a fruitful theme:
A theme, fair ——! doubly kind to me,
Since satirizing those is praising thee;
Who wouldst not bear, too modestly refin'd,
A panegyric of a grosser kind.
Britannia's daughters, much more fair than nice,
Too fond of admiration, lose their price;
Worn in the public eye, give cheap delight
To throngs, and tarnish to the sated sight:
As unreserv'd, and beauteous, as the sun,
Through every sign of vanity they run;
Assemblies, parks, coarse feasts in city-halls,
Lectures, and trials, plays, committees, balls,
Wells, bedlams, executions, Smithfield scenes,
And fortune-tellers' caves, and lions' dens,
Taverns, exchanges, bridewells, drawing-rooms,
Installments, pillories, coronations, tombs,
Tumblers, and funerals, puppet-shows, reviews,
Sales, races, rabbits, (and still stranger!) pews.
Clarinda's bosom burns, but burns for fame;
And love lies vanquish'd in a nobler flame;
Warm gleams of hope she, now, dispenses; then,
Like April suns, dives into clouds again:
With all her lustre, now, her lover warms;
Then, out of ostentation, hides her charms:
'Tis, next, her pleasure sweetly to complain,
And to be taken with a sudden pain;

Then, she starts up, all ecstasy and bliss,
And is, sweet soul! just as sincere in this:
O how she rolls her charming eyes in spite!
And looks delightfully with all her might!
But, like our heroes, much more brave than wise,
She conquers for the triumph, not the prize.
Zara resembles Ætna crown'd with snows;
Without she freezes, and within she glows:
Twice ere the sun descends, with zeal inspir'd,
From the vain converse of the world retir'd,
She reads the psalms and chapters for the day,
In —— Cleopatra, or the last new play.
Thus gloomy Zara, with a solemn grace,
Deceives mankind, and hides behind her face.
Nor far beneath her in renown, is she,
Who, through good breeding, is ill company;
Whose manners will not let her larum cease,
Who thinks you are unhappy, when at peace;
To find you news, who racks her subtle head,
And vows — that her great-grandfather is dead.
A dearth of words a woman need not fear,
But 'tis a task indeed to learn — to hear:
In that the skill of conversation lies;
That shows, or makes, you both polite and wise.
Xantippe cries, "Let nymphs, who nought can say,
Be lost in silence, and resign the day;
And let the guilty wife her guilt confess,
By tame behaviour, and a soft address;"
Through virtue, she refuses to comply

With all the dictates of humanity;
Through wisdom, she refuses to submit
To wisdom's rules, and raves to prove her wit;
Then, her unblemish'd honour to maintain,
Rejects her husband's kindness with disdain:
But if, by chance, an ill-adapted word
Drops from the lip of her unwary lord,
Her darling china, in a whirlwind sent,
Just intimates the lady's discontent.
Wine may indeed excite the meekest dame;
But keen Xantippe, scorning borrow'd flame,
Can vent her thunders, and her lightnings play,
O'er cooling gruel, and composing tea:
Nor rests by night, but, more sincere than nice,
She shakes the curtains with her kind advice:
Doubly, like echo, sound is her delight,
And the last word is her eternal right.
Is 't not enough, plagues, wars, and famines rise
To lash our crimes, but must our wives be wise?
Famine, plague, war, and an unnumber'd throng
Of guilt-avenging ills, to man belong:
What black, what ceaseless cares besiege our state!
What strokes we feel from fancy, and from fate!
If fate forbears us, fancy strikes the blow;
We make misfortune; suicides in woe.
Superfluous aid! unnecessary skill!
Is nature backward to torment, or kill?
How oft the noon, how oft the midnight, bell,
(That iron tongue of death!) with solemn knell,

On folly's errands as we vainly roam,
Knocks at our hearts, and finds our thoughts from
home!
Men drop so fast, ere life's mid stage we tread,
Few know so many friends alive, as dead.
Yet, as immortal, in our up-hill chase
We press coy fortune with unslacken'd pace;
Our ardent labours for the toys we seek,
Join night to day, and Sunday to the week:
Our very joys are anxious, and expire
Between satiety and fierce desire.
Now what reward for all this grief and toil?
But one; a female friend's endearing smile;
A tender smile, our sorrows' only balm,
And, in life's tempest, the sad sailor's calm.
How have I seen a gentle nymph draw nigh,
Peace in her air, persuasion in her eye;
Victorious tenderness! it all o'ercame,
Husbands look'd mild, and savages grew tame.
The Sylvan race our active nymphs pursue;
Man is not all the game they have in view:
In woods and fields their glory they complete;
Their Master Betty leaps a five-barr'd gate;
While fair Miss Charles to toilets is confin'd,
Nor rashly tempts the barb'rous sun and wind.
Some nymphs affect a more heroic breed,
And volt from hunters to the manag'd steed;
Command his prancings with a martial air,
And Fobert has the forming of the fair.
More than one steed must Delia's empire feel,

Who sits triumphant o'er the flying wheel;
And as she guides it thro' th' admiring throng,
With what an air she smacks the silken thong!
Graceful as John, she moderates the reins,
And whistles sweet her diuretic strains;
Sesostris like, such charioteers as these
May drive six harness'd monarchs, if they please:
They drive, row, run, with love of glory smit,
Leap, swim, shoot flying, and pronounce on wit.
O'er the belle-lettre lovely Daphne reigns;
Again the god Apollo wears her chains:
With legs toss'd high, on her sophee she sits
Vouchsafing audience to contending wits:
Of each performance she 's the final test;
One act read o'er, she prophesies the rest;
And then, pronouncing with decisive air,
Fully convinces all the town — she 's fair.
Had lovely Daphne Hecatessa's face,
How would her elegance of taste decrease!
Some ladies' judgment in their features lies,
And all their genius sparkles from their eyes.
"But hold," she cries, "lampooner! have a care;
Must I want common sense, because I 'm fair?"
O no: see Stella; her eyes shine as bright
As if her tongue was never in the right;
And yet what real learning, judgment, fire!
She seems inspir'd, and can herself inspire:
How then (if malice rul'd not all the fair)
Could Daphne publish, and could she forbear?

We grant that beauty is no bar to sense,
Nor is 't a sanction for impertinence.
  Sempronia lik'd her man ; and well she might;
The youth in person, and in parts, was bright;
Possess'd of every virtue, grace, and art,
That claims just empire o'er the female heart:
He met her passion, all her sighs return'd,
And, in full rage of youthful ardour, burn'd:
Large his possessions, and beyond her own :
Their bliss the theme, and envy of the town :
The day was fix'd, when, with one acre more,
In stepp'd deform'd, debauch'd, diseas'd threescore.
The fatal sequel I, through shame, forbear:
Of pride, and av'rice, who can cure the fair ?
  Man's rich with little, were his judgment true;
Nature is frugal, and her wants are few ;
Those few wants answer'd, bring sincere delights;
But fools create themselves new appetites :
Fancy, and pride, seek things at vast expense,
Which relish not to reason, nor to sense.
When surfeit, or unthankfulness, destroys,
In nature's narrow sphere, our solid joys,
In fancy's airy land of noise and show,
Where nought but dreams, no real pleasures, grow;
Like cats in air-pumps, to subsist we strive
On joys too thin to keep the soul alive.
Lemira 's sick ; make haste ; the doctor call:
He comes; but where 's his patient ? At the ball.
The doctor stares; her woman curtsies low,
And cries, "My lady, Sir, is always so:

Diversions put her maladies to flight:
True, she can't stand, but she can dance all night:
I 've known my lady (for she loves a tune)
For fevers take an opera in June:
And, tho' perhaps you 'll think the practice bold,
A midnight park is sov'reign for a cold:
With cholics, breakfasts of green fruit agree;
With indigestions, supper just at three."
A strange alternative, replies Sir Hans,
Must women have a doctor, or a dance?
Though sick to death, abroad they safely roam,
But droop and die, in perfect health, at home:
For want — but not of health, are ladies ill;
And tickets cure beyond the doctor's pill.
  Alas, my heart! how languishingly fair
Yon lady lolls! with what a tender air!
Pale as a young dramatic author, when,
O'er darling lines, fell Cibber waves his pen.
Is her lord angry, or has * Veny chid?
Dead is her father, or the mask forbid?
"Late sitting up has turn'd her roses white."
Why went she not to bed? "Because 'twas night."
Did she then dance, or play? "Nor this, nor that."
Well, night soon steals away in pleasing chat.
"No, all alone, her prayers she rather chose,
Than be that wretch to sleep till morning rose."
Then lady Cynthia, mistress of the shade,
Goes, with the fashionable owls, to bed:

* Lap-dog.

This her pride covets, this her health denies;
Her soul is silly, but her body 's wise.
Others, with curious arts, dim charms revive,
And triumph in the bloom of fifty-five.
You, in the morning, a fair nymph invite;
To keep her word, a brown one comes at night:
Next day she shines in glossy black; and then
Revolves into her native red again:
Like a dove's neck, she shifts her transient charms,
And is her own dear rival in your arms.
But one admirer has the painted lass;
Nor finds that one, but in her looking-glass:
Yet Laura 's beautiful to such excess,
That all her art scarce makes her please us less.
To deck the female cheek, he only knows,
Who paints less fair the lily, and the rose.
How gay they smile! Such blessings nature pours,
O'erstock'd mankind enjoy but half her stores:
In distant wilds, by human eyes unseen,
She rears her flowers, and spreads her velvet green:
Pure gurgling rills the lonely desert trace,
And waste their music on the savage race.
Is nature then a niggard of her bliss?
Repine we guiltless in a world like this?
But our lewd tastes her lawful charms refuse,
And painted art's depraved allurements choose.
Such Fulvia's passion for the town; fresh air
(An odd effect!) gives vapours to the fair;
Green fields, and shady groves, and crystal springs,

And larks, and nightingales, are odious things;
But smoke, and dust, and noise, and crowds,
delight;
And to be press'd to death, transports her quite:
Where silver riv'lets play through flow'ry meads,
And woodbines give their sweets, and limes their
shades,
Black kennels' absent odours she regrets,
And stops her nose at beds of violets.
Is stormy life preferr'd to the serene?
Or is the public to the private scene?
Retir'd, we tread a smooth and open way;
Through briers and brambles in the world we stray;
Stiff opposition, and perplex'd debate,
And thorny care, and rank and stinging hate,
Which choke our passage, our career control,
And wound the firmest temper of our soul.
O sacred solitude! divine retreat!
Choice of the prudent! envy of the great!
By thy pure stream, or in thy waving shade,
We court fair wisdom, that celestial maid:
The genuine offspring of her lov'd embrace,
(Strangers on earth!) are innocence and peace:
There, from the ways of men laid safe ashore,
We smile to hear the distant tempest roar;
There, bless'd with health, with business unper-
plex'd,
This life we relish, and ensure the next;
There too the muses sport; these numbers free,
Pierian Eastbury! I owe to thee.

There sport the muses; but not there alone:
Their sacred force Amelia feels in town.
Nought but a genius can a genius fit;
A wit herself, Amelia weds a wit:
Both wits! though miracles are said to cease,
Three days, three wondrous days! they liv'd in peace;
With the fourth sun a warm dispute arose,
On Durfey's poesy, and Bunyan's prose:
The learned war both wage with equal force,
And the fifth morn concluded the divorce.

Phœbe, though she possesses nothing less,
Is proud of being rich in happiness:
Laboriously pursues delusive toys,
Content with pains, since they 're reputed joys.
With what well-acted transport will she say,
"Well, sure, we were so happy yesterday!
And then that charming party for to-morrow!"
Though, well she knows, 'twill languish into sorrow:
But she dares never boast the present hour;
So gross that cheat, it is beyond her power:
For such is or our weakness, or our curse,
Or rather such our crime, which still is worse,
The present moment, like a wife, we shun,
And ne'er enjoy, because it is our own.

Pleasures are few, and fewer we enjoy;
Pleasure, like quicksilver, is bright, and coy;
We strive to grasp it with our utmost skill,
Still it eludes us, and it glitters still:

If seiz'd at last, compute your mighty gains;
What is it, but rank poison in your veins?
As Flavia in her glass an angel spies,
Pride whispers in her ear pernicious lies;
Tells her, while she surveys a face so fine,
There's no satiety of charms divine:
Hence, if her lover yawns, all chang'd appears
Her temper, and she melts (sweet soul!) in tears:
She, fond and young, last week, her wish enjoy'd,
In soft amusement all the night employ'd;
The morning came, when Strephon, waking, found
(Surprising sight!) his bride in sorrow drown'd.
"What miracle," says Strephon, "makes thee weep?"
"Ah, barb'rous man!" she cries, "how could you —— sleep?"
Men love a mistress, as they love a feast;
How grateful one to touch, and one to taste!
Yet sure there is a certain time of day,
We wish our mistress, and our meat, away:
But soon the sated appetites return,
Again our stomachs crave, our bosoms burn:
Eternal love let man, then, never swear;
Let women never triumph, nor despair;
Nor praise, nor blame, too much, the warm, or chill;
Hunger and love are foreign to the will.
There is indeed a passion more refin'd,
For those few nymphs whose charms are of the mind:
But not of that unfashionable set

Is Phyllis; Phyllis and her Damon met.
Eternal love exactly hits her taste;
Phyllis demands eternal love at least.
Embracing Phyllis with soft smiling eyes,
Eternal love I vow, the swain replies:
But say, my all, my mistress, and my friend!
What day next week th' eternity shall end?
  Some nymphs prefer astronomy to love:
Elope from mortal man, and range above.
The fair philosopher to Rowley flies,
Where, in a box, the whole creation lies:
She sees the planets in their turns advance,
And scorns, Poitier, thy sublunary dance;
Of Desagulier she bespeaks fresh air;
And Whiston has engagements with the fair.
What vain experiments Sophronia tries!
'Tis not in air-pumps the gay colonel dies.
But though to-day this rage of science reigns,
(O fickle sex!) soon end her learned pains.
Lo! Pug from Jupiter her heart has got,
Turns out the stars, and Newton is a sot.
  To ——— turn; she never took the height
Of Saturn, yet is ever in the right.
She strikes each point with native force of mind,
While puzzled learning blunders far behind,
Graceful to sight, and elegant to thought,
The great are vanquish'd, and the wise are taught.
Her breeding finish'd, and her temper sweet,
When serious, easy; and when gay, discreet;
In glittering scenes, o'er her own heart, sincere;

In crowds, collected; and in courts, severe;
Sincere, and warm, with zeal well understood,
She takes a noble pride in doing good;
Yet not superior to her sex's cares,
The mode she fixes by the gown she wears;
Of silks and china she 's the last appeal;
In these great points she leads the commonweal;
And if disputes of empire rise between
Mechlin the queen of lace, and colberteen,
'Tis doubt! 'tis darkness! till suspended fate
Assumes her nod, to close the grand debate.
When such her mind, why will the fair express
Their emulation only in their dress?
　But, oh! the nymph that mounts above the skies,
And, gratis, clears religious mysteries,
Resolv'd the church's welfare to ensure,
And make her family a sine-cure:
The theme divine at cards she 'll not forget,
But takes in texts of Scripture at picquet;
In those licentious meetings acts the prude,
And thanks her Maker that her cards are good.
What angels would those be, who thus excel
In theologics, could they sew as well!
Yet why should not the fair her text pursue?
Can she more decently the doctor woo?
'Tis hard, too, she who makes no use but chat
Of her religion, should be barr'd in that.
　Isaac, a brother of the canting strain,
When he has knock'd at his own skull in vain,
To beauteous Marcia often will repair

With a dark text, to light it at the fair.
O how his pious soul exults to find
Such love for holy men in woman-kind!
Charm'd with her learning, with what rapture he
Hangs on her bloom, like an industrious bee!
Hums round about her, and with all his power
Extracts sweet wisdom from so fair a flower!
The young and gay declining, Appia flies
At nobler game, the mighty and the wise:
By nature more an eagle than a dove,
She impiously prefers the world to love.
Can wealth give happiness? look round, and see
What gay distress! what splendid misery!
Whatever fortune lavishly can pour,
The mind annihilates, and calls for more!
Wealth is a cheat; believe not what it says;
Like any lord it promises — and pays.
How will the miser startle, to be told
Of such a wonder, as insolvent gold!
What nature wants has an intrinsic weight;
All more, is but the fashion of the plate,
Which, for one moment, charms the fickle view;
It charms us now; anon we cast anew;
To some fresh birth of fancy more inclin'd:
Then wed not acres, but a noble mind.
Mistaken lovers, who make worth their care,
And think accomplishments will win the fair:
The fair, 'tis true, by genius should be won,
As flow'rs unfold their beauties to the sun;
And yet in female scales a fop outweighs,

And wit must wear the willow and the bays.
Nought shines so bright in vain Liberia's eye
As riot, impudence, and perfidy;
The youth of fire, that has drunk deep, and play'd,
And kill'd his man, and triumph'd o'er his maid;
For him, as yet unhang'd, she spreads her charms,
Snatches the dear destroyer to her arms;
And amply gives (though treated long amiss)
The man of merit his revenge in this,
If you resent, and wish a woman ill,
But turn her o'er one moment to her will.
The languid lady next appears in state,
Who was not born to carry her own weight;
She lolls, reels, staggers, till some foreign aid
To her own stature lifts the feeble maid.
Then, if ordain'd to so severe a doom,
She, by just stages, journeys round the room:
But, knowing her own weakness, she despairs
To scale the Alps — that is, ascend the stairs.
My fan! let others say, who laugh at toil;
Fan! hood! glove! scarf! is her laconic style;
And that is spoke with such a dying fall,
That Betty rather sees, than hears the call:
The motion of her lips, and meaning eye,
Piece out th' idea her faint words deny.
O listen with attention most profound!
Her voice is but the shadow of a sound.
And help! oh help! her spirits are so dead,
One hand scarce lifts the other to her head.
If, there, a stubborn pin it triumphs o'er,

She pants! she sinks away! and is more.
Let the robust and the gigantic carve,
Life is not worth so much, she 'd rather starve;
But chew she must herself; ah cruel fate!
That Rosalinda can't by proxy eat.
  An antidote in female caprice lies
(Kind heaven!) against the poison of their eyes.
  Thalestris triumphs in a manly mien;
Loud is her accent, and her phrase obscene.
In fair and open dealing where 's the shame?
What nature dares to give, she dares to name.
This honest fellow is sincere and plain,
And justly gives the jealous husband pain.
(Vain is the task to petticoats assign'd,
If wanton language shows a naked mind.)
And now and then, to grace her eloquence,
An oath supplies the vacancies of sense.
Hark! the shrill notes transpierce the yielding air,
And teach the neighb'ring echoes how to swear.
By Jove, is faint, and for the simple swain;
She, on the Christian system, is profane.
But though the volley rattles in your ear,
Believe her dress, she 's not a grenadier.
If thunder 's awful, how much more our dread,
When Jove deputes a lady in his stead?
A lady! pardon my mistaken pen,
A shameless woman is the worst of men.
  Few to good breeding make a just pretence;
Good breeding is the blossom of good sense;
The last result of an accomplish'd mind,

With outward grace, the body's virtue, join'd.
A violated decency now reigns;
And nymphs for failings take peculiar pains.
With Chinese painters modern toasts agree,
The point they aim at is deformity:
They throw their persons with a hoyden air
Across the room, and toss into the chair.
So far their commerce with mankind is gone,
They, for our manners, have exchang'd their own.
The modest look, the castigated grace,
The gentle movement, and slow measur'd pace,
For which her lovers died, her parents pray'd,
Are indecorums with the modern maid.
Stiff forms are bad; but let not worse intrude,
Nor conquer art and nature, to be rude.
Modern good-breeding carry to its height,
And lady D——'s self will be polite.
  Ye rising fair! ye bloom of Britain's isle!
When high-born Anna, with a soften'd smile,
Leads on your train, and sparkles at your head,
What seems most hard, is, not to be well bred.
Her bright example with success pursue,
And all, but adoration, is your due.
  But adoration! give me something more,
Cries Lyce, on the borders of threescore:
Nought treads so silent as the foot of time;
Hence we mistake our autumn for our prime;
'Tis greatly wise to know, before we 're told,
The melancholy news, that we grow old.
Autumnal Lyce carries in her face

Memento mori to each public place.
O how your beating breast a mistress warms,
Who looks through spectacles to see your charms!
While rival undertakers hover round,
And with his spade the sexton marks the ground,
Intent not on her own, but others' doom,
She plans new conquests, and defrauds the tomb.
In vain the cock has summon'd sprites away,
She walks at noon, and blasts the bloom of day.
Gay rainbow silks her mellow charms infold,
And nought of Lyce but herself is old.
Her grizzled locks assume a smirking grace,
And art has levell'd her deep-furrow'd face.
Her strange demand no mortal can approve,
We 'll ask her blessing, but can't ask her love.
She grants, indeed, a lady may decline
(All ladies but herself) at ninety-nine.
O how unlike her is the sacred age
Of prudent Portia! her gray hairs engage;
Whose thoughts are suited to her life's decline:
Virtue 's the paint that can with wrinkles shine.
That, and that only, can old age sustain;
Which yet all wish, nor know they wish for pain.
Not num'rous are our joys, when life is new;
And yearly some are falling of the few;
But when we conquer life's meridian stage,
And downward tend into the vale of age,
They drop apace; by nature some decay,
And some the blasts of fortune sweep away;

Till naked quite of happiness, aloud
We call for death, and shelter in a shroud.
  Where 's Portia now?—But Portia left behind
Two lovely copies of her form and mind.
What heart untouch'd their early grief can view,
Like blushing rose-buds dipp'd in morning dew?
Who into shelter takes their tender bloom,
And forms their minds to flee from ills to come?
The mind, when turn'd adrift, no rules to guide,
Drives at the mercy of the wind and tide;
Fancy and passion toss it to and fro;
Awhile torment, and then quite sink in woe.
Ye beauteous orphans, since in silent dust
Your best example lies, my precepts trust.
Life swarms with ills; the boldest are afraid;
Where then is safety for a tender maid?
Unfit for conflict, round beset with woes,
And man, whom least she fears, her worst of foes!
When kind, most cruel; when oblig'd the most,
The least obliging; and by favours lost.
Cruel by nature, they for kindness hate;
And scorn you for those ills themselves create.
If on your fame your sex a blot has thrown,
'Twill ever stick, through malice of your own.
Most hard! in pleasing your chief glory lies;
And yet from pleasing your chief dangers rise:
Then please the best; and know, for men of sense,
Your strongest charms are native innocence.
Art on the mind, like paint upon the face,
Fright him, that 's worth your love, from your embrace.

In simple manners all the secret lies;
Be kind and virtuous, you 'll be blest and wise.
Vain show and noise intoxicate the brain,
Begin with giddiness, and end in pain.
Affect not empty fame, and idle praise,
Which, all those wretches I describe, betrays.
Your sex's glory 'tis, to shine unknown;
Of all applause, be fondest of your own.
Beware the fever of the mind! that thirst
With which the age is eminently curst:
To drink of pleasure, but inflames desire;
And abstinence alone can quench the fire;
Take pain from life, and terror from the tomb;
Give peace in hand; and promise bliss to come.

SATIRE VI. ON WOMEN.

INSCRIBED TO THE RIGHT HONOURABLE THE LADY ELIZABETH GERMAIN.

Interdum tamen et tollit comœdia vocem.—HOR.

I SOUGHT a patroness, but sought in vain.
Apollo whisper'd in my ear—"Germain."—
I know her not.—"Your reason 's somewhat odd;
Who knows his patron, now?" replied the god.
"Men write, to me, and to the world, unknown;
Then steal great names, to shield them from the town.
Detected worth, like beauty disarray'd,

To covert flies, of praise itself afraid:
Should she refuse to patronize your lays,
In vengeance write a volume in her praise.
Nor think it hard so great a length to run;
When such the theme, 'twill easily be done."
  Ye fair! to draw your excellence at length,
Exceeds the narrow bounds of human strength;
You, here, in miniature your picture see;
Nor hope from Zincks more justice than from me.
My portraits grace your mind, as his your side;
His portraits will inflame, mine quench, your pride.
He 's dear, you frugal; choose my cheaper lay;
And be your reformation all my pay.
  Lavinia is polite, but not profane;
To church as constant as to Drury Lane.
She decently, in form, pays heaven its due;
And makes a civil visit to her pew.
Her lifted fan, to give a solemn air,
Conceals her face, which passes for a prayer:
Curtsies to curtsies, then, with grace, succeed;
Not one the fair omits, but at the creed.
Or if she joins the service, 'tis to speak;
Thro' dreadful silence the pent heart might break;
Untaught to bear it, women talk away
To God himself, and fondly think they pray.
But sweet their accent, and their air refin'd;
For they 're before their Maker — and mankind:
When ladies once are proud of praying well,
Satan himself will toll the parish bell.
  Acquainted with the world, and quite well bred,

Drusa receives her visitants in bed;
But, chaste as ice, this Vesta, to defy
The very blackest tongue of calumny,
When from the sheets her lovely form she lifts,
She begs you just would turn you, while she shifts.
Those charms are greatest which decline the sight,
That makes the banquet poignant and polite.
There is no woman, where there 's no reserve;
And 'tis on plenty your poor lovers starve.
But with a modern fair, meridian merit
Is a fierce thing, they call a nymph of spirit.
Mark well the rollings of her flaming eye;
And tread on tiptoe, if you dare draw nigh.
"Or if you take a lion by the beard,*
Or dare defy the fell Hyrcanian pard,
Or arm'd rhinoceros, or rough Russian bear,"
First make your will, and then converse with her.
This lady glories in profuse expense;
And thinks distraction is magnificence.
To beggar her gallant, is some delight;
To be more fatal still, is exquisite;
Had ever nymph such reason to be glad?
In duel fell two lovers; one run mad.
Her foes their honest execrations pour;
Her lovers only should detest her more.
Flavia is constant to her old gallant,
And generously supports him in his want;
But marriage is a fetter, is a snare,

* Shakespeare.

A hell, no lady so polite can bear.
She 's faithful, she 's observant, and with pains
Her angel brood of bastards she maintains.
Nor least advantage has the fair to plead,
But that of guilt, above the marriage-bed.
  Amasia hates a prude, and scorns restraint;
Whate'er she is, she 'll not appear a saint:
Her soul superior flies formality;
So gay her air, her conduct is so free,
Some might suspect the nymph not over good —
Nor would they be mistaken, if they should.
  Unmarried Abra puts on formal airs;
Her cushion 's threadbare with her constant prayers.
Her only grief is, that she cannot be
At once engag'd in prayer and charity.
And this, to do her justice, must be said,
"Who would not think that Abra was a maid?"
  Some ladies are too beauteous to be wed;
For where 's the man that 's worthy of their bed?
If no disease reduce her pride before,
Lavinia will be ravish'd at threescore.
Then she submits to venture in the dark;
And nothing now is wanting — but her spark.
  Lucia thinks happiness consists in state;
She weds an idiot, but she eats in plate.
The goods of fortune, which her soul possess,
Are but the ground of unmade happiness;
The rude material: wisdom add to this,
Wisdom, the sole artificer of bliss;

She from herself, if so compell'd by need,
Of thin content can draw the subtle thread;
But (no detraction to her sacred skill)
If she can work in gold, 't is better still.
If Tullia had been blest with half her sense,
None could too much admire her excellence:
But since she can make error shine so bright,
She thinks it vulgar to defend the right.
With understanding she is quite o'errun;
And by too great accomplishments undone:
With skill she vibrates her eternal tongue,
For ever most divinely in the wrong.
Naked in nothing should a woman be;
But veil her very wit with modesty:
Let man discover, let not her display,
But yield her charms of mind with sweet delay.
For pleasure form'd, perversely some believe,
To make themselves important, men must grieve.
Lesbia the fair, to fire her jealous lord,
Pretends, the fop she laughs at, is ador'd.
In vain she 's proud of secret innocence;
The fact she fains were scarce a worse offence.
Mira, endow'd with every charm to bless,
Has no design, but on her husband's peace:
He lov'd her much; and greatly was he mov'd
At small inquietudes in her he lov'd.
"How charming this!"—The pleasure lasted long;
Now every day the fits come thick and strong:
At last he found the charmer only feign'd;
And was diverted when he should be pain'd.

What greater vengeance had the gods in store?
How tedious life, now she can plague no more!
She tries a thousand arts; but none succeed:
She 's forc'd a fever to procure indeed:
Thus strictly prov'd this virtuous, loving wife,
Her husband's pain was dearer than her life.
  Anxious Melania rises to my view,
Who never thinks her lover pays his due:
Visit, present, treat, flatter, and adore;
Her majesty, to-morrow, calls for more.
His wounded ears complaints eternal fill,
As unoil'd hinges, querulously shrill.
"You went last night with Celia to the ball."
You prove it false. "Not go! that 's worst of all."
Nothing can please her, nothing not inflame;
And arrant contradictions are the same.
Her lover must be sad, to please her spleen;
His mirth is an inexpiable sin:
For of all rivals that can pain her breast,
There 's one, that wounds far deeper than the rest;
To wreck her quiet, the most dreadful shelf
Is if her lover dares enjoy himself.
  And this, because she 's exquisitely fair:
Should I dispute her beauty, how she 'd stare!
How would Melania be surpris'd to hear
She 's quite deform'd! And yet the case is clear;
What 's female beauty, but an air divine,
Thro' which the mind's all gentle graces shine?
They, like the sun, irradiate all between;
The body charms because the soul is seen.

Hence, men are often captives of a face,
They know not why, of no peculiar grace:
Some forms, tho' bright, no mortal man can bear;
Some, none resist, tho' not exceeding fair.
  Aspasia 's highly born, and nicely bred,
Of taste refin'd, in life and manners read;
Yet reaps no fruit from her superior sense,
But to be teaz'd by her own excellence.
"Folks are so awkward! things so unpolite!"
She 's elegantly pain'd from morn till night.
Her delicacy 's shock'd where'er she goes;
Each creature's imperfections are her woes.
Heaven by its favour has the fair distrest,
And pour'd such blessings—that she can't be blest.
  Ah! why so vain, though blooming in thy spring,
Thou shining, frail, ador'd, and wretched thing?
Old age will come; disease may come before;
Fifteen is full as mortal as threescore.
Thy fortune, and thy charms, may soon decay:
But grant these fugitives prolong their stay,
Their basis totters, their foundation shakes;
Life, that supports them, in a moment breaks;
Then wrought into the soul let virtues shine;
The ground eternal, as the work divine.
  Julia 's a manager; she 's born for rule;
And knows her wiser husband is a fool;
Assemblies holds, and spins the subtle thread
That guides the lover to his fair one's bed:
For difficult amours can smooth the way,
And tender letters dictate, or convey.

But if depriv'd of such important cares,
Her wisdom condescends to less affairs.
For her own breakfast she 'll project a scheme,
Nor take her tea without a stratagem ;
Presides o'er trifles with a serious face ;
Important by the virtue of grimace.
  Ladies supreme among amusements reign ;
By nature born to soothe, and entertain.
Their prudence in a share of folly lies :
Why will they be so weak, as to be wise ?
  Syrena is for ever in extremes,
And with a vengeance she commends, or blames.
Conscious of her discernment, which is good,
She strains too much to make it understood.
Her judgment just, her sentence is too strong ;
Because she 's right, she 's ever in the wrong.
  Brunetta 's wise in actions great, and rare ;
But scorns on trifles to bestow her care.
Thus ev'ry hour Brunetta is to blame,
Because th' occasion is beneath her aim,
Think nought a trifle, though it small appear ;
Small sands the mountain, moments make the year,
And trifles life. Your care to trifles give,
Or you may die, before you truly live.
  Go breakfast with Alicia, there you 'll see,
Simplex munditiis, to the last degree :
Unlac'd her stays, her night-gown is untied,
And what she has of head-dress is aside.
She drawls her words, and waddles in her pace ;
Unwash'd her hands, and much besnuff'd her face.

A nail uncut, and head uncomb'd, she loves;
And would draw on jack-boots, as soon as gloves.
Gloves by Queen Bess's maidens might be miss'd;
Her blessed eyes ne'er saw a female fist.
Lovers, beware! to wound how can she fail
With scarlet finger, and long jetty nail?
For Harvey the first wit she cannot be,
Nor, cruel Richmond, the first toast for thee.
Since full each other station of renown,
Who would not be the greatest trapes in town?
Women were made to give our eyes delight;
A female sloven is an odious sight.
Fair Isabella is so fond of fame,
That her dear self is her eternal theme;
Through hopes of contradiction, oft she 'll say,
"Methinks I look so wretchedly to-day!"
When most the world applauds you, most beware;
'Tis often less a blessing than a snare.
Distrust mankind; with your own heart confer;
And dread even there to find a flatterer.
The breath of others raises our renown;
Our own as surely blows the pageant down.
Take up no more than you by worth can claim,
Lest soon you prove a bankrupt in your fame.
But own I must, in this perverted age,
Who most deserve, can't always most engage.
So far is worth from making glory sure,
It often hinders what it should procure.
Whom praise we most? The virtuous, brave, and
wise?

No; wretches, whom, in secret, we despise.
And who so blind, as not to see the cause?
No rivals rais'd by such discreet applause;
And yet, of credit it lays in a store,
By which our spleen may wound true worth the
more.

Ladies there are who think one crime is all:
Can women, then, no way but backward fall?
So sweet is that one crime they don't pursue,
To pay its loss, they think all others few.
Who hold that crime so dear, must never claim
Of injur'd modesty the sacred name.

But Clio thus: "What! railing without end?
Mean task! how much more gen'rous to commend!"
Yes, to commend as you are wont to do,
My kind instructor, and example too.
"Daphnis," says Clio, "has a charming eye:
What pity 'tis her shoulder is awry!
Aspasia's shape indeed — but then her air —
The man has parts who finds destruction there.
Almeria's wit has something that 's divine;
And wit 's enough — how few in all things shine!
Selina serves her friends, relieves the poor —
Who was it said Selina 's near threescore?
At Lucia's match I from my soul rejoice;
The world congratulates so wise a choice;
His lordship's rent-roll is exceeding great —
But mortgages will sap the best estate.
In Sherley's form might cherubims appear;
But then — she has a freckle on her ear."

Without a but, Hortensia she commends,
The first of women, and the best of friends;
Owns her in person, wit, fame, virtue, bright:
But how comes this to pass?— She died last night.
  Thus nymphs commend, who yet at satire rail:
Indeed that 's needless, if such praise prevail.
And whence such praise? Our virulence is thrown
On others' fame, thro' fondness for our own.
  Of rank and riches proud, Cleora frowns;
For are not coronets akin to crowns?
Her greedy eye, and her sublime address,
The height of avarice and pride confess.
You seek perfections worthy of her rank;
Go, seek for her perfections at the bank.
By wealth unquench'd, by reason uncontrol'd,
For ever burns her sacred thirst of gold.
As fond of five-pence, as the veriest cit;
And quite as much detested as a wit.
  Can gold calm passion, or make reason shine?
Can we dig peace, or wisdom, from the mine?
Wisdom to gold prefer; for 'tis much less
To make our fortune, than our happiness.
That happiness which great ones often see,
With rage and wonder, in a low degree;
Themselves unblest. The poor are only poor;
But what are they who droop amid their store?
Nothing is meaner than a wretch of state;
The happy only are the truly great.
Peasants enjoy like appetites with kings;
And those best satisfied with cheapest things.

Could both our Indies buy but one new sense,
Our envy would be due to large expense.
Since not, those pomps which to the great belong,
Are but poor arts to mark them from the throng.
See how they beg an alms of flattery!
They languish! oh support them with a lie!
A decent competence we fully taste;
It strikes our sense, and gives a constant feast:
More, we perceive by dint of thought alone;
The rich must labor to possess their own,
To feel their great abundance; and request
Their humble friends to help them to be blest;
To see their treasures, hear their glory told,
And aid the wretched impotence of gold.
But some, great souls! and touch'd with warmth divine,
Give gold a price, and teach its beams to shine.
All hoarded treasures they repute a load;
Nor think their wealth their own, till well bestow'd.
Grand reservoirs of public happiness,
Through secret streams diffusively they bless;
And, while their bounties glide conceal'd from view,
Relieve our wants, and spare our blushes too.
But satire is my task; and these destroy
Her gloomy province, and malignant joy.
Help me, ye misers! help me to complain,
And blast our common enemy, Germain:
But our invectives must despair success;
For next to praise, she values nothing less.
What picture 's yonder, loosen'd from its frame?

Or is 't Asturia? that affected dame.
The brightest forms, through affectation, fade
To strange new things, which nature never made.
Frown not, ye fair! so much your sex we prize,
We hate those arts that take you from our eyes.
In Albucinda's native grace is seen
What you, who labour at perfection, mean.
Short is the rule, and to be learnt with ease,
Retain your gentle selves, and you must please.
Here might I sing of Memmia's mincing mien,
And all the movements of the soft machine:
How two red lips affected zephyrs blow,
To cool the Bohea, and inflame the beau:
While one white finger, and a thumb, conspire
To lift the cup, and make the world admire.
Tea! how I tremble at thy fatal stream!
As Lethe, dreadful to the love of fame.
What devastations on thy banks are seen!
What shades of mighty names which once have been!
An hecatomb of characters supplies
Thy painted altars' daily sacrifice.
H——, P——, B——, aspers'd by thee, decay,
As grains of finest sugars melt away,
And recommend thee more to mortal taste:
Scandal 's the sweet'ner of a female feast.
But this inhuman triumph shall decline,
And thy revolting naiads call for wine;
Spirits no longer shall serve under thee;
But reign in thy own cup, exploded tea!

Citronia's nose declares thy ruin nigh,
And who dares give Citronia's nose the lie?*
  The ladies long at men of drink exclaim'd,
And what impair'd both health and virtue, blam'd;
At length, to rescue man, the generous lass
Stole from her consort the pernicious glass;
As glorious as the British queen renown'd,
Who suck'd the poison from her husband's wound.
  Nor to the glass alone are nymphs inclin'd,
But every bolder vice of bold mankind.
  O Juvenal! for thy severer rage!
To lash the ranker follies of our age.
  Are there, among the females of our isle,
Such faults, at which it is a fault to smile?
There are. Vice, once by modest nature chain'd
And legal ties, expatiates unrestrain'd;
Without thin decency held up to view,
Naked she stalks o'er law and gospel too.
Our matrons lead such exemplary lives,
Men sigh in vain for none, but for their wives;
Who marry to be free, to range the more,
And wed one man to wanton with a score.
Abroad too kind, at home 'tis steadfast hate,
And one eternal tempest of debate.
What foul eruptions, from a look most meek!
What thunders bursting, from a dimpled cheek!
Their passions bear it with a lofty hand!

* —— Solem quis dicere falsum
Audeat? VIRG.

But then, their reason is at due command.
Is there whom you detest, and seek his life?
Trust no soul with the secret — but his wife.
Wives wonder that their conduct I condemn,
And ask, what kindred is a spouse to them?
  What swarms of am'rous grandmothers I see!
And misses, ancient in iniquity?
What blasting whispers, and what loud declaiming!
What lying, drinking, bawding, swearing, gaming!
Friendship so cold, such warm incontinence;
Such griping av'rice, such profuse expense;
Such dead devotion, such a zeal for crimes;
Such licens'd ill, such masquerading times;
Such venal faith, such misapplied applause;
Such flatter'd guilt, and such inverted laws;
Such dissolution through the whole I find,
'Tis not a world, but chaos of mankind.
  Since Sundays have no balls, the well-dress'd belle
Shines in the pew, but smiles to hear of hell;
And casts an eye of sweet disdain on all,
Who listens less to Collins than St. Paul.
Atheists have been but rare; since nature's birth,
Till now, she-atheists ne'er appear'd on earth.
Ye men of deep researches, say, whence springs
This daring character, in timorous things?
Who start at feathers, from an insect fly,
A match for nothing — but the Deity.
  But, not to wrong the fair, the muse must own
In this pursuit they court not fame alone;

But join to that a more substantial view,
" From thinking free, to be free agents too."
They strive with their own hearts, and keep them down,
In complaisance to all the fools in town.
O how they tremble at the name of prude!
And die with shame at thought of being good!
For what will Artimis, the rich and gay,
What will the wits, that is, the coxcombs say?
They heaven defy, to earth's vile dregs a slave;
Thro' cowardice, most execrably brave.
With our own judgments durst we to comply,
In virtue should we live, in glory die.
Rise then, my muse, in honest fury rise;
They dread a satire, who defy the skies.
Atheists are few: most nymphs a Godhead own;
And nothing but his attributes dethrone.
From Atheists far, they steadfastly believe
God is, and is Almighty —— to forgive.
His other excellence they 'll not dispute;
But mercy, sure, is his chief attribute.
Shall pleasures of a short duration chain
A lady's soul in everlasting pain?
Will the great Author us poor worms destroy,
For now and then a sip of transient joy?
No, he 's for ever in a smiling mood;
He 's like themselves, or how could he be good?
And they blaspheme, who blacker schemes suppose. —
Devoutly, thus, Jehovah they depose,

The pure! the just! and set up, in his stead,
A deity, that 's perfectly well bred.
"Dear Tillotson! be sure the best of men;
Nor thought he more, than thought great Origen,
Though once upon a time he misbehav'd;
Poor Satan! doubtless, he 'll at length be sav'd.
Let priests do something for their one in ten;
It is their trade; so far they 're honest men.
Let them cant on, since they have got the knack,
And dress their notions, like themselves, in black;
Fright us, with terrors of a world unknown,
From joys of this, to keep them all their own.
Of earth's fair fruits, indeed, they claim a fee;
But then they leave our untith'd virtue free.
Virtue 's a pretty thing to make a show:
Did ever mortal write like Rochefocaut?"
Thus pleads the devil's fair apologist,
And, pleading, safely enters on his list.
Let angel-forms angelic truths maintain;
Nature disjoins the beauteous and profane.
For what 's true beauty, but fair virtue's face?
Virtue made visible in outward grace?
She, then, that 's haunted with an impious mind,
The more she charms, the more she shocks mankind.
But charms decline: the fair long vigils keep:
They sleep no more! * quadrille has murder'd sleep.

* Shakespeare.

"Poor K—p! cries Livia; I have not been there
These two nights; the poor creature will despair.
I hate a crowd — but to do good, you know —
And people of condition should bestow."
Convinc'd, o'ercome, to K—p's grave matrons run;
Now set a daughter, and now stake a son;
Let health, fame, temper, beauty, fortune, fly;
And beggar half their race — thro' charity.
 Immortal were we, or else mortal quite,
I less should blame this criminal delight:
But since the gay assembly's gayest room
Is but the upper story of some tomb,
Methinks, we need not our short beings shun,
And, thought to fly, contend to be undone.
We need not buy our ruin with our crime,
And give eternity to murder time.
 The love of gaming is the worst of ills;
With ceaseless storms the blacken'd soul it fills;
Inveighs at heaven, neglects the ties of blood;
Destroys the power and will of doing good;
Kills health, pawns honour, plunges in disgrace,
And, what is still more dreadful — spoils your face.
 See yonder set of thieves that live on spoil,
The scandal, and the ruin of our isle!
And see, (strange sight!) amid that ruffian band,
A form divine high wave her snowy hand;
That rattles loud a small enchanted box,
Which, loud as thunder, on the board she knocks.
And as fierce storms, which earth's foundation
 shook,

From Æolus's cave impetuous broke,
From this small cavern a mix'd tempest flies,
Fear, rage, convulsion, tears, oaths, blasphemies!
For men, I mean, — the fair discharges none;
She (guiltless creature!) swears to heaven alone.
See her eyes start! cheeks glow! and muscles swell!
Like the mad maid in the Cumean cell.
Thus that divine one her soft nights employs!
Thus tunes her soul to tender nuptial joys!
And when the cruel morning calls to bed,
And on her pillow lays her aching head,
With the dear images her dreams are crown'd,
The die spins lovely, or the cards go round;
Imaginary ruin charms her still;
Her happy lord is cuckol'd by spadille:
And if she 's brought to bed, 'tis ten to one,
He marks the forehead of her darling son.
O scene of horror, and of wild despair,
Why is the rich Atrides' splended heir
Constrain'd to quit his ancient lordly seat,
And hide his glories in a mean retreat?
Why that drawn sword? And whence that dismal cry?
Why pale distraction thro' the family?
See my lord threaten, and my lady weep,
And trembling servants from the tempest creep.
Why that gay son to distant regions sent?
What fiends that daughter's destin'd match prevent?

Why the whole house in sudden ruin laid?
O nothing, but last night — my lady play'd.
But wanders not my satire from my theme?
Is this too owing to the love of fame?
Though now your hearts on lucre are bestow'd,
'Twas first a vain devotion to the mode;
Nor cease we here, since 'tis a vice so strong,
The torrent sweeps all womankind along;
This may be said, in honour of our times,
That none now stand distinguish'd by their crimes.
If sin you must, take nature for your guide:
Love has some soft excuse to soothe your pride:
Ye fair apostates from love's ancient power!
Can nothing ravish, but a golden shower?
Can cards alone your glowing fancy seize;
Must Cupid learn to punt, ere he can please?
When you 're enamour'd of a lift or cast,
What can the preacher more, to make us chaste?
Why must strong youths unmarried pine away?
They find no woman disengag'd —— from play.
Why pine the married — O severer fate!
They find from play no disengag'd — estate.
Flavia, at lovers false, untouch'd and hard,
Turns pale, and trembles at a cruel card.
Nor Arria's Bible can secure her age;
Her threescore years are shuffling with her page.
While death stands by, but till the game is done,
To sweep that stake, in justice, long his own;
Like old cards ting'd with sulphur, she takes fire;
Or, like snuffs sunk in sockets, blazes higher.

Ye gods! with new delights inspire the fair;
Or give us sons, and save us from despair.
Sons, brothers, fathers, husbands, tradesmen, close
In my complaint, and brand your sins in prose:
Yet I believe, as firmly as my creed,
In spite of all our wisdom, you 'll proceed:
Our pride so great, our passion is so strong,
Advice to right confirms us in the wrong.
I hear you cry, "This fellow 's very odd."
When you chastise, who would not kiss the rod?
But I 've a charm your anger shall control,
And turn your eyes with coldness on the vole.
The charm begins! To yonder flood of light,
That bursts o'er gloomy Britain, turn your sight.
What guardian power o'erwhelms your souls with awe?
Her deeds are precepts, her example law;
'Midst empire's charms, how Carolina's heart
Glows with the love of virtue, and of art!
Her favour is diffus'd to that degree,
Excess of goodness! it has dawn'd on me:
When in my page, to balance numerous faults,
Or godlike deeds were shown, or gen'rous thoughts,
She smil'd, industrious to be pleas'd, nor knew
From whom my pen the borrow'd lustre drew.
*Thus the majestic mother of mankind,
To her own charms most amiably blind,

* Milton.

On the green margin innocently stood,
And gaz'd indulgent on the crystal flood;
Survey'd the stranger in the painted wave,
And, smiling, prais'd the beauties which she gave.

SATIRE VII.

TO THE RIGHT HONOURABLE SIR ROBERT WALPOLE.

Carmina tum melius, cum venerit ipse, canemus. VIRG.

On this last labour, this my closing strain,
Smile, Walpole! or the Nine inspire in vain:
To thee, 'tis due; that verse how justly thine,
Where Brunswick's glory crowns the whole design!
That glory, which thy counsels make so bright;
That glory, which on thee reflects a light.
Illustrious commerce, and but rarely known!
To give, and take, a lustre from the throne.
Nor think that thou art foreign to my theme;
The fountain is not foreign to the stream.
How all mankind will be surprised, to see
This flood of British folly charg'd on thee!
Say, Britain! whence this caprice of thy sons,
Which thro' their various ranks with fury runs?
The cause is plain, a cause which we must bless;
For caprice is the daughter of success,
(A bad effect, but from a pleasing cause!)
And gives our rulers undesign'd applause;

Tells how their conduct bids our wealth increase,
And lulls us in the downy lap of peace.
  While I survey the blessings of our isle,
Her arts triumphant in the royal smile,
Her public wounds bound up, her credit high,
Her commerce spreading sails in every sky,
The pleasing scene recalls my theme again,
And shows the madness of ambitious men,
Who, fond of bloodshed, draw the murd'ring sword,
And burn to give mankind a single lord.
  The follies past are of a private kind;
Their sphere is small; their mischief is confin'd:
But daring men there are (Awake, my muse,
And raise thy verse!) who bolder frenzy choose;
Who stung by glory, rave, and bound away;
The world their field, and humankind their prey.
  The Grecian chief, th' enthusiast of his pride,
With rage and terror stalking by his side,
Raves round the globe; he soars into a god!
Stand fast, Olympus! and sustain his nod.
The pest divine in horrid grandeur reigns,
And thrives on mankind's miseries and pains,
What slaughter'd hosts! what cities in a blaze!
What wasted countries! and what crimson seas!
With orphans' tears his impious bowl o'erflows,
And cries of kingdoms lull him to repose.
  And cannot thrice ten hundred years unpraise
The boist'rous boy, and blast his guilty bays?
Why want we then encomiums on the storm,
Or famine, or volcano? They perform

Their mighty deeds: they, hero-like, can slay,
And spread their ample desarts in a day.
O great alliance! O divine renown!
With dearth, and pestilence, to share the crown.
When men extol a wild destroyer's name,
Earth's builder and preserver they blaspheme.
One to destroy, is murder by the law;
And gibbets keep the lifted hand in awe;
To murder thousands, takes a specious name,
War's glorious art, and gives immortal fame.
When, after battle, I the field have seen
Spread o'er with ghastly shapes, which once were men;
A nation crush'd, a nation of the brave!
A realm of death! and on this side the grave!
Are there, said I, who from this sad survey,
This human chaos, carry smiles away?
How did my heart with indignation rise!
How honest nature swell'd into my eyes!
How was I shock'd to think the hero's trade
Of such materials, fame and triumph made!
How guilty these! Yet not less guilty they,
Who reach false glory by a smoother way:
Who wrap destruction up in gentle words,
And bows, and smiles, more fatal than their swords;
Who stifle nature, and subsist on art;
Who coin the face, and petrify the heart;
All real kindness for the show discard,
As marble polish'd, and as marble hard;

Who do for gold what Christians do thro' grace,
"With open arms their enemies embrace:"
Who give a nod when broken hearts repine;
"The thinnest food on which a wretch can dine:"
Or, if they serve you, serve you disinclin'd,
And, in their height of kindness, are unkind.
Such courtiers were, and such again may be,
Walpole! when men forget to copy thee.
Here cease, my muse! the catalogue is writ;
Nor one more candidate for fame admit,
Tho' disappointed thousands justly blame
Thy partial pen, and boast an equal claim:
Be this their comfort, fools, omitted here,
May furnish laughter for another year.
Then let Crispino, who was ne'er refused
The justice yet of being well abus'd,
With patience wait; and be content to reign
The pink of puppies in some future strain.
Some future strain, in which the muse shall tell
How science dwindles, and how volumes swell.
How commentators each dark passage shun,
And hold their farthing candle to the sun.
How tortur'd texts to speak our sense are made,
And every vice is to the scripture laid.
How misers squeeze a young voluptuous peer;
His sins to Lucifer not half so dear.
How Verres is less qualified to steal
With sword and pistol, than with wax and seal.
How lawyers' fees to such excess are run,
That clients are redress'd till they 're undone.

How one man's anguish is another's sport;
And ev'n denials cost us dear at court.
How man eternally false judgments makes,
And all his joys and sorrows are mistakes.
This swarm of themes that settles on my pen,
Which I, like summer flies, shake off again,
Let others sing; to whom my weak essay
But sounds a prelude, and points out their prey:
That duty done, I hasten to complete
My own design; for Tonson 's at the gate.
The love of fame in its effect survey'd,
The muse has sung; be now the cause display'd:
Since so diffusive, and so wide its sway,
What is this power, whom all mankind obey?
Shot from above, by heaven's indulgence, came
This generous ardour, this unconquer'd flame,
To warm, to raise, to deify, mankind,
Still burning brightest in the noblest mind.
By large-soul'd men, for thirst of fame renown'd,
Wise laws were fram'd, and sacred arts were found;
Desire of praise first broke the patriot's rest,
And made a bulwark of the warrior's breast;
It bids Argyll in fields and senate shine.
What more can prove its origin divine?
But, oh! this passion planted in the soul,
On eagle's wings to mount her to the pole,
The flaming minister of virtue meant,
Set up false gods, and wrong'd her high descent.
Ambition, hence, exerts a doubtful force,
Of blots, and beauties, an alternate source;

Hence Gildon rails, that raven of the pit,
Who thrives upon the carcasses of wit;
And in art-loving Scarborough is seen
How kind a pattern Pollio might have been.
Pursuit of fame with pedants fills our schools,
And into coxcombs burnishes our fools;
Pursuit of fame makes solid learning bright,
And Newton lifts above a mortal height;
That key of nature, by whose wit she clears
Her long, long secrets of five thousand years.
Would you then fully comprehend the whole,
Why, and in what degrees, pride sways the soul?
(For though in all, not equally, she reigns,)
Awake to knowledge, and attend my strains.
Ye doctors! hear the doctrine I disclose,
As true, as if 't were writ in dullest prose;
As if a letter'd dunce had said, "'Tis right,"
And imprimatur usher'd it to light.
Ambition, in the truly noble mind,
With sister virtue is for ever join'd;
As in fam'd Lucrece, who, with equal dread,
From guilt, and shame, by her last conduct, fled:
Her virtue long rebell'd in firm disdain,
And the sword pointed at her heart in vain;
But, when the slave was threaten'd to be laid
Dead by her side, her love of fame obey'd.
In meaner minds ambition works alone;
But with such art puts virtue's aspect on,
That not more like in feature and in mien,

* The god and mortal in the comic scene.
False Julius, ambush'd in this fair disguise,
Soon made the Roman liberties his prize.
No mask in basest minds ambition wears,
But in full light pricks up her ass's ears:
All I have sung are instances of this,
And prove my theme unfolded not amiss.
Ye vain! desist from your erroneous strife;
Be wise, and quit the false sublime of life,
The true ambition there alone resides,
Wehre justice vindicates, and wisdom guides;
Where inward dignity joins outward state;
Our purpose good, as our achievement great;
Where public blessings public praise attend;
Where glory is our motive, not our end.
Wouldst thou be fam'd? Have those high deeds in view
Brave men would act, though scandal should ensue.
Behold a prince! whom no swoln thoughts inflame;
No pride of thrones, no fever after fame!
But when the welfare of mankind inspires,
And death in view to dear-bought glory fires,
Proud conquests then, then regal pomps delight;
Then crowns, then triumphs, sparkle in his sight;
Tumult and noise are dear, which with them bring
His people's blessings to their ardent king:
But, when those great heroic motives cease,

* Amphitryon.

His swelling soul subsides to native peace;
From tedious grandeur's faded charms withdraws,
A sudden foe to splendour and applause;
Greatly deferring his arrears of fame,
Till men and angels jointly shout his name.
O pride celestial! which can pride disdain;
O blest ambition! which can ne'er be vain.
From one fam'd Alpine hill, which props the sky,
In whose deep womb unfathom'd waters lie,
Here burst the Rhone, and sounding Po; there shine,
In infant rills, the Danube and the Rhine;
From the rich store one fruitful urn supplies,
Whole kingdoms smile, a thousand harvests rise.
In Brunswick such a source the muse adores,
Which public blessings thro' half Europe pours.
When his heart burns with such a godlike aim,
Angels and George are rivals for the fame;
George! who in foes can soft affections raise,
And charm envenom'd satire into praise.
*Nor human rage alone his power perceives,
But the mad winds, and the tumultuous waves.
Ev'n storms (death's fiercest ministers!) forbear,
And, in their own wild empire, learn to spare.
Thus, nature's self, supporting man's decree,
Styles Britain's sovereign, sovereign of the sea.
While sea and air, great Brunswick! shook our state,
And sported with a king's and kingdom's fate,

* The king in danger by sea.

Depriv'd of what she lov'd, and press'd by fear
Of ever losing what she held most dear,
How did Britannia, like *Achilles, weep,
And tell her sorrows to the kindred deep!
Hang o'er the floods, and, in devotion warm,
Strive, for thee, with the surge, and fight the storm
  What felt thy Walpole, pilot of the realm!
Our Palinurus † slept not at the helm;
His eye ne'er clos'd; long since inur'd to wake,
And out-watch every star for Brunswick's sake:
By thwarting passions tost, by cares opprest,
He found the tempest pictur'd in his breast:
But, now, what joys that gloom of heart dispel,
No powers of language — but his own, can tell:
His own, which nature and the graces form,
At will, to raise, or hush, the civil storm.

* Hom. Il. lib. I.

† Ecce Deus ramum Lethæo rore madentem, &c.
VIRG. lib. 1

OCEAN: AN ODE,

OCCASIONED BY HIS MAJESTY'S ROYAL ENCOURAGEMENT OF THE SEA SERVICE.

TO WHICH IS PREFIXED AN ODE TO THE KING; AND A DISCOURSE ON ODE.

I THINK myself obliged to recommend to you a consideration of the greatest importance; and I should look upon it as a great happiness, if, at the beginning of my reign, I could see the foundation laid of so great and necessary a work, as the increase and encouragement of our seamen in general; that they may be invited, rather than compelled by force and violence, to enter into the service of their country, as oft as occasion shall require it: a consideration worthy the representatives of a people great and flourishing in trade and navigation. This leads me to mention to you the case of Greenwich Hospital, that care may be taken, by some addition to that fund, to render comfortable and effectual that charitable provision, for the support and maintenance of our seamen, worn out, and become decrepit by age and infirmities, in the service of their country. [Speech, Jan. 27, 1727–8.]

TO THE KING.—1728.

OLD ocean's praise
Demands my lays;
A truly British theme I sing;
A theme so great,
I dare complete,
And join with ocean, ocean's king.

The Roman ode
Majestic flow'd:
Its stream divinely clear, and strong;
In sense, and sound,
Thebes roll'd profound;
The torrent roar'd and foam'd along.

Let Thebes, nor Rome,
So fam'd, presume
To triumph o'er a northern isle;
Late time shall know
The north can glow,
If dread Augustus deign to smile.

The naval crown
Is all his own!
Our fleet, if war, or commerce, call,
His will performs
Through waves and storms,
And rides in triumph round the ball.

No former race,
With strong embrace,
This theme to ravish durst aspire;
With virgin charms
My soul it warms,
And melts melodious on my lyre.

My lays I file
With cautious toil;
Ye graces! turn the glowing lines;

On anvils neat
Your strokes repeat;
At every stroke the work refines!

How music charms!
How metre warms!
Parent of actions, good and brave!
How vice it tames!
And worth inflames!
And holds proud empire o'er the grave!

Jove mark'd for man
A scanty span,
But lent him wings to fly his doom;
Wit scorns the grave;
To wit he gave
The life of gods! immortal bloom!

Since years will fly,
And pleasures die,
Day after day, as years advance;
Since, while life lasts,
Joy suffers blasts
From frowning fate, and fickle chance;

Nor life is long;
But soon we throng,
Like autumn leaves, death's pallid shore;
We make, at least,
Of bad the best,
If in life's phantom, fame, we soar.

Our strains divide
The laurel's pride;
With those we lift to life, to live;
By fame enroll'd
With heroes bold,
And share the blessings which we give.

What hero's praise
Can fire my lays,
Like his, with whom my lay begun?
" Justice sincere,
And courage clear,
Rise the two columns of his throne.

" How form'd for sway!
Who look, obey;
They read the monarch in his port:
Their love and awe
Supply the law;
And his own lustre makes the court:"

On yonder height,
What golden light
Triumphant shines? and shines alone?
Unrivall'd blaze!
The nations gaze!
'Tis not the sun; 'tis Britain's throne.

Our monarch, there,
Rear'd high in air,
Should tempests rise, disdains to bend;

Like British oak,
Derides the stroke;
His blooming honours far extend!

Beneath them lies,
With lifted eyes,
Fair Albion, like an amorous maid;
While interest wings
Bold foreign kings
To fly, like eagles, to his shade.

At his proud foot
The sea, pour'd out,
Immortal nourishment supplies;
Thence wealth and state,
And power and fate,
Which Europe reads in George's eyes.

From what we view,
We take the clue,
Which leads from great to greater thing
Men doubt no more,
But gods adore,
When such resemblance shines in kings.

ON LYRIC POETRY.

How imperfect soever my own composition may be, yet am I willing to speak a word or two, of the nature of lyric poetry; to show that I have, at least, some idea of perfection in that kind of poem in which I am engaged; and that I do not think myself poet enough entirely to rely on inspiration for success in it.

To our having, or not having, this idea of perfection in the poem we undertake, is chiefly owing the merit or demerit of our performances, as also the modesty or vanity of our opinions concerning them. And in speaking of it I shall show how it unavoidably comes to pass, that bad poets, that is, poets in general, are esteemed, and really are, the most vain, the most irritable, and most ridiculous set of men upon earth. But poetry in its own nature is certainly

Non hos quæsitum munus in usus. — Virg.

He that has an idea of perfection in the work he undertakes may fail in it; he that has not, must: and yet he will be vain. For every little degree of beauty, how short or improper soever, will be looked on fondly by him; because it is all pure gains, and more than he promised to himself; and because he has no test, or standard in his judgment, with which to chastise his opinion of it.

Now this idea of perfection is, in poetry, more refined than in other kinds of writing; and because more refined, therefore more difficult; and because more difficult, therefore more rarely attained; and the non-attainment of it is, as I have said, the source of our vanity. Hence the poetic clan are more obnoxious to vanity than others. And from vanity consequently flows that great sensibility of disrespect, that quick resentment, that tinder of the mind that kindles at every spark, and justly marks them out for the genus irritabile among mankind. And from this combustible temper, this serious anger for no very serious things, things looked on by most as foreign to the important points of life, as consequentially flows that inheritance of ridicule, which devolves on them, from generation to generation. As soon as they become authors, they become like Ben Jonson's angry boy, and learn the art of quarrel.

> Concordes animæ — dum nocte prementur;
> Heu! quantum inter se bellum, si lumina vitæ
> Attigerint, quantas acies stragemque ciebunt!
> Qui Juvenes! quantas ostentant, aspice, vires.
> Ne, pueri! ne tanta animis assuescite bella.
> Tuque prior, tu parce, genus qui ducis Olympo,
> Sidereo flagrans clypeo, et cœlestibus armis,
> Projice tela manu, sanguis meus!
> Nec te ullæ facies, non terruit ipse Typhœus
> Arduus, arma tenens; non te Messapus et Ufens,
> Contemtorque Deûm Mezentius. VIRG.

But to return. He that has this idea of perfection in the work he undertakes, however successful he is, will yet be modest; because to rise up to that idea, which he proposed for his model, is almost, if not absolutely, impossible.

These two observations account for what may seem as strange, as it is infallibly true; I mean, they show us why good writers have the lowest, and bad writers the highest, opinion of their own performances. They who have only a partial idea of this perfection, as their portion of ignorance or knowledge of it is greater or less, have proportionable degrees of modesty or conceit.

Nor, though natural good understanding makes a tolerably just judgment in things of this nature, will the reader judge the worse, for forming to himself a notion of what he ought to expect from the piece he has in hand, before he begins his perusal of it.

The ode, as it is the eldest kind of poetry, so it is more spiritous, and more remote from prose, than any other, in sense, sound, expression, and conduct. Its thoughts should be uncommon, sublime, and moral; its numbers full, easy, and most harmonious; its expression pure, strong, delicate, yet unaffected; and of a curious felicity beyond other poems; its conduct should be rapturous, somewhat abrupt, and immethodical to a vulgar eye. That apparent order, and connexion, which gives form and life to some compositions, takes away the very soul of this. Fire, elevation, and select thought, are indispensable; an humble, tame, and vulgar ode is the most pitiful error a pen can commit.

> Musa dedit fidibus divos, puerosque deorum.

And as its subjects are sublime, its writer's genius should be so too; otherwise it becomes the meanest thing in writing, viz. an involuntary burlesque.

It is the genuine character, and true merit of the ode, a little to startle some apprehensions. Men of cold complexions are very apt to mistake a want of vigour in their imaginations, for a delicacy of taste in their judgments; and, like persons of a tender sight, they look on bright objects, in their natural lustre, as too glaring; what is most delightful to a stronger eye, is painful to them. Thus Pindar, who has as much logic at the bottom as Aristotle or Euclid, to some critics has appeared as mad; and must appear so to all who enjoy no portion of his own divine spirit. Dwarf understandings, measuring others by their own standard, are apt to think they see a monster, when they see a man.

And indeed it seems to be the amends which nature makes to those whom she has not blessed with an elevation of mind, to indulge them in the comfortable mistake, that all is wrong, which falls not within the narrow limits of their own comprehensions and relish.

Judgment, indeed, that masculine power of the mind, in ode, as in all compositions, should bear the supreme sway; and a beautiful imagination, as its mistress, should be subdued to its dominion. Hence, and hence only, can proceed the fairest offspring of the human mind.

But then in ode, there is this difference from other kinds of poetry; that, there, the imagination, like a very beautiful mistress, is indulged in the appearance of domineering; though the judgment, like an artful lover, in reality carries its point; and the less it is suspected of it, it shows the more masterly conduct, and deserves the greater commendation.

It holds true in this province of writing, as in war, "The more danger, the more honour." It must be very enterprising: it must, in Shakespeare's style, have hairbreadth 'scapes; and often tread the very brink of error: nor can it ever deserve the applause of the real judge, unless it renders itself obnoxious to the misapprehensions of the contrary.

Such is Casimire's strain among the moderns, whose lively wit, and happy fire, is an honour to them. And Buchanan might justly be much admired, if any thing more than the sweetness of his numbers, and the purity of his diction, were his own: his original, from which I have taken my motto, through all the disadvantages of a northern prose translation, is still admirable; and,

Cowley says, as preferable in beauty to Buchanan, as Judæa is to Scotland.

Pindar, Anacreon, Sappho, and Horace, are the great masters of lyric poetry among Heathen writers. Pindar's muse, like Sacharissa, is a stately, imperious, and accomplished beauty; equally disdaining the use of art, and the fear of any rival; so intoxicating that it was the highest commendation that could be given an ancient, that he was not afraid to taste of her charms;

> Pindarici fontis qui non expalluit haustus;

a danger which Horace declares he durst not run.

Anacreon's Muse is like Amoret, most sweet, natural, and delicate; all over flowers, graces, and charms; inspiring complacency, not awe; and she seems to have good nature enough to admit a rival, which she cannot find.

Sappho's Muse, like Lady ——, is passionately tender, and glowing; like oil set on fire, she is soft, and warm, in excess. Sappho has left us a few fragments only; time has swallowed the rest; but that little which remains, like the remaining jewel of Cleopatra, after the other was dissolved at her banquet, may be esteemed (as was that jewel) a sufficient ornament for the goddess of beauty herself.

Horace's Muse (like one I shall not presume to name) is correct, solid, and moral; she joins all the sweetness and majesty, all the sense and the fire of the former, in the justest proportions and degrees; superadding a felicity of dress entirely her own. She moreover is distinguishable by this particularity, that she abounds in hidden graces, and secret charms, which none but the discerning can discover; nor are any capable of doing full justice, in their opinion to her excellencies, without giving the world, at the same time, an incontestable proof of refinement in their own understandings.

But, after all, to the honour of our own country I must add, that I think Mr. Dryden's Ode on St. Cecilia's Day inferior to no composition of this kind. Its chief beauty consists in adapting the numbers most happily to the variety of the occasion. Those by which he has chosen to express majesty, (viz.)

> Assumes the God,
> Affects to nod,
> And seems to shake the spheres,

are chosen in the following ode, because the subject of it is great.

For the more harmony likewise, I chose the frequent return of rhyme; which laid me under great difficulties. But difficulties overcome give grace and pleasure. Nor can I account for the pleasure of rhyme in general (of which the moderns are too fond) but from this truth.

But then the writer must take care that the difficulty is overcome. That is, he must make rhyme consistent with as perfect sense, and expression, as could be expected if he was free from that shackle. Otherwise, it gives neither grace to the work, nor pleasure to the reader, nor, consequently, reputation to the poet.

To sum the whole: ode should be peculiar, but not strained; moral, but not flat; natural, but not obvious; delicate, but not affected; noble, but not ambitious; full, but not obscure; fiery, but not mad; thick, but not loaded in its numbers, which should be most harmonious, without the least sacrifice of expression, or of sense. Above all, in this, as in every work of genius, somewhat of an original spirit should be, at least attempted; otherwise the poet, whose character disclaims mediocrity, makes a secondary praise his ultimate ambition; which has something of a contradiction in it. Originals only have true life, and differ as much from the best imitations, as men from the most animated pictures of them. Nor is what I say at all inconsistent with a due deference for the great standards of antiquity; nay, that very deference is an argument for it, for doubtless their example is on my side in this matter. And we should rather imitate their example in the general motives, and fundamental methods of their working, than in their works themselves. This is a distinction, I think, not hitherto made, and a distinction of consequence. For the first may make us their equals; the second must pronounce us their inferiors even in our utmost success. But the first of these prizes is not so readily taken by the moderns; as valuables too massy for easy carriage are not so liable to the thief.

The ancients had a particular regard to the choice of their subjects; which were generally national and great. My subject is, in its own nature, noble; most proper for an Englishman; never more proper than on this occasion; and (what is strânge) hitherto unsung.

If I stand not absolutely condemned by my own rules; if I have hit the spirit of ode in general; if I cannot think with Mr. Cowley, that "Music alone, sometimes, makes an excellent ode;"

> Versus inopes rerum, nugæque canoræ;

if there is any thought, enthusiasm, and picture, which are as the body, soul, and robe of poetry; in a word, if in any degree I have provided rather food for men, than air for wits; I hope smaller faults will meet indulgence for the sake of the design, which is the glory of my country and my king.

And indeed, this may be said, in general, that great subjects are above being nice; that dignity and spirit ever suffer from scrupulous exactness; And that the minuter cares effeminate a composition. Great masters of poetry, painting, and statuary, in their nobler works, have even affected the contrary: and justly; for a truly masculine air partakes more of the negligent, than of the neat, both in writings, and in life —

Grandis oratio haberet majestatis suæ pondus. — PETRON.

A poem, like a criminal, under too severe correction, may lose all its spirit, and expire. We know it was Faberrimus, that was such an artist at a hair or a nail. And we know the cause was

Quia ponere totum
Nescius. HOR.

To close: if a piece of this nature wants an apology, I must own, that those who have strength of mind sufficient profitably to devote the whole of their time to the severer studies, I despair of imitating, I can only envy and admire. The mind is relieved and strengthened by variety; and he that sometimes is sporting with his pen, is only taking the most effectual means of giving a general importance to it. This truth is clear from the knowledge of human nature, and of history; from which I could cite very celebrated instances, did I not fear that, by citing them, I should condemn myself, who am so little qualified to follow their example in its full extent.

OCEAN. AN ODE.

Let the sea make a noise, let the floods clap their hands.
PSALM XCVIII.

SWEET rural scene!
Of flocks and green!
At careless ease my limbs are spread;
All nature still,
But yonder rill;
And list'ning pines nod o'er my head:

In prospect wide,
The boundless tide!
Waves cease to foam, and winds to roar;
Without a breeze,
The curling seas
Dance on, in measure to the shore.

Who sings the source
Of wealth and force?
Vast field of commerce, and big war,
Where wonders dwell!
Where terrors swell!
And Neptune thunders from his car?

Where? where are they,
Whom Pæan's ray
Has touch'd, and bid divinely rave?—

What! none aspire?
I snatch the lyre,
And plunge into the foaming wave.

The wave resounds!
The rock rebounds!
The Nereids to my song reply!
I lead the choir,
And they conspire,
With voice and shell, to lift it high.

They spread in air
Their bosoms fair,
Their verdant tresses pour behind:
The billows beat
With nimble feet,
With notes triumphant swell the wind.

Who love the shore,
Let those adore
The god Apollo, and his Nine,
Parnassus' hill,
And Orpheus' skill;
But let Arion's harp be mine.

The main! the main!
Is Britain's reign;
Her strength, her glory, is her fleet:
The main! the main!
Be Britain's strain;
As Tritons strong, as Syrens sweet.

Thro' nature wide
Is nought descried
So rich in pleasure or surprise;
When all-serene,
How sweet the scene!
How dreadful, when the billows rise;

And storms deface
The fluid glass,
In which erewhile Britannia fair
Look'd down with pride,
Like Ocean's bride,
Adjusting her majestic air!

When tempests cease,
And, hush'd in peace,
The flatten'd surges smoothly spread,
Deep silence keep,
And seem to sleep
Recumbent on their oozy bed;

With what a trance,
The level glance,
Unbroken, shoots along the seas!
Which tempt from shore
The painted oar;
And every canvass courts the breeze!

When rushes forth
The frowning north
On black'ning billows, with what dread

My shuddering soul
Beholds them roll,
And hears their roarings o'er my head!

With terror mark
Yon flying bark!
Now center-deep descend the brave;
Now, toss'd on high,
It takes the sky,
A feather on the tow'ring wave!

Now spins around
In whirls profound:
Now whelm'd; now pendant near the clouds;
Now stunn'd, it reels
'Midst thunder's peals:
And now fierce lightning fires the shrouds.

All ether burns!
Chaos returns!
And blends, once more, the seas and skies:
No space between
Thy bosom green,
O deep! and the blue concave, lies.

The northern blast,
The shatter'd mast,
The syrt, the whirlpool, and the rock,
The breaking spout,
The stars gone out,
The boiling streight, the monsters shock,

Let others fear;
To Britain dear
Whate'er promotes her daring claim;
Those terrors charm,
Which keep her warm
In chase of honest gain, or fame.

The stars are bright
To cheer the night,
And shed, thro' shadows, temper'd fire;
And Phœbus' flames,
With burnish'd beams,
Which some adore, and all admire.

Are then the seas
Outshone by these?
Bright Thetis! thou art not outshone;
With kinder beams,
And softer gleams,
Thy bosom wears them as thy own.

There, set in green,
Gold stars are seen,
A mantle rich! thy charms to wrap;
And when the sun
His race has run,
He falls enamour'd in thy lap.

Those clouds, whose dyes
Adorn the skies,
That silver snow, that pearly rain,

Has Phœbus stole
To grace the pole,
The plunder of th' invaded main!

The gaudy bow,
Whose colours glow,
Whose arch with so much skill is bent,
To Phœbus' ray,
Which paints so gay,
By thee the wat'ry woof was lent.

In chambers deep,
Where waters sleep,
What unknown treasures pave the floor!
The pearl, in rows,
Pale lustre throws;
The wealth immense, which storms devour.

From Indian mines,
With proud designs,
The merchant, swoln, digs golden ore;
The tempests rise,
And seize the prize,
And toss him breathless on the shore.

His son complains
In pious strains,
"Ah cruel thirst of gold!" he cries;
Then ploughs the main,
In zeal for gain,
The tears yet swelling in his eyes.

Thou wat'ry vast!
What mounds are cast
To bar thy dreadful flowings o'er!
Thy proudest foam
Must know its home;
But rage of gold disdains a shore.

Gold pleasure buys;
But pleasure dies,
Too soon the gross fruition cloys;
Tho' raptures court,
The sense is short;
But virtue kindles living joys;

Joys felt alone!
Joys ask'd of none!
Which time's and fortune's arrows miss:
Joys that subsist,
Tho' fates resist,
An unprecarious, endless bliss!

The soul refin'd
Is most inclin'd
To every moral excellence;
All vice is dull,
A knave 's a fool;
And virtue is the child of sense.

The virtuous mind,
Nor wave, nor wind,
Nor civil rage, nor tyrant's frown,

The shaken ball,
Nor planet's fall,
From its firm basis can dethrone.

This Britain knows,
And therefore glows
With gen'rous passions, and expends
Her wealth and zeal
On public weal,
And brightens both by god-like ends.

What end so great
As that which late
Awoke the genius of the main;
Which tow'ring rose
With George to close,
And rival great Eliza's reign?

A voice has flown
From Britain's throne
To re-inflame a grand design;
That voice shall rear
Yon *fabric fair,
As nature's rose at the divine.

When nature sprung,
Blest angels sung,
And shouted o'er the rising ball;

* A new fund for Greenwich hospital, recommended from the throne.

For strains as high
As man's can fly,
These sea-devoted honours call.

From boist'rous seas,
The lap of ease
Receives our wounded, and our old;
High domes ascend!
Stretch'd arches bend!
Proud columns swell! wide gates unfold!

Here, soft reclin'd,
From wave, from wind,
And fortune's tempest safe ashore,
To cheat their care,
Of former war
They talk the pleasing shadows o'er.

In lengthen'd tales,
Our fleet prevails;
In tales the lenitives of age!
And o'er the bowl,
They fire the soul
Of list'ning youth, to martial rage.

Unhappy they!
And falsely gay!
Who bask for ever in success;
A constant feast
Quite palls the taste,
And long enjoyment is distress.

When, after toil,
His native soil
The panting mariner regains,
What transport flows
From bare repose!
We reap our pleasure from our pains.

Ye warlike slain!
Beneath the main,
Wrapt in a wat'ry winding sheet;
Who bought with blood
Your country's good,
Your country's *full-blown glory greet.

What pow'rful charm
Can death disarm?
Your long, your iron slumbers break?
By Jove, by Fame,
By George's name,
Awake! awake! awake! awake!

With spiral shell,
Full blasted, tell,
That all your wat'ry realms should ring;
Your pearl alcoves,
Your coral groves,
Should echo theirs, and Britain's king.

* Written soon after King George the First's accession.

As long as stars
Guide mariners,
As Carolina's virtues please,
Or suns invite
The ravish'd sight,
The British flag shall sweep the seas.

Peculiar both!
Oúr soil's strong growth,
And our bold natives' hardy mind;
Sure heaven bespoke
Our hearts and oak,
To give a master to mankind.

That noblest birth
Of teeming earth,
Of forests fair, that daughter proud,
To foreign coasts
Our grandeur boasts,
And Britain's pleasure speaks aloud:

Now big with war,
Sends fate from far,
If rebel realms their fate demand,
Now, sumptuous spoils
Of foreign soils
Pours in the bosom of our land.

Hence Britain lays
In scales, and weighs
The fate of kingdoms, and of kings;

And as she frowns,
Or smiles, on crowns
A night, or day of glory, springs.

Thus ocean swells
The streams and rills,
And to their borders lifts them high;
Or else withdraws
The mighty cause,
And leaves their famish'd channels dry.

How mixt, how frail,
How sure to fail,
Is every pleasure of mankind!
A damp destroys
My blooming joys,
While Britain's glory fires my mind.

For who can gaze
On restless seas,
Unstruck with life's more restless state?
Where all are tost,
And most are lost,
By tides of passion, blasts of fate?

The world 's the main,
How vext! how vain!
Ambition swells, and anger foams;
May good men find,
Beneath the wind,
A noiseless shore, unruffled homes!

The public scene
Of harden'd men
Teach me, O teach me to despise!
The world few know
But to their woe,
Our crimes with our experience rise;

All tender sense
Is banish'd thence,
All maiden nature's first alarms
What shock'd before
Disgust no more,
And what disgusted has its charms.

In landscapes green
True bliss is seen,
With innocence, in shades, she sports;
In wealthy towns
Proud labour frowns,
And painted sorrow smiles in courts.

These scenes untried
Seduc'd my pride,
To fortune's arrows bar'd my breast;
Till wisdom came,
A hoary dame!
And told me pleasure was in rest.

"O may I steal
Along the vale
Of humble life, secure from foes!

My friend sincere!
My judgment clear!
And gentle business my repose!

"My mind be strong
To combat wrong!
Grateful, O king! for favours shown!
Soft to complain
For others' pain!
And bold to triumph o'er my own!

"(When fortune 's kind)
Acute to find,
And warm to relish every boon!
And wise to still
Fantastic ill,
Whose frightful spectres stalk at noon!

"No fruitless toils!
No brainless broils!
Each moment levell'd at the mark!
Our day so short
Invites to sport;
Be sad and solemn when 'tis dark.

"Yet, prudence, still
Rein thou my will!
What 's most important, make most dear!
For 'tis in this
Resides true bliss;
True bliss, a deity severe!

"When temper leans
To gayer scenes,
And serious life void moments spares,
The sylvan chase
My sinews brace!
Or song unbend my mind from cares!

"Nor shun, my soul!
The genial bowl,
Where mirth, good nature, spirit, flow!
Ingredients these,
Above, to please
The laughing gods, the wise, below.

"Though rich the vine,
More wit than wine,
More sense than wit, good-will than art,
May I provide!
Fair truth, my pride!
My joy, the converse of the heart!

"The gloomy brow,
The broken vow,
To distant climes, ye gods! remove!
The nobly soul'd
Their commerce hold
With words of truth and looks of love!

"O glorious aim!
O wealth supreme!
Divine benevolence of soul!

That greatly glows,
And freely flows,
And in one blessing grasps the whole;

"Prophetic schemes,
And golden dreams,
May I, unsanguine, cast away!
Have, what I have!
And live, not leave,
Enamour'd of the present day!

"My hours my own!
My faults unknown!
My chief revenue in content!
Then, leave one beam
Of honest fame!
And scorn the labour'd monument!

"Unhurt my urn!
Till that great turn
When mighty nature's self shall die!
Time cease to glide,
With human pride,
Sunk in the ocean of eternity."

A PARAPHRASE ON PART OF THE BOOK OF JOB.*

TO THE RIGHT HONOURABLE THOMAS LORD PARKER, BARON OF MACCLESFIELD, LORD HIGH CHANCELLOR OF GREAT BRITAIN, ETC. ETC.

MY LORD,

THOUGH I have not the honour of being known to your lordship, I presume to take a privilege which men of retirement are apt to think themselves in possession of, as being the only method they have of making their way to persons of your lordship's high station without struggling through multitudes for access. I may possibly fail in my respect to your lordship, even while I endeavour to show it most; but if I err, it is because I imagined I ought not to make my first approach to one of your lordship's exalted character with less ceremony than that of a dedication. It is annexed to the condition of eminent merit, not to suffer more from the malice of its enemies, than from the importunity of its admirers; and per-

* It is disputed amongst the critics who was the author of the book of Job; some give it to Moses, some to others. As I was engaged in this little performance, some arguments occurred to me which favour the former of those opinions; which arguments I have flung into the following notes, where little else is to be expected.

haps it would be unjust, that your lordship should hope to be exempted from the troubles, when you possess all the talents, of a patron.

I have here a fair occasion to celebrate those sublime qualities, of which a whole nation is sensible, were it not inconsistent with the design of my present application. By the just discharge of your great employments, your lordship may well deserve the prayers of the distressed, the thanks of your country, and the approbation of your royal master: this indeed is a reason why every good Briton should applaud your lordship; but it is equally a reason why none should disturb you in the execution of your important affairs by works of fancy and amusement. I was therefore induced to make this address to your lordship, by considering you rather in the amiable light of a person distinguished for a refined taste of the polite arts, and the candour that usually attends it, than in the dignity of your public character.

The greatness and solemnity of the subjects treated of in the following work cannot fail in some measure to recommend it to a person who holds in the utmost veneration those sacred books from which it is taken; and would at the same time justify to the world my choice of the great name prefixed to it, could I be assured that the undertaking had not suffered in my hands. Thus much I think myself obliged to say; that if this little performance had not been very indulgently spoken of by some, whose judgment is universally allowed in writings of this nature, I had not dared to gratify my ambition in offering it to your lordship: I am sensible that I am endeavouring to excuse one vanity by another; but I hope I shall meet with pardon for it, since it is visibly intended to show the great submission and respect with which I am, my lord, your lordship's most obedient and most humble servant,

EDWARD YOUNG.

THRICE happy Job* long liv'd in regal state,
Nor saw the sumptuous East a prince so great;
Whose worldly stores in such abundance flow'd,
Whose heart with such exalted virtue glow'd.
At length misfortunes take their turn to reign,
And ills on ills succeed; a dreadful train!
What now but deaths, and poverty, and wrong,

* The Almighty's speech, chapter xxxviii. &c. which is what I paraphrase in this little work, is by much the finest part of the noblest and most ancient poem in the world. Bishop Patrick says, its grandeur is as much above all other poetry, as thunder is louder than a whisper. In order to set this distinguished part of the poem in a fuller light, and give the reader a clearer conception of it, I have abridged the preceding and subsequent parts of the poem, and joined them to it; so that this piece is a sort of an epitome of the whole book of Job.

I use the word paraphrase, because I want another which might better answer to the uncommon liberties I have taken. I have omitted, added, and transposed. The mountain, the comet, the sun, and other parts, are entirely added: those

The sword wide-wasting, the reproachful tongue,
And spotted plagues, that mark'd his limbs all o'er
So thick with pains, they wanted room for more?
A change so sad what mortal heart could bear?
Exhausted woe had left him nought to fear;
But gave him all to grief. Low earth he prest,
Wept in the dust, and sorely smote his breast.
His friends around the deep affliction mourn'd,
Felt all his pangs, and groan for groan return'd;
In anguish of their hearts their mantles rent,
And seven long days in solemn silence spent;
A debt of rev'rence to distress so great!
Then Job contain'd no more; but cursed his fate.
His day of birth, its inauspicious light
He wishes sunk in shades of endless night,
And blotted from the year; nor fears to crave
Death, instant death; impatient for the grave,
That seat of bliss, that mansion of repose,
Where rest and mortals are no longer foes;

upon the peacock, the lion, &c. are much enlarged; and I have thrown the whole into a method more suited to our notions of regularity. The judicious, if they compare this piece with the original, will, I flatter myself, find the reasons for the great liberties I have indulged myself in through the whole.

Longinus has a chapter on interrogations, which shows that they contribute much to the sublime. This speech of the Almighty is made up of them. Interrogation seems indeed the proper style of majesty incensed. It differs from other manner of reproof, as bidding a person execute himself does from a common execution; for he that asks the guilty a proper question, makes him, in effect, pass sentence on himself.

Where counsellors are hush'd, and mighty kings
(O happy turn!) no more are wretched things.
His words were daring, and displeas'd his friends;
His conduct they reprove, and he defends;
And now they kindled into warm debate,
And sentiments oppos'd with equal heat;
Fix'd in opinion, both refuse to yield,
And summon all their reason to the field:
So high at length their arguments were wrought,
They reach'd the last extent of human thought:
A pause ensu'd. — When, lo! Heaven interpos'd,
And awfully the long contention clos'd.
Full o'er their heads, with terrible surprise,
A sudden whirlwind blacken'd all the skies:
(They saw, and trembled!*) From the darkness broke
A dreadful voice, and thus th' Almighty spoke.
Who gives his tongue a loose so bold and vain,
Censures my conduct, and reproves my reign?
Lifts up his thoughts against me from the dust,
And tells the world's Creator what is just?

* The book of Job is well known to be dramatic, and, like the tragedies of old Greece, is fiction built on truth. Probably this most noble part of it, the Almighty speaking out of the whirlwind, (so suitable to the after-practice of the Greek stage, when there happened *dignus vindice nodus*,) is fictitious; but is a fiction more agreeable to the time in which Job lived, than to any since. Frequent before the law were the appearances of the Almighty after this manner, Exod. c. xix. Ezek. c. i. &c. Hence is he said to "dwell in thick darkness: and have his way in the whirlwind."

Of late so brave, now lift a dauntless eye,
Face my demand, and give it a reply:
Where didst thou dwell at nature's early birth?
Who laid foundations for the spacious earth?
Who on its surface did extend the line,
Its form determine, and its bulk confine?
Who fix'd the corner-stone? What hand, declare,
Hung it on nought, and fasten'd it on air;
When the bright morning stars in concert sung,
When heaven's high arch with loud hosannas rung;
When shouting sons of God the triumph crown'd,
And the wide concave thunder'd with the sound?
Earth's num'rous kingdoms, hast thou view'd them all?
And can thy span of knowledge grasp the ball?
Who heav'd the mountain, which sublimely stands,
And casts its shadow into distant lands?

Who, stretching forth his sceptre o'er the deep,
Can that wide world in due subjection keep?
I broke the globe, I scoop'd its hollow'd side,
And did a bason for the floods provide;
I chain'd them with my word; the boiling sea,
Work'd up in tempests, hears my great decree;
"* Thus far, thy floating tide shall be convey'd;
And here, O main, be thy proud billows stay'd."

* There is a very great air in all that precedes, but this is signally sublime. We are struck with admiration to see the vast and ungovernable ocean receiving commands, and punctually obeying them; to find it like a managed horse, raging, tossing, and foaming, but by the rule and direction of its master. This passage yields in sublimity to that of "Let there be

Hast thou explor'd the secrets of the deep,
Where, shut from use, unnumber'd treasures sleep?
Where, down a thousand fathoms from the day,
Springs the great fountain, mother of the sea?
Those gloomy paths did thy bold foot e'er tread,
Whole worlds of waters rolling o'er thy head?
Hath the cleft centre open'd wide to thee?
Death's inmost chambers didst thou ever see?
E'er knock at his tremendous gate, and wade
To the black portal through th' incumbent shade?
Deep are those shades; but shades still deeper hide
My counsels from the ken of human pride.
Where dwells the light? In what refulgent dome?
And where has darkness made her dismal home?
Thou know'st, no doubt, since thy large heart is fraught
With ripen'd wisdom, through long ages brought;
Since nature was call'd forth when thou wast by,
And into being rose beneath thine eye!
Are mists begotten? Who their father knew?
From whom descend the pearly drops of dew?
To bind the stream by night, what hand can boast,
Or whiten morning with the hoary frost?
Whose powerful breath, from northern regions blown,
Touches the sea, and turns it into stone?

light," &c., so much only as the absolute government of nature yields to the creation of it.

The like spirit in these two passages is no bad concurrent argument, that Moses is author of the book of Job.

A sudden desart spreads o'er realms defac'd,
And lays one half of the creation waste?
Thou know'st me not; thy blindness cannot see
How vast a distance parts thy God from thee.
Canst thou in whirlwinds mount aloft? Canst thou
In clouds and darkness wrap thy awful brow?
And, when day triumphs in meridian light,
Put forth thy hand, and shade the world with night?
Who launch'd the clouds in air, and bid them roll
Suspended seas aloft, from pole to pole?
Who can refresh the burning sandy plain,
And quench the summer with a waste of rain?
Who, in rough desarts, far from human toil,
Made rocks bring forth, and desolation smile?
There blooms the rose, where human face ne'er shone,
And spreads its beauties to the sun alone.
To check the shower, who lifts his hand on high,
And shuts the sluices of th' exhausted sky
When earth no longer mourns her gaping veins,
Her naked mountains, and her russet plains;
But, new in life, a cheerful prospect yields
Of shining rivers, and of verdant fields;
When groves and forests lavish all their bloom,
And earth and heaven are fill'd with rich perfume?
Hast thou e'er scal'd my wintry skies, and seen
Of hail and snows my northern magazine?
These the dread treasures of mine anger are,
My funds of vengeance for the day of war,

When clouds rain death, and storms, at my command,
Rage through the world, or waste a guilty land.
Who taught the rapid winds to fly so fast,
Or shakes the centre with his eastern blast?
Who from the skies can a whole deluge pour?
Who strikes through nature with the solemn roar
Of dreadful thunder, points it where to fall,
And in fierce lightning wraps the flying ball?
Not he who trembles at the darted fires,
Falls at the sound, and in the flash expires.
Who drew the comet out to such a size,
And pour'd his flaming train o'er half the skies?
Did thy resentment hang him out? Does he
Glare on the nations, and denounce, from thee?
Who on low earth can moderate the rein,
That guides the stars along th' ethereal plain?
Appoint their seasons, and direct their course,
Their lustre brighten, and supply their force?
Canst thou the skies' benevolence restrain,
And cause the Pleiades to shine in vain?
Or, when Orion sparkles from his sphere,
Thaw the cold season, and unbind the year?
Bid Mazzaroth his destin'd station know,
And teach the bright Arcturus where to glow?
Mine is the night, with all her stars; I pour
Myriads, and myriads I reserve in store.
Dost thou pronounce where day-light shall be born,
And draw the purple curtain of the morn;
Awake the sun, and bid him come away,

And glad thy world with his obsequious ray?
Hast thou, inthron'd in flaming glory, driven
Triumphant round the spacious ring of heaven?
That pomp of light, what hand so far displays,
That distant earth lies basking in the blaze?
Who did the soul with her rich powers invest,
And light up reason in the human breast?
To shine, with fresh increase of lustre, bright,
When stars and sun are set in endless night?
To these my various questions make reply.
Th' Almighty spoke; and, speaking, shook the sky.
What then, Chaldæan sire, was thy surprise!
Thus thou, with trembling heart, and downcast eyes:
"Once and again, which I in groans deplore,
My tongue has err'd; but shall presume no more.
My voice is in eternal silence bound,
And all my soul falls prostrate to the ground."
He ceas'd: when, lo! again th' Almighty spoke;
The same dread voice from the black whirlwind broke.
Can that arm measure with an arm divine?
And canst thou thunder with a voice like mine?
Or in the hollow of thy hand contain
The bulk of waters, the wide-spreading main,
When, mad with tempests, all the billows rise
In all their rage, and dash the distant skies?
Come forth, in beauty's excellence array'd;
And be the grandeur of thy power display'd;
Put on omnipotence, and, frowning, make
The spacious round of the creation shake;

Dispatch thy vengeance, bid it overthow
Triumphant vice, lay lofty tyrants low,
And crumble them to dust. When this is done,
I grant thy safety lodg'd in thee alone;
Of thee thou art, and mayst undaunted stand
Behind the buckler of thine own right hand.
Fond man! the vision of a moment made!
Dream of a dream! and shadow of a shade!
What worlds hast thou produc'd, what creatures fram'd,
What insects cherish'd, that thy God is blam'd?
When *pain'd with hunger, the wild raven's brood
Loud calls on God, importunate for food,
Who hears their cry, who grants their hoarse request,
And stills the clamour of the craving nest?
Who in the stupid ostrich† has subdu'd

* Another argument that Moses was the author, is, that most of the creatures here mentioned are Egyptian. The reason given why the raven is particularly mentioned as an object of the care of Providence, is, because by her clamorous and importunate voice, she particularly seems always calling upon it; thence κοράσσω, à κόραξ, Ælian. l. ii. c. 48, is "to ask earnestly." And since there were ravens on the bank of the Nile more clamorous than the rest of that species, those probably are meant in that place.

† There are many instances of this bird's stupidity: let two suffice. First, it covers its head in the reeds, and thinks itself all out of sight,

Stat lumine clauso
Ridendum revoluta caput, creditque latere
Quæ non ipsa videt. CLAUD.

Secondly, they that go in pursuit of them, draw the skin of

A parent's care, and fond inquietude?
While far she flies, her scatter'd eggs are found,
Without an owner, on the sandy ground;
Cast out on fortune, they at mercy lie,
And borrow life from an indulgent sky;
Adopted by the sun, in blaze of day,
They ripen under his prolific ray.
Unmindful she, that some unhappy tread
May crush her young in their neglected bed.
*What time she skims along the field with speed,
†She scorns the rider, and pursuing steed.

an ostrich's neck on one hand, which proves a sufficient lure to take them with the other.

They have so little brain, that Heliogabalus had six hun dred heads for his supper.

Here we may observe, that our judicious as well as sublime author, just touches the great points of distinction in each creature, and then hastens to another. A description is exact when you cannot add, but what is common to another thing; nor withdraw, but something peculiarly belonging to the thing described. A likeness is lost in too much description, as a meaning often in too much illustration.

* Here is marked another peculiar quality of this creature, which neither flies nor runs directly, but has a motion composed of both, and, using its wings as sails, makes great speed.

Vasta velut Libyæ venantûm vocibus ales
Cum premitur, calidas cursu transmittit arenas,
Inque modum veli sinuatis flamine pennis
Pulverulenta volat. CLAUD. in Eutr.

† Xenophon says, Cyrus had horses that could overtake the goat and the wild ass; but none that could reach this creature. A thousand golden ducats, or a hundred camels, was the stated price of a horse that could equal their speed.

How rich the peacock! * what bright glories run
From plume to plume, and vary in the sun!
He proudly spreads them, to the golden ray
Gives all his colours, and adorns the day;
With conscious state the specious round displays,
And slowly moves amid the waving blaze.
Who taught the hawk to find, in seasons wise,
Perpetual summer, and a change of skies?
When clouds deform the year, she mounts the wind,
Shoots to the south, nor fears the storm behind;
The sun returning, she returns again,
Lives in his beams, and leaves ill days to men.
Tho' strong the hawk,† tho' practis'd well to fly,
An eagle drops her in a lower sky;
An eagle, when, deserting human sight,
She seeks the sun in her unwearied flight:
Did thy command her yellow pinion lift
So high in air, and set her on the clift,
Where far above thy world she dwells alone,
And proudly makes the strength of rocks her own;

* Though this bird is but just mentioned in my author, I could not forbear going a little farther, and spreading those beautiful plumes (which are there shut up) in half a dozen lines. The circumstance I have marked of his opening his plumes to the sun is true. Expandit colores adverso maxime sole, quia sic fulgentius radiant. PLIN. l. x. c. 20.

† Thyanus (de Re Accip.) mentions a hawk that flew from Paris to London in a night.

And the Egyptians, in regard to its swiftness, made it their symbol for the wind; for which reason we may suppose the hawk, as well as the crow above, to have been a bird of note in Egypt.

*Thence wide o'er nature takes her dread survey,
And with a glance predestinates her prey?
She feasts her young with blood; and, hov'ring o'er
Th' unslaughter'd host, enjoys the promis'd gore.
†Know'st thou how many moons, by me assign'd,
Roll o'er the mountain goat, and forest hind,
While pregnant they a mother's load sustain?
They bend in anguish, and cast forth their pain.
Hale are their young, from human frailties freed;
Walk unsustain'd, and unassisted feed;
They live at once; forsake the dam's warm side;
Take the wide world, with nature for their guide;
Bound o'er the lawn, or seek the distant glade;
And find a home in each delightful shade.
Will the tall reem, which knows no lord but me,

* The eagle is said to be of so acute a sight, that when she is so high in air that man cannot see her, she can discern the smallest fish under water. My author accurately understood the nature of the creatures he describes, and seems to have been a naturalist as well as a poet, which the next note will confirm.

† The meaning of this question is, Knowest thou the time and circumstances of their bringing forth? For to know the time only was easy, and had nothing extraordinary in it; but the circumstances had something peculiarly expressive of God's providence, which makes the question proper in this place. Pliny observes, that the hind with young is by instinct directed to a certain herb called Seselis, which facilitates the birth. Thunder also (which looks like the more immediate hand of Providence) has the same effect. Ps. xxix. In so early an age to observe these things, may style our author a naturalist.

Low at the crib, and ask an alms of thee;
Submit his unworn shoulder to the yoke,
Break the stiff clod, and o'er thy furrow smoke?
Since great his strength, go trust him, void of care;
Lay on his neck the toil of all the year;
Bid him bring home the seasons to thy doors,
And cast his load among thy gather'd stores.
Didst thou from service the wild ass discharge,
And break his bonds, and bid him live at large,
Through the wide waste, his ample mansion, roam,
And lose himself in his unbounded home?
By nature's hand magnificently fed,
His meal is on the range of mountains spread;
As in pure air aloft he bounds along,
He sees in distant smoke the city throng;
Conscious of freedom, scorns the smother'd train,
The threat'ning driver, and the servile rein.
Survey the warlike horse! didst thou invest
With thunder his robust distended chest?
No sense of fear his dauntless soul allays;
'Tis dreadful to behold his nostrils blaze;
To paw the vale he proudly takes delight,
And triumphs in the fulness of his might;
High rais'd he snuffs the battle from afar,
And burns to plunge amid the raging war;
And mocks at death, and throws his foam around,
And in a storm of fury shakes the ground.
How does his firm, his rising heart, advance
Full on the brandish'd sword, and shaken lance;
While his fix'd eyeballs meet the dazzling shield,

Gaze, and return the lightning of the field!
He sinks the sense of pain in gen'rous pride,
Nor feels the shaft that trembles in his side;
But neighs to the shrill trumpet's dreadful blast
Till death; and when he groans, he groans his last.
But, fiercer still, the lordly lion stalks,
Grimly majestic in his lonely walks;
When round he glares, all living creatures fly;
He clears the desart with his rolling eye.
Say, mortal, does he rouse at thy command,
And roar to thee, and live upon thy hand?
Dost thou for him in forests bend thy bow,
And to his gloomy den the morsel throw,
Where bent on death lie hid his tawny brood,
And, couch'd in dreadful ambush, pant for blood;
Or, stretch'd on broken limbs, consume the day,
In darkness wrapt, and slumber o'er their prey?
*By the pale moon they take their destin'd round,
And lash their sides, and furious tear the ground.
Now shrieks, and dying groans, the desart fill;
They rage, they rend; their rav'nous jaws distill
With crimson foam; and, when the banquet 's o'er,
They stride away, and paint their steps with gore;
In flight alone the shepherd puts his trust,
And shudders at the talon in the dust.
Mild is my behemoth, though large his frame;

* Pursuing their prey by night is true of most wild beasts, particularly the lion. Ps. cvi. 20. The Arabians have one among their five hundred names for the lion, which signifies "the hunter by moonshine."

Smooth is his temper, and represt his flame,
While unprovok'd. This native of the flood
Lifts his broad foot, and puts ashore for food;
Earth sinks beneath him, as he moves along
To seek the herbs, and mingle with the throng.
See with what strength his harden'd loins are
bound,
All over proof and shut against a wound.
How like a mountain cedar moves his tail!
Nor can his complicated sinews fail.
Built high and wide, his solid bones surpass
The bars of steel; his ribs are ribs of brass;
His port majestic, and his armed jaw,
Give the wide forest, and the mountain, law.
The mountains feed him; there the beasts admire
The mighty stranger, and in dread retire:
At length his greatness nearer they survey,
Graze in his shadow, and his eye obey.
The fens and marshes are his cool retreat,
His noontide shelter from the burning heat;
Their sedgy bosoms his wide couch are made,
And groves of willows give him all their shade.
His eye drinks Jordan up, when, fir'd with
drought,
He trusts to turn its current down his throat;
In lessen'd waves it creeps along the plain:
* He sinks a river, and he thirsts again.

* Cephissi glaciale caput, quo suetus anhelam
Ferre sitim Python, amnemque avertere ponto.
STAT. Theb. vii. 349.

* Go to the Nile, and, from its fruitful side,
Cast forth thy line into the swelling tide:
With slender hair leviathan command,
And stretch his vastness on the loaded strand.
Will he become thy servant? Will he own
Thy lordly nod, and tremble at thy frown?
Or with his sport amuse thy leisure day,
And, bound in silk, with thy soft maidens play?
Shall pompous banquets swell with such a prize?
And the bowl journey round his ample size?
Or the debating merchants share the prey,
And various limbs to various marts convey?
Thro' his firm skull what steel its way can win?
What forceful engine can subdue his skin?
Fly far, and live; tempt not his matchless might:
The bravest shrink to cowards in his sight;
† The rashest dare not rouse him up: Who then
Shall turn on me, among the sons of men?
Am I a debtor? Hast thou ever heard

Qui spiris tegeret montes, hauriret hiatu
Flumina, &c. CLAUD. Pref. in Ruf.

Let not then this hyperbole seem too much for an eastern poet, though some commentators of name strain hard in this place for a new construction, through fear of it.

* The taking the crocodile is most difficult. Diodorus says, they are not to be taken but by iron nets. When Augustus conquered Egypt, he struck a medal, the impress of which was a crocodile chained to a palm-tree, with this inscription, Nemo antea religavit.

† This alludes to a custom of this creature, which is, when sated with fish, to come ashore and sleep among the reeds.

Whence come the gifts that are on me conferr'd?
My lavish fruit a thousand valleys fills,
And mine the herds, that graze a thousand hills:
Earth, sea, and air, all nature is my own;
And stars and sun are dust beneath my throne.
And dar'st thou with the world's great Father vie,
Thou, who dost tremble at my creature's eye?
At full my huge leviathan shall rise,
Boast all his strength, and spread his wondrous size.
Who, great in arms, e'er stripp'd his shining mail,
Or crown'd his triumph with a single scale?
Whose heart sustains him to draw near? * Behold,
Destruction yawns; his spacious jaws unfold,
And, marshall'd round the wide expanse, disclose
Teeth edg'd with death, and crowding rows on rows:
What hideous fangs on either side arise!
And what a deep abyss between them lies!
Mete with thy lance, and with thy plummet sound,
The one how long, the other how profound.
His bulk is charg'd with such a furious soul,
That clouds of smoke from his spread nostrils roll,

* The crocodile's mouth is exceeding wide. When he gapes, says Pliny, sic totum os. Martial says to his old woman,

Cum comparata rictibus tuis ora
Niliacus habet crocodilus angusta.

So that the expression there is barely just.

As from a furnace; and, when rous'd his ire,
* Fate issues from his jaws in streams of fire.
The rage of tempests, and the roar of seas,
Thy terror, this thy great superior please;
Strength on his ample shoulder sits in state;
His well-join'd limbs are dreadfully complete;
His flakes of solid flesh are slow to part;
As steel his nerves, as adamant his heart.
When, late awak'd, he rears him from the floods,
And, stretching forth his stature to the clouds,
Writhes in the sun aloft his scaly height,
And strikes the distant hills with transient light,
Far round are fatal damps of terror spread,
The mighty fear, nor blush to own their dread.
† Large is his front; and, when his burnish'd eyes
Lift their broad lids, the morning seems to rise.

* This too is nearer the truth than at first view may be imagined. The crocodile, say the naturalists, lying long under water, and being there forced to hold its breath, when it emerges, the breath long represt is hot, and bursts out so violently, that it resembles fire and smoke. The horse suppresses not his breath by any means so long, neither is he so fierce and animated; yet the most correct of poets ventures to use the same metaphor concerning him:

Collectumque premens volvit sub naribus ignem.

By this and the foregoing note I would caution against a false opinion of the eastern boldness, from passages in them ill understood.

† "His eyes are like the eyelids of the morning." I think this gives us as great an image of the thing it would express

In vain may death in various shapes invade,
The swift-wing'd arrow, the descending blade;
His naked breast their impotence defies;
The dart rebounds, the brittle fauchion flies.
Shut in himself, the war without he hears,
Safe in the tempest of their rattling spears;
The cumber'd strand their wasted volleys strow;
His sport, the rage and labour of the foe.
His pastimes like a cauldron boil the flood,
And blacken ocean with the rising mud;
The billows feel him, as he works his way;
His hoary footsteps shine along the sea;

as can enter the thought of man. It is not improbable that the Egyptians stole their hieroglyphic for the morning, which is the crocodile's eye, from this passage, though no commentator, I have seen, mentions it. It is easy to conceive how the Egyptians should be both readers and admirers of the writings of Moses, whom I suppose the author of this poem.

I have observed already that three or four of the creatures here described are Egyptian; the two last are notoriously so, they are the river-horse and the crocodile, those celebrated inhabitants of the Nile; and on these two it is that our author chiefly dwells. It would have been expected from an author more remote from that river than Moses, in a catalogue of creatures produced to magnify their Creator, to have dwelt on the two largest works of his hand, viz. the elephant and the whale. This is so natural an expectation, that some commentators have rendered behemoth and leviathan, the elephant and whale, though the descriptions in our author will not admit of it; but Moses being, as we may well suppose, under an immediate terror of the hippopotamus and crocodile, from their daily mischiefs and ravages around him, it is very accountable why he should permit them to take place.

The foam high-wrought, with white divides the
green,
And distant sailors point where death has been.
His like earth bears not on her spacious face:
Alone in nature stands his dauntless race,
For utter ignorance of fear renown'd,
In wrath he rolls his baleful eye around:
Makes every swoln, disdainful heart, subside,
And holds dominion o'er the sons of pride.
Then the Chaldæan eas'd his lab'ring breast,
With full conviction of his crime opprest.
"Thou canst accomplish all things, Lord of
might:
And every thought is naked to thy sight.
But, oh! thy ways are wonderful, and lie
Beyond the deepest reach of mortal eye.
Oft have I heard of thine Almighty power;
But never saw thee till this dreadful hour.
O'erwhelm'd with shame, the Lord of life I see,
Abhor myself, and give my soul to thee.
Nor shall my weakness tempt thine anger more:
Man is not made to question, but adore."

ON MICHAEL ANGELO'S FAMOUS PIECE OF THE CRUCIFIXION;

WHO IS SAID TO HAVE STABBED A PERSON THAT HE MIGHT DRAW IT MORE NATURALLY.*

Whilst his Redeemer on his canvass dies,
Stabb'd at his feet his brother weltering lies:
The daring artist, cruelly serene,
Views the pale cheek and the distorted mien;
He drains off life by drops, and, deaf to cries,
Examines every spirit as it flies:
He studies torment, dives in mortal woe,
To rouse up every pang repeats his blow;
Each rising agony, each dreadful grace,
Yet warm transplanting to his Saviour's face.
Oh glorious theft! oh nobly wicked draught!
With its full charge of death each feature fraught,
Such wondrous force the magic colours boast,
From his own skill he starts in horror lost.

* Though the report was propagated without the least truth, it may be sufficient ground to justify a poetical fancy's en larging on it.

TO MR. ADDISON,

ON THE TRAGEDY OF CATO.

WHAT do we see? Is Cato then become
A greater name in Britain than in Rome?
Does mankind now admire his virtues more,
Though Lucan, Horace, Virgil, wrote before?
How will posterity this truth explain?
"Cato begins to live in Anna's reign."
The world's great chiefs, in council or in arms,
Rise in your lines with more exalted charms;
Illustrious deeds in distant nations wrought,
And virtues by departed heroes taught,
Raise in your soul a pure immortal flame,
Adorn your life, and consecrate your fame;
To your renown all ages you subdue,
And Cæsar fought, and Cato bled for you.

All Souls Coll. Oxon.

HISTORICAL EPILOGUE TO THE BROTHERS.

A TRAGEDY.

AN Epilogue, through custom, is your right,
But ne'er perhaps was needful till this night:

To-night the virtuous falls, the guilty flies,
Guilt's dreadful close our narrow scene denies.
In history's authentic record read
What ample vengeance gluts Demetrius' shade;
Vengeance so great, that, when his tale is told,
With pity some e'en Perseus may behold.
  Perseus surviv'd, indeed, and fill'd the throne,
But ceaseless cares in conquest made him groan:
Nor reign'd he long; from Rome swift thunder flew,
And headlong from his throne the tyrant threw:
Thrown headlong down, by Rome in triumph led,
For this night's deed his perjur'd bosom bled:
His brother's ghost each moment made him start,
And all his father's anguish rent his heart.
  When, rob'd in black, his children round him hung,
And their rais'd arms in early sorrow wrung;
The younger smil'd, unconscious of their woe;
At which thy tears, O Rome! began to flow;
So sad the scene! What then must Perseus feel,
To see Jove's race attend the victor's wheel:
To see the slaves of his worst foes increase,
From such a source! — An emperor's embrace!
He sicken'd soon to death; and, what is worse,
He well deserv'd, and felt, the coward's curse;
Unpitied, scorn'd, insulted his last hour,
Far, far from home, and in a vassal's power:
His pale cheek rested on his shameful chain,
No friend to mourn, no flatterer to feign;

No suit retards, no comfort soothes his doom,
And not one tear bedews a monarch's tomb.
Nor ends it thus — dire vengeance to complete,
His ancient empire falling shares his fate:
His throne forgot! his weeping country chain'd!
And nations ask — where Alexander reign'd.
As public woes a prince's crime pursue,
So public blessings are his virtue's due.
Shout, Britons, shout — auspicious fortune bless!
And cry, Long live — Our title to success!

EPITAPH

ON LORD AUBREY BEAUCLERK,* IN WESTMINSTER ABBEY, 1740.

WHILST Britain boasts her empire o'er the deep,
This marble shall compel the brave to weep:
As men, as Britons, and as soldiers, mourn;
'Tis dauntless, loyal, virtuous Beauclerk's urn.
Sweet were his manners, as his soul was great,
And ripe his worth, though immature his fate;

* Lord Aubrey Beauclerk was the eighth son of the Duke of St. Albans, who was one of the sons of King Charles the Second. He was born in the year 1711; and, being regularly bred to the sea service, in 1731 he was appointed to the command of his majesty's ship the Ludlow Castle; and he commanded the Prince Frederick at the attack of the harbour of Carthagena, March 24, 1741. This young nobleman was one

Each tender grace that joy and love inspires,
Living, he mingled with his martial fires:
Dying, he bid Britannia's thunders roar;
And Spain still felt him, when he breath'd no more.

EPITAPH AT WELWYN, HERTFORDSHIRE.

If fond of what is rare, attend!
Here lies an honest man,
Of perfect piety,
Of lamblike patience,
My friend, James Barker;
To whom I pay this mean memorial,
For what deserves the greatest.
An example
Which shone through all the clouds of fortune,
Industrious in low estate,
The lesson and reproach of those above him.
To lay this little stone
Is my ambition;
While others rear

of the most promising commanders in the king's service. When on the desperate attack of the castle of Bocca Chica, at the entrance of the said harbour, he lost his life, both his legs being first shot off. The prose part of the inscription on his monument was the production of Mrs. Mary Jones of Oxford; who also wrote a poem on his death, printed in her Miscellanies, 8vo, 1752. — *R.*

The polish'd marbles of the great!
Vain pomp;
A turf o'er virtue charms us more.
E. Y. 1749.

A LETTER TO MR. TICKELL,

OCCASIONED BY THE DEATH OF THE RIGHT HON. JOSEPH ADDISON, ESQ., 1719.

—— Tu nunc eris alter ab illo. — VIRG.

O LONG with me in Oxford groves confin'd,
In social arts and sacred friendship join'd;
Fair Isis' sorrow, and fair Isis' boast,
Lost from her side, but fortunately lost;
Thy wonted aid, my dear companion! bring,
And teach me thy departed friend to sing:
A darling theme! once powerful to inspire,
And now to melt, the muses' mournful choir:
Now, and now first, we freely dare commend
His modest worth, nor shall our praise offend.
Early he bloom'd amid the learned train,
And ravish'd Isis listen'd to his strain.
"See, see," she cried, "old Maro's muse appears,
Wak'd from her slumber of two thousand years:
Her finish'd charms to Addison she brings,
Thinks in his thought, and in his numbers sings.

All read transported his pure classic page;
Read, and forget their climate and their age."
The state, when now his rising fame was known,
Th' unrival'd genius challeng'd for her own,
Nor would that one, for scenes for action strong,
Should let a life evaporate in song.
As health and strength the brightest charms dispense,
Wit is the blossom of the soundest sense:
Yet few, how few, with lofty thoughts inspir'd,
With quickness pointed, and with rapture fir'd,
In conscious pride their own importance find,
Blind to themselves, as the hard world is blind!
Wit they esteem a gay but worthless power,
The slight amusement of a leisure hour;
Unmindful that, conceal'd from vulgar eyes,
Majestic wisdom wears the bright disguise.
Poor Dido fondled thus, with idle joy,
Dread Cupid, lurking in the Trojan boy;
Lightly she toy'd, and trifled with his charms,
And knew not that a god was in her arms.
Who greatest excellence of thought could boast,
In action, too, have been distinguish'd most:
This Sommers* knew, and Addison sent forth
From the malignant regions of the north,
To be matur'd in more indulgent skies,
Where all the vigour of the soul can rise;
Thro' warmer veins where sprightlier spirits run,

* Lord Sommers procured a pension for Mr. Addison, which enabled him to prosecute his travels. — *R.*

And sense enliven'd sparkles in the sun.
With secret pain the prudent patriot gave
The hopes of Britain to the rolling wave,
Anxious, the charge to all the stars resign'd,
And plac'd a confidence in sea and wind.
Ausonia soon receiv'd her wondering guest,
And equal wonder in her turn confess'd,
To see her fervours rival'd by the pole,
Her lustre beaming from a northern soul:
In like surprise was her Æneas lost,
To find his picture grace a foreign coast.
Now the wide field of Europe he surveys,
Compares her kings, her thrones and empires weighs,
In ripen'd judgment and consummate thought;
Great work! by Nassau's favour cheaply bought.
He now returns to Britain a support,
Wise in her senate, graceful in her court;
And when the public welfare would permit,
The source of learning, and the soul of wit.
O Warwick! (whom the muse is fond to name,
And kindles, conscious of her future theme,)
O Warwick! by divine contagion bright!
How early didst thou catch his radiant light!
By him inspir'd, how shine before thy time,
And leave thy years, and leap into thy prime!
On some warm bank, thus, fortunately born,
A rose-bud opens to a summer's morn,
Full-blown ere noon her fragrant pride displays,
And shows th' abundance of her purple rays.

Wit, as her bays, was once a barren tree;
We now, surpris'd, her fruitful branches see;
Or, orange-like, till his auspicious time
It grew indeed, but shiver'd in our clime:
He first the plant to richer gardens led,
And fix'd, indulgent, in a warmer bed:
The nation, pleas'd, enjoys the rich produce,
And gathers from her ornament her use.
When loose from public cares the grove he sought,
And fill'd the leisure interval with thought,
The various labours of his easy page,
A chance amusement, polish'd half an age.
Beyond this truth old bards could scarce invent,
Who durst to frame a world by accident.
What he has sung, how early and how well,
The Thames shall boast, and Roman Tiber tell.
A glory more sublime remains in store,
Since such his talents, that he sung no more.
No fuller proof of power th' Almighty gave,
Making the sea, than curbing her proud wave.
Nought can the genius of his works transcend,
But their fair purpose and important end;
To rouse the war for injur'd Europe's laws,
To steel the patriot in great Brunswick's cause;
With virtue's charms to kindle sacred love,
Or paint th' eternal bowers of bliss above.
Where hadst thou room, great author! where to roll
The mighty theme of an immortal soul?
Through paths unknown, unbeaten, whence were
brought

Thy proofs so strong for immaterial thought?
One let me join, all other may excel.
"How could a mortal essence think so well?"
But why so large in the great writer's praise?
More lofty subjects should my numbers raise;
In him (illustrious rivalry!) contend
The statesman, patriot, Christian, and the friend!
His glory such, it borders on disgrace
To say he sung the best of human race.
In joy once join'd, in sorrow now for years,
Partner in grief, and brother of my tears,
Tickell! accept this verse, thy mournful due;
Thou further shalt the sacred theme pursue;
And, as thy strain describes the matchless man,
Thy life shall second what thy muse began.
Though sweet the numbers, though a fire divine
Dart through the whole, and burn in every line,
Who strives not for that excellence he draws,
Is stain'd by fame, and suffers from applause.
But haste to thy illustrious task; prepare
The noble work well trusted to thy care,
The gift* bequeath'd by Addison's command,
To Craggs made sacred by his dying hand.
Collect the labours, join the various rays,
The scatter'd light in one united blaze;
Then bear to him so true, so truly lov'd,
In life distinguish'd, and in death approv'd,
Th' immortal legacy. He hangs awhile

* The publication of his Works.

In generous anguish o'er the glorious pile;
With anxious pleasure the known page reviews,
And the dear pledge with falling tears bedews.
What though thy tears, pour'd o'er thy godlike
friend,
Thy other cares for Britain's weal suspend?
Think not, O patriot! while thy eyes o'erflow,
Those cares suspended for a private woe;
Thy love to him is to thy country shown;
He mourns for her who mourns for Addison.

REFLECTIONS ON THE PUBLIC SITUATION OF THE KINGDOM

INSCRIBED TO THE DUKE OF NEWCASTLE.

Holles! immortal in far more than fame!
Be thou illustrious in far more than power.
Great things are small when greater rise to view
Tho' station'd high, and press'd with public cares,
Disdain not to peruse my serious song,
Which peradventure may push by the world:
Of a few moments rob Britannia's weal,
And leave Europa's counsels less mature!
For thou art noble, and the theme is great.
Nor shall or Europe or Britannia blame
Thine absent ear, but gain by the delay.

Long vers'd in senates and in cabinets,
States' intricate demands and high debates!
As thou of use to those, so this to thee;
And in a point that empire far outweighs,
That far outweighs all Europe's thrones in one.
Let greatness prove its title to be great.
'Tis power's supreme prerogative to stamp
On other minds an image of its own.
Bend the strong influence of high place, to stem
The stream that sweeps away the country's weal;
The Stygian stream, the torrent of our guilt.
Far as thou mayst give life to virtue's cause;
Let not the ties of personal regard
Betray the nation's trust to feeble hands:
Let not fomented flames of private pique
Prey on the vitals of the public good:
Let not our streets with blasphemies resound,
Nor lewdness whisper where the laws can reach:
Let not best laws, the wisdom of our sires,
Turn satires on their sunk degenerate sons,
The bastards of their blood! and serve no point
But with more emphasis to call them fools:
Let not our rank enormities unhinge
Britannia's welfare from divine support.
Such deeds the minister, the prince adorn;
No power is shown but in such deeds as these:
All, all is impotence but acting right;
And where 's the statesman but would show his power?
To prince and people thou, of equal zeal!

Be it henceforward but thy second care
To grace thy country, and support the throne;
Though this supported, that adorn'd so well,
A throne superior our first homage claims;
To Cæsar's Cæsar our first tribute due:
A tribute which, unpaid, makes specious wrong
And splendid sacrilege of all beside:
Illustrious followers; we must first be just;
And what so just as awe for the supreme?
Less fear we rugged ruffians of the north,
Than virtue's well-clad rebels nearer home
Less Loyola's disguis'd, all-aping sons,
Than traitors lurking in our appetites;
Less all the legions Seine and Tagus send,
Than unrein'd passions rushing on our peace:
You savage mountaineers are tame to these.
Against those rioters send forth the laws,
And break to reason's yoke their wild careers.
  Prudence for all things points the proper hour,
Though some seem more importunate and great.
Tho' Britain's generous views and interests spread
Beyond the narrow circle of her shores,
And their grand entries make on distant lands;
Though Britain's genius the wide wave bestrides,
And, like a vast Colossus, towering stands
With one foot planted on the continent;
Yet be not wholly wrapp'd in public cares,
Tho' such high cares should call as call'd of late;
The cause of kings and emperors adjourn,
And Europe's little balance drop awhile;

For greater drop it: ponder and adjust
The rival interests and contending claims
Of life and death, of now and of for-ever;
Sublimest theme; and needful as sublime.
Thus great Eliza's oracles renown'd,
Thus Walsingham and Raleigh, (Britain's boasts!)
Thus every statesman thought that ever — died.
There 's inspiration in a sable hour,
And Death's approach makes politicians wise.
When thunderstruck, that eagle Wolsey fell;
When royal favour, as an ebbing sea,
Like a leviathan, his grandeur left,
His gasping grandeur! naked on the strand,
Naked of human, doubtful of divine,
Assistance; no more wallowing in his wealth,
Spouting proud foams of insolence no more,
On what, then, smote his heart, uncardinal'd,
And sunk beneath the level of a man!
On the grand article, the sum of things!
The point of the first magnitude! that point
Tubes mounted in a court, but rarely reach;
Some painted cloud still intercepts their sight.
First right to judge; then choose; then persevere,
Steadfast, as if a crown or mistress call'd. —
These, these are politics will stand the test,
When finer politics their masters sting,
And statesmen fain would shrink to common men.
These, these are politics will answer now,
(When common men would fain to statesmen swell,)
Beyond a Machiavel's or Tencin's scheme.

All safety rests on honest counsels : these
Immortalize the statesman, bless the state,
Make the prince triumph, and the people smile;
In peace rever'd, or terrible in arms,
Close-leagued with an invincible ally,
Which honest counsels never fail to fix
In favour of an unabandon'd land ;
A land — that starts at such a land as this,
A parliament, so principled, will sink
All ancient schools of empire in disgrace,
And Britain's glory, rising from the dead,
Will fill the world, loud fame's superior song.
Britain ! — that word pronounc'd is an alarm ;
It warms the blood, though frozen in our veins ;
Awakes the soul, and sends her to the field,
Enamour'd of the glorious face of Death.
Britain ! —there 's noble magic in the sound.
O what illustrious images arise !
Embattled, round me, blaze the pomps of war !
By sea, by land, at home, in foreign climes,
What full-blown laurels on our fathers' brows !
Ye radiant trophies ! and imperial spoils !
Ye scenes ! — astonishing to modern sight !
Let me, at least, enjoy you in a dream.
Why vanish ? Stay, ye godlike strangers ! stay :
Strangers ! — I wrong my countrymen : they wake ;
High beats the pulse : the noble pulse of war
Beats to that ancient measure, that grand march
Which then prevail'd, when Britain highest soar'd,

And every battle paid for heroes slain.
No more our great forefathers stain our cheeks
With blushes; their renown our shame no more.
In military garb, and sudden arms,
Up starts old Britain; crosiers are laid by;
Trade wields the sword, and agriculture leaves
Her half-turn'd furrow: other harvests fire
A nobler avarice, avarice of renown!
And laurels are the growth of every field.
In distant courts is our commotion felt;
And less like gods sit monarchs on their thrones.
What arm can want or sinews or success,
Which, lifted from an honest heart, descends,
With all the weight of British wrath, to cleave
The papal mitre, or the Gallic chain,
At every stroke, and save a sinking land?
Or death or victory must be resolv'd;
To dream of mercy, O how tame! how mad!
Where, o'er black deeds the crucifix display'd,
Fools think Heaven purchas'd by the blood they shed;
By giving, not supporting, pains and death!
Nor simple death! where they the greatest saints
Who most subdue all tenderness of heart;
Students in torture! where, in zeal to him,
Whose darling title is the Prince of Peace,
The best turn ruthless butchers, for our sakes;
To save us in a world they recommend,
And yet forbear, themselves with earth content;
What modesty! — such virtues Rome adorn!

And chiefly those who Rome's first honours wear,
Whose name from Jesus, and whose hearts from hell!
And shall a pope-bred princeling crawl ashore,
Replete with venom, guiltless of a sting,
And whistle cut-throats, with those swords that scrap'd
Their barren rocks for wretched sustenance,
To cut his passage to the British throne?
One that has suck'd in malice with his milk,
Malice, to Britain, liberty, and truth?
Less savage was his brother-robber's nurse,
The howling nurse of plundering Romulus,
Ere yet far worse than pagan harbour'd there.
Hail to the brave! be Britain Britain still:
Britain! high favour'd of indulgent Heaven!
Nature's anointed empress of the deep!
The nurse of merchants, who can purchase crowns!
Supreme in commerce! that exuberant source
Of wealth, the nerve of war; of wealth, the blood,
The circling current in a nation's veins,
To set high bloom on the fair face of peace!
This once so celebrated seat of power,
From which escap'd the mighty Cæsar triumph'd!
Of Gallic lilies this eternal blast!
This terror of armadas! this true bolt,
Ethereal-temper'd, to repress the vain
Salmonean thunders from the papal chair!
This small isle wide-realm'd monarchs eye with awe!
Which says to their ambition's foaming waves,

"Thus far, nor farther!" — Let her hold, in life,
Nought dear disjoin'd from freedom and renown;
Renown, our ancestors' great legacy,
To be transmitted to their latest sons.
By thoughts inglorious, and un-British deeds,
Their cancel'd will is impiously profan'd.
Inhumanly disturb'd their sacred dust.

Their sacred dust with recent laurels crown,
By your own valour won. This sacred isle,
Cut from the continent, that world of slaves;
This temple built by Heaven's peculiar care,
In a recess from the contagious world,
With ocean pour'd around it for its guard,
And dedicated, long, to liberty,
That health, that strength, that bloom, of civil life!
This temple of still more divine; of faith
Sifted from errors, purified by flames,
Like gold, to take anew truth's heavenly stamp,
And (rising both in lustre and in weight)
With her bless'd Master's unmaim'd image shine;
Why should she longer droop? why longer act
As an accomplice with the plots of Rome?
Why longer lend an edge to Bourbon's sword,
And give him leave, among his dastard troops,
To muster that strong succour, Albion's crimes?
Send his self-impotent ambition aid,
And crown the conquest of her fiercest foes?
Where are her foes most fatal? Blushing truth,
"In her friends' vices," — with a sigh replies.
Empire on virtue's rock unshaken stands;

Flux as the billows, when in vice dissolv'd.
If Heaven reclaims us by the scourge of war,
What thanks are due to Paris and Madrid?
Would they a revolution? — Aid their aim,
But be the revolution — in our hearts!
Wouldst thou (whose hand is at the helm) the bark,
The shaken bark of Britain, should outride
The present blast, and every future storm?
Give it that ballast which alone has weight
With Him whom wind, and waves, and war, obey,
Persist. Are others subtle? Thou be wise:
Above the Florentine's court-science raise;
Stand forth a patriot of the moral world;
The pattern, and the patron, of the just:
Thus strengthen Britain's military strength;
Give its own terror to the sword she draws.
Ask you, "What mean I?" — The most obvious truth;
Armies and fleets alone ne'er won the day.
When our proud arms are once disarm'd, disarm'd
Of aid from Him by whom the mighty fall;
Of aid from Him by whom the feeble stand;
Who takes away the keenest edge of battle,
Or gives the sword commission to destroy;
Who blasts, or bids the martial laurel bloom —
Emasculated, then, most manly might;
Or, though the might remains, it nought avails:
Then wither'd weakness foils the sinewy arm
Of man's meridian and high-hearted power:

Our naval thunders, and our tented fields
With travel'd banners fanning southern climes,
What do they? This; and more what can they do?
When heap'd the measure of a kingdom's crimes,
The prince most dauntless, the first plume of war,
By such bold inroads into foreign lands,
Such elongation of our armaments,
But stretches out the guilty nation's neck,
While Heaven commands her executioner,
Some less abandon'd nation, to discharge
Her full-ripe vengeance in a final blow,
And tell the world, "Not strong is human strength;
And that the proudest empire holds of Heaven."
O Britain! often rescued, often crown'd,
Beyond thy merit and most sanguine hopes,
With all that 's great in war, or sweet in peace!
Know from what source thy signal blessings flow.
Though bless'd with spirits ardent in the field,
Though cover'd various oceans with thy fleets,
Though fenc'd with rocks, and moated by the main,
Thy trust repose in a far stronger guard;
In Him, who thee, though naked, could defend;
Tho' weak, could strengthen; ruin'd, could restore.
How oft, to tell what arm defends thine isle,
To guard her welfare, and yet check her pride,
Have the winds snatch'd the victory from war?
Or, rather, won the day, when war despair'd?
How oft has providential succour aw'd,
Aw'd while it bless'd us, conscious of our guilt;

Struck dead all confidence in human aid,
And, while we triumph'd, made us tremble too!
Well may we tremble now; what manners reign?
But wherefore ask we, when a true reply
Would shock too much? Kind Heaven! avert events
Whose fatal nature might reply too plain!
Heaven's half-bar'd arm of vengeance has been wav'd
In northern skies, and pointed to the south.
Vengeance delay'd but gathers and ferments;
More formidably blackens in the wind;
Brews deeper draughts of unrelenting wrath,
And higher charges the suspended storm.
"That public vice portends a public fall" —
Is this conjecture of adventurous thought!
Or pious coward's pulpit cushion'd dream;
Far from it. This is certain; this is fate.
What says experience, in her awful chair
Of ages, her authentic annals spread
Around her? What says reason eagle-eyed?
Nay, what says common sense, with common care
Weighing events, and causes, in her scale?
All give one verdict, one decision sign;
And this the sentence Delphos could not mend:
"Whatever secondary props may rise
From politics, to build the public peace,
The basis is the manners of the land.
When rotten these, the politician's wiles
But struggle with destruction, as a child

With giants huge, or giants with a Jove.
The statesman's arts to conjure up a peace,
Or military phantoms void of force,
But scare away the vultures for an hour;
The scent cadaverous (for, oh! how rank
The stench of profligates!) soon lures them back
On the proud flutter of a Gallic wing
Soon they return; soon make their full descent;
Soon glut their rage, and riot in our ruin;
Their idols grac'd and gorgeous with our spoils,
Of universal empire sure presage!
Till now repell'd by seas of British blood."
 And whence the manners of the multitude?
The colours of their manners, black or fair,
Falls from above; from the complexion falls
Of state Othellos, or white men in power:
And from the greater height example falls,
Greater the weight, and deeper its impress
In ranks inferior, passive to the stroke:
From the court-mint, of hearts the current coin,
The pupil presses, but the pattern drives.
What bonds then, bonds how manifold, and stron;
To duty, double duty, are the great!
And are there Samsons that can burst them all?
Yes; and great minds that stand in need of none,
Whose pulse beats virtues, and whose generous blood
Aids mental motives to push on renown,
In emulation of their glorious sires,
From whom rolls down the consecrated stream.

Some sow good seeds in the glad people's hearts,
Some cursed tares, like Satan in the text:
This makes a foe most fatal to the state;
A foe who (like a wizard in his cell)
In his dark cabinet of crooked schemes,
Resembling Cuma's gloomy grot, the forge
Of boasted oracles, and real lies,
(Aided, perhaps, by second-sighted Scots,
French magi, relics riding post from Rome,
A gothic hero * rising from the dead,
And changing for spruce plaid his dirty shroud,
With succour suitable from lower still,)
A foe who, these concurring to the charm,
Excites those storms that shall o'erturn the state,
Rend up her ancient honours by the root,
And lay the boast of ages, the rever'd
Of nations, the dear-bought with sumless wealth
And blood illustrious, (spite of her La Hogues,
Her Cresseys, and her Blenheims,) in the dust.
How must this strike a horror thro' the breast,
Thro' every generous breast where honour reigns,
Thro' every breast where honour claims a share!
Yes, and thro' every breast of honour void!
This thought might animate the dregs of men;
Ferment them into spirit; give them fire
To fight the cause, the black opprobrious cause,
Foul core of all! — corruption at our hearts.

* The invader affects the character of Charles XII. of Sweden.

What wreck of empire has the stream of time
Swept, with her vices, from the mountain height
Of grandeur, deified by half mankind,
To dark oblivion's melancholy lake,
Or flagrant infamy's eternal brand!
Those names, at which surrounding nations shook,
Those names ador'd, a nuisance! or forgot!
Nor this the caprice of a doubtful die,
But Nature's course; no single chance against it.
For know, my lord! 'tis writ in adamant,
'Tis fixt, as is the basis of the world,
Whose kingdoms stand or fall by the decree.
What saw these eyes, surpris'd! — Yet why surpris'd —
For aid divine the crisis seem'd to call,
And how divine was the monition given!
As late I walk'd the night in troubled thought,
My peace disturb'd by rumours from the north,
While thunder o'er my head, portentous, roll'd,
As giving signal of some strange event,
And ocean groan'd beneath for her he lov'd,
Albion the fair! so long his empire's queen,
Whose reign is, now, contested by her foes,
On her white cliffs (a tablet broad and bright,
Strongly reflecting the pale lunar ray)
By fate's own iron pen I saw it writ,
And thus the title ran:

THE STATESMAN'S CREED.

"Ye states! and empires! nor of empires least,
Though least in size, hear, Britain! thou whose lot,
Whose final lot, is in the balance laid,
Irresolutely play the doubtful scales,
Nor know'st thou which will win. — Know then from me,
As govern'd well or ill, states sink or rise:
State ministers, as upright or corrupt,
Are balm or poison in a nation's veins!
Health or distemper, hasten or retard
The period of her pride, her day of doom:
And though, for reasons obvious to the wise,
Just Providence deals otherwise with men,
Yet believe, Britons! nor too late believe,
'Tis fix'd! by fate irrevocably fix'd!
Virtue and vice are empire's life and death."

Thus it is written — Heard you not a groan?
Is Britain on her death-bed? — No, that groan
Was utter'd by her foes — but soon the scale,
If this divine monition is despis'd,
May turn against us. Read it, ye who rule!
With reverence read; with steadfastness believe;
With courage act as such belief inspires;
Then shall your glory stand like fate's decree;
Then shall your name in adamant be writ,
In records that defy the tooth of time,
By nations sav'd, resounding your applause.

While deep beyond your monument's proud base,
In black oblivion's kennel, shall be trod
Their execrable names, who, high in power,
And deep in guilt, most ominously shine,
(The meteors of the state!) give vice her head,
To license lewd let loose the public rein;
Quench every spark of conscience in the land,
And triumph in the profligate's applause:
Or who to the first bidder sell their souls,
Their country sell, sell all their fathers bought
With funds exhausted and exhausted veins,
To demons, by his holiness ordain'd
To propagate the gospel — penn'd at Rome;
Hawk'd through the world by consecrated bulls;
And how illustrated? — by Smithfield flames:
Who plunge (but not like Curtius) down the gulf,
Down narrow-minded self's voracious gulf,
Which gapes and swallows all they swore to save:
Hate all that lifted heroes into gods,
And hug the horrors of a victor's chain:
Of bodies politic that destin'd hell,
Inflicted here, since here their beings end;
And fall from foes detested and despis'd,
On disbelievers — of the statesman's creed.
Note, here, my lord, (unnoted yet it lies
By most, or all,) these truths political
Serve more than public ends: this creed of states
Seconds, and irresistibly supports,
The Christian creed. Are you surpris'd? — Attend
And on the statesman's build a nobler name.

This punctual justice exercis'd on states,
With which authentic chronicle abounds,
As all men know, and therefore must believe ;
This vengeance pour'd on nations ripe in guilt,
Pour'd on them here, where only they exist,
What is it but an argument of sense,
Or rather demonstration, to support
Our feeble faith — "That they who states compose,
That men who stand not bounded by the grave,
Shall meet like measure at their proper hour ?"
For God is equal, similarly deals
With states and persons, or he were not God !
What means a rectitude immutable ?
A pattern here of universal right.
What, then, shall rescue an abandon'd man ?
Nothing, it is replied. Replied, by whom ?
Replied by politicians well as priests :
Writ sacred set aside, mankind's own writ,
The whole world's annals ; these pronounce his doom.
Thus (what might seem a daring paradox)
E'en politics advance divinity :
True masters there are better scholars here,
Who travel history in quest of schemes
To govern nations, or perhaps oppress,
May there start truths that other aims inspire,
And, like Candace's eunuch, as they read,
By Providence turn Christians on their road :
Digging for silver, they may strike on gold ;

May be surpris'd with better than they sought,
And entertain an angel unawares.
Nor is divinity ungrateful found.
As politics advance divinity,
Thus, in return, divinity promotes
True politics, and crowns the statesman's praise.
All wisdoms are but branches of the chief,
And statesmen found but shoots of honest men.
Are this world's witchcrafts pleaded in excuse
For deviations in our moral line?
This, and the next world, view'd with such an eye
As suits a statesman, such as keeps in view
His own exalted science, both conspire
To recommend and fix us in the right.
If we reward the politics of Heaven,
The grand administration of the whole,
What 's the next world? A supplement of this:
Without it, justice is defective here;
Just as to states, defective as to men:
If so, what is this world? As sure as right
Sits in Heaven's throne, a prophet of the next.
Prize you the prophet? then believe him too:
His prophecy more precious than his smile.
How comes it then to pass, with most on earth,
That this should charm us, that should discompose?
Long as the statesman finds this case his own,
So long his politics are uncomplete;
In danger he; nor is the nation safe,
But soon must rue his inauspicious power.

What hence results? a truth that should resound
For ever awful in Britannia's ear:
" Religion crowns the statesman and the man,
Sole source of public and of private peace."
This truth all men must own, and therefore will,
And praise and preach it too: — and when that's done,
Their compliment is paid, and 'tis forgot.
What highland pole-axe half so deep can wound?
But how dare I, so mean, presume so far?
Assume my seat in the dictator's chair?
Pronounce, predict (as if indeed inspir'd),
Promulge my censures, lay out all my throat,
Till hoarse in clamour on enormous crimes?
Two mighty columns rise in my support;
In their more awful and authentic voice,
Record profane and sacred, drown the muse,
Tho' loud, and far out-thread her threatening song.
Still further, Holles! suffer me to plead
That I speak freely, as I speak to thee:
Guilt only startles at the name of guilt;
And truth, plain truth, is welcome to the wise.
Thus what seem'd my presumption is thy praise.
Praise, and immortal praise, is virtue's claim;
And virtue's sphere is action: yet we grant
Some merit to the trumpet's loud alarm,
Whose clangour kindles cowards into men.
Nor shall the verse, perhaps, be quite forgot,
Which talks of immortality, and bids,

In every British breast, true glory rise,
As now the warbling lark awakes the morn.
To close, my lord! with that which all should close
And all begin, and strike us every hour,
Though no war wak'd us, no black tempest frown'd.
The morning rises gay; yet gayest morn
Less glorious after night's incumbent shades;
Less glorious far bright nature, rich array'd
With golden robes, in all the pomp of noon,
Than the first feeble dawn of moral day?
Sole day, (let those whom statesmen serve attend,)
Though the sun ripens diamonds for their crowns;
Sole day worth his regard whom Heaven ordains,
Undarken'd, to behold noon dark, and date,
From the sun's death, and every planet's fall,
His all-illustrious and eternal year;
Where statesmen and their monarchs, (names of awe
And distance here,) shall rank with common men,
Yet own their glory never dawn'd before.

RESIGNATION.

IN TWO PARTS.

My soul shall be satisfied even as it were with marrow and fatness, when my mouth praiseth thee with joyful lips.

Psalm lxiii. 6.

ADVERTISEMENT.

This was not intended for the public; there were many and strong reasons against it, and are so still; but some extracts of it, from the few copies which were given away, being got into the printed papers, it was thought necessary to publish something, lest a copy still more imperfect than this should fall into the press: and it is hoped, that this unwelcome occasion of publication may be some excuse for it.

As for the following stanzas, God Almighty's infinite power, and marvellous goodness to man, is dwelt on, as the most just and cogent reason for our cheerful and absolute resignation to his will; nor are any of those topics declined, which have a just tendency to promote that supreme virtue: such as the vanity of this life, the value of the next, the approach of death, &c.

PART I.

The days how few, how short the years
Of man's too rapid race!
Each leaving, as it swiftly flies,
A shorter in its place.

They who the longest lease enjoy,
  Have told us with a sigh,
That to be born seems little more
  Than to begin to die.

Numbers there are who feel this truth
  With fears alarm'd; and yet,
In life's delusions lull'd asleep,
  This weighty truth forget:

And am not I to these akin?
  Age slumbers o'er the quill;
Its honour blots, whate'er it writes,
  And am I writing still?

Conscious of nature in decline,
  And languor in my thoughts;
To soften censure, and abate
  Its rigour on my faults

Permit me, madam! ere to you
  The promis'd verse I pay,
To touch on felt infirmity,
  Sad sister of decay.

One world deceas'd, another born,
  Like Noah they behold,
O'er whose white hairs, and furrow'd brows,
  Too many suns have roll'd:

Happy the patriarch! he rejoic'd
  His second world to see:
My second world, though gay the scene,
  Can boast no charms for me.

To me this brilliant age appears
  With desolation spread;
Near all with whom I liv'd, and smil'd,
  Whilst life was life, are dead;

And with them died my joys; the grave
  Has broken nature's laws;
And clos'd, against this feeble frame,
  Its partial cruel jaws;

Cruel to spare! condemn'd to life!
  A cloud impairs my sight;
My weak hand disobeys my will,
  And trembles as I write.

What shall I write? Thalia, tell;
  Say, long abandon'd muse!
What field of fancy shall I range?
  What subject shall I choose?

A choice of moment high inspire,
  And rescue me from shame,
For doting on thy charms so late,
  By grandeur in my theme.

Beyond the themes, which most admire,
 Which dazzle, or amaze,
Beyond renown'd exploits of war,
 Bright charms, or empire's blaze,

Are themes, which, in a world of woe
 Can best appease our pain;
And, in an age of gaudy guilt,
 Gay folly's flood restrain;

Amidst the storms of life support
 A calm, unshaken mind;
And with unfading laurels crown
 The brow of the resign'd.

O resignation! yet unsung,
 Untouch'd by former strains;
Though claiming every muse's smile,
 And every poet's pains,

Beneath life's evening, solemn shade,
 I dedicate my page
To thee, thou safest guard of youth!
 Thou sole support of age!

All other duties crescents are
 Of virtue faintly bright,
The glorious consummation, thou!
 Which fills her orb with light:

How rarely fill'd! the love divine
  In evils to discern,
This the first lesson which we want,
  The latest, which we learn;

A melancholy truth! for know,
  Could our proud hearts resign,
The distance greatly would decrease
  'Twixt human and divine.

But though full noble is my theme,
  Full urgent is my call
To soften sorrow, and forbid
  The bursting tear to fall:

The task I dread; dare I to leave
  Of humble prose the shore,
And put to sea? a dangerous sea?
  What throngs have sunk before!

How proud the poet's billow swells!
  The God! the God! his boast:
A boast how vain! What wrecks abound!
  Dead bards stench every coast.

What then am I? Shall I presume,
  On such a moulten wing,
Above the general wreck to rise,
  And in my winter, sing;

When nightingales, when sweetest bards
   Confine their charming song
To summer's animating heats,
   Content to warble young?

Yet write I must; a lady * sues;
   How shameful her request!
My brain in labour for dull rhyme!
   Hers teeming with the best!

But you a stranger will excuse,
   Nor scorn his feeble strain;
To you a stranger, but, through fate,
   No stranger to your pain.

The ghost of grief deceas'd ascends,
   His old wound bleeds anew;
His sorrows are recall'd to life
   By those he sees in you;

Too well he knows the twisting strings
   Of ardent hearts combin'd
When rent asunder, how they bleed,
   How hard to be resign'd:

Those tears you pour, his eyes have shed;
   The pang you feel, he felt;
Thus nature, loud as virtue, bids
   His heart at yours to melt.

* Mrs. M——.

But what can heart, or head, suggest?
  What sad experience say?
Through truths austere, to peace we work
  Our rugged, gloomy way:

What are we? whence? for what? and whither?
  Who know not, needs must mourn;
But thought, bright daughter of the skies!
  Can tears to triumph turn.

Thought is our armour, 'tis the mind's
  Impenetrable shield,
When, sent by fate, we meet our foes,
  In sore affliction's field;

It plucks the frightful mask from ills,
  Forbids pale fear to hide,
Beneath that dark disguise, a friend,
  Which turns affection's tide.

Affection frail! train'd up by sense,
  From reason's channel strays:
And whilst it blindly points at peace,
  Our peace to pain betrays.

Thought winds its fond, erroneous stream
  From daily dying flowers,
To nourish rich immortal blooms,
  In amaranthine bowers;

Whence throngs, in ecstasy, look down
  On what once shock'd their sight;
And thank the terrors of the past
  For ages of delight.

All withers here; who most possess
  Are losers by their gain,
Stung by full proof, that, bad at best,
  Life's idle all is vain:

Vain, in its course, life's murmuring stream;
  Did not its course offend,
But murmur cease; life, then, would seem
  Still vainer, from its end.

How wretched! who, through cruel fate,
  Have nothing to lament!
With the poor alms this world affords
  Deplorably content!

Had not the Greek his world mistook,
  His wish had been most wise;
To be content with but one world,
  Like him, we should despise.

Of earth's revenue would you state
  A full account and fair?
We hope; and hope; and hope; then cast
  The total up ———

Despair.

Since vain all here, all future, vast,
  Embrace the lot assign'd;
Heaven wounds to heal; its frowns are friends;
  Its stroke severe, most kind.

But in laps'd nature rooted deep,
  Blind error domineers;
And on fools' errands, in the dark,
  Sends out our hopes and fears;

Bids us for ever pains deplore,
  Our pleasures overprize;
These oft persuade us to be weak;
  Those urge us to be wise.

From virtue's rugged path to right
  By pleasure are we brought,
To flowery fields of wrong, and there
  Pain chides us for our fault:

Yet whilst it chides, it speaks of peace
  If folly is withstood;
And says, time pays an easy price,
  For our eternal good.

In earth's dark cot, and in an hour,
  And in delusion great,
What an economist is man
  To spend his whole estate,

And beggar an eternity!
  For which as he was born,
More worlds than one against it weigh'd,
  As feathers he should scorn.

Say not, your loss in triumph leads
  Religion's feeble strife;
Joys future amply reimburse
  Joys bankrupts of this life.

But not deferr'd your joy so long,
  It bears an early date;
Affliction's ready pay in hand,
  Befriends our present state;

What are the tears, which trickle down
  Her melancholy face,
Like liquid pearl? Like pearls of price,
  They purchase lasting peace.

Grief softens hearts, and curbs the will,
  Impetuous passion tames,
And keeps insatiate, keen desire
  From launching in extremes.

Through time's dark womb, our judgment right,
  If our dim eye was thrown,
Clear should we see, the will divine
  Has but forestall'd our own;

At variance with our future wish,
Self-sever'd we complain;
If so, the wounded, not the wound,
Must answer for the pain:

The day shall come, and swift of wing,
Though you may think it slow,
When, in the list of fortune's smiles,
You 'll enter frowns of woe.

For mark the path of Providence;
This course it has pursued —
"Pain is the parent, woe the womb,
Of sound, important good:"

Our hearts are fasten'd to this world
By strong and endless ties:
And every sorrow cuts a string,
And urges us to rise:

'Twill sound severe — Yet rest assur'd
I'm studious of your peace;
Though I should dare to give you joy —
Yes, joy of his decease:

An hour shall come, (you question this,)
An hour, when you shall bless,
Beyond the brightest beams of life,
Dark days of your distress.

Hear then without surprise a truth,
  A daughter truth to this,
Swift turns of fortune often tie
  A bleeding heart to bliss:

Esteem you this a paradox?
  My sacred motto read;
A glorious truth! divinely sung
  By one, whose heart had bled;

To resignation swift he flew,
  In her a friend he found,
A friend, which bless'd him with a smile
  When gasping with his wound.

On earth nought precious is obtain'd
  But what is painful too;
By travel, and to travel born,
  Our sabbaths are but few:

To real joy we work our way,
  Encountering many a shock,
Ere found what truly charms; as found
  A Venus in the block.

In some disaster, some severe
  Appointment for our sins,
That mother blessing, (not so call'd,)
  True happiness, begins.

No martyr e'er defied the flames,
By stings of life unvext;
First rose some quarrel with this world,
Then passion for the next.

You see, then, pangs are parent pangs,
The pangs of happy birth;
Pangs, by which only can be born
True happiness on earth.

The peopled earth look all around,
Or through time's records run!
And say, what is a man unstruck?
It is a man undone.

This moment, am I deeply stung —
My bold pretence is tried;
When vain man boasts, heaven puts to proof
The vauntings of his pride;

Now need I, madam! your support. —
How exquisite the smart;
How critically tim'd the news *
Which strikes me to the heart!

The pangs of which I spoke, I feel:
If worth like thine is born,

* Whilst the author was writing this, he received the news of Mr. Samuel Richardson's death, who was then printing the former part of the poem.

O long-belov'd! I bless the blow,
And triumph, whilst I mourn.

Nor mourn I long; by grief subdued,
By reason's empire shown;
Deep anguish comes by heaven's decree,
Continues by our own;

And when continued past its point,
Indulg'd in length of time,
Grief is disgrac'd, and, what was fate,
Corrupts into a crime:

And shall I, criminally mean,
Myself and subject wrong?
No; my example shall support
The subject of my song.

Madam! I grant your loss is great;
Nor little is your gain?
Let that be weigh'd; when weigh'd aright,
It richly pays your pain:

When heaven would kindly set us free,
And earth's enchantment end;
It takes the most effectual means,
And robs us of a friend.

But such a friend! and sigh no more?
'Tis prudent; but severe:

Heaven aid my weakness, and I drop
All sorrow — with this tear.

Perhaps your settled grief to soothe,
I should not vainly strive,
But with soft balm your pain assuage,
Had he been still alive;

Whose frequent aid brought kind relief,
In my distress of thought,
Ting'd with his beams my cloudy page,
And beautified a fault:

To touch our passions' secret springs
Was his peculiar care;
And deep his happy genius div'd
In bosoms of the fair;

Nature, which favours to the few,
All art beyond, imparts,
To him presented, at his birth,
The key of human hearts.

But not to me by him bequeath'd
His gentle, smooth address;
His tender hand to touch the wound
In throbbing of distress;

Howe'er, proceed I must, unbless'd
With Esculapian art:

Know, love sometimes, mistaken love!
  Plays disaffection's part:

Nor lands, nor seas, nor suns, nor stars,
  Can soul from soul divide;
They correspond from distant worlds,
  Though transports are denied:

Are you not, then, unkindly kind?
  Is not your love severe?
O! stop that crystal source of woe;
  Nor wound him with a tear.

As those above from human bliss
  Receive increase of joy;
May not a stroke from human woe,
  In part, their peace destroy?

He lives in those he left; — to what?
  Your, now, paternal care,
Clear from its cloud your brighten'd eye,
  It will discern him there;

In features, not of form alone,
  But those, I trust, of mind;
Auspicious to the public weal,
  And to their fate resign'd.

Think on the tempests he sustain'd;
  Revolve his battles won;

And let those prophesy your joy
  From such a father's son:

Is consolation what you seek?
  Fan, then, his martial fire:
And animate to flame the sparks
  Bequeath'd him by his sire:

As nothing great is born in haste,
  Wise nature's time allow;
His father's laurels may descend,
  And flourish on his brow.

Nor, madam! be surpris'd to hear
  That laurels may be due
Not more to heroes of the field,
  (Proud boasters!) than to you:

Tender as is the female frame,
  Like that brave man you mourn,
You are a soldier, and to fight
  Superior battles born;

Beneath a banner nobler far
  Than ever was unfurl'd
In fields of blood; a banner bright!
  High wav'd o'er all the world.

It, like a streaming meteor, casts
  A universal light;

Sheds day, sheds more, eternal day
On nations whelm'd in night.

Beneath that banner, what exploit
Can mount our glory higher,
Than to sustain the dreadful blow,
When those we love expire?

Go forth a moral Amazon;
Arm'd with undaunted thought;
The battle won, though costing dear,
You 'll think it cheaply bought:

The passive hero, who sits down
Unactive, and can smile
Beneath affliction's galling load,
Out-acts a Cæsar's toil:

The billows stain'd by slaughter'd foes
Inferior praise afford;
Reason 's a bloodless conqueror,
More glorious than the sword.

Nor can the thunders of huzzas,
From shouting nations, cause
Such sweet delight, as from your heart
Soft whispers of applause:

The dear deceas'd so fam'd in arms,
With what delight he 'll view

His triumphs on the main outdone,
  Thus conquer'd, twice, by you.

Share his delight; take heed to shun
  Of bosoms most diseas'd
That odd distemper, an absurd
  Reluctance to be pleas'd:

Some seem in love with sorrow's charms,
  And that foul fiend embrace:
This temper let me justly brand,
  And stamp it with disgrace:

Sorrow! of horrid parentage!
  Thou second-born of hell!
Against heaven's endless mercies pour'd
  How dar'st thou to rebel?

From black and noxious vapours bred,
  And nurs'd by want of thought,
And to the door of phrensy's self
  By perseverance brought,

Thy most inglorious, coward tears
  From brutal eyes have ran:
Smiles, incommunicable smiles!
  Are radiant marks of man;

They cast a sudden glory round
  Th' illumin'd human face;

And light in sons of honest joy
  Some beams of Moses' face:

Is resignation's lesson hard?
  Examine, we shall find
That duty gives up little more
  Than anguish of the mind;

Resign; and all the load of life
  That moment you remove,
Its heavy tax, ten thousand cares
  Devolve on one above;

Who bids us lay our burthen down
  On his almighty hand,
Softens our duty to relief,
  To blessing a command.

For joy what cause! how every sense
  Is courted from above
The year around, with presents rich,
  The growth of endless love!

But most o'erlook the blessings pour'd,
  Forget the wonders done,
And terminate, wrapp'd up in sense,
  Their prospect at the sun;

From that, their final point of view,
  From that their radiant goal,

On travel infinite of thought,
  Sets out the nobler soul,

Broke loose from time's tenacious ties,
  And earth's involving gloom,
To range at last its vast domain,
  And talk with worlds to come :

They let unmark'd, and unemploy'd,
  Life's idle moments run;
And doing nothing for themselves,
  Imagine nothing done;

Fatal mistake! their fate goes on,
  Their dread account proceeds,
And their not doing is set down
  Amongst their darkest deeds;

Though man sits still, and takes his ease;
  God is at work on man;
No means, no moment unemploy'd,
  To bless him, if he can.

But man consents not, boldly bent
  To fashion his own fate;
Man, a mere bungler in the trade,
  Repents his crime too late;

Hence loud laments: let me thy cause,
  Indulgent father! plead;

Of all the wretches we deplore,
  Not one by thee was made.

What is thy whole creation fair?
  Of love divine the child;
Love brought it forth; and, from its birth,
  Has o'er it fondly smil'd:

Now, and through periods distant far,
  Long ere the world began,
Heaven is, and has in travail been,
  Its birth the good of man;

Man holds in constant service bound
  The blustering winds and seas;
Nor suns disdain to travel hard
  Their master, man, to please:

To final good the worst events
  Through secret channels run;
Finish for man their destin'd course,
  As 'twas for man begun.

One point (observ'd, perhaps, by few)
  Has often smote, and smites
My mind, as demonstration strong;
  That heaven in man delights:

What's known to man of things unseen,
  Of future worlds, or fates?

So much, nor more, than what to man's
  Sublime affairs relates;

What's revelation then? a list,
  An inventory just
Of that poor insect's goods, so late
  Call'd out of night and dust.

What various motives to rejoice!
  To render joy sincere,
Has this no weight? our joy is felt
  Beyond this narrow sphere:

Would we in heaven new heaven create,
  And double its delight?
A smiling world, when heaven looks down,
  How pleasing in its sight!

Angels stoop forward from their thrones
  To hear its joyful lays;
As incense sweet enjoy, and join,
  Its aromatic praise:

Have we no cause to fear the stroke
  Of heaven's avenging rod,
When we presume to counteract
  A sympathetic God?

If we resign, our patience makes
  His rod an armless wand;

If not, it darts a serpent's sting,
Like that in Moses' hand;

Like that, it swallows up whate'er
Earth's vain magicians bring,
Whose baffled arts would boast below
Of joys a rival spring.

Consummate love! the list how large
Of blessings from thy hand!
To banish sorrow, and be blest,
Is thy supreme command.

Are such commands but ill obey'd?
Of bliss, shall we complain?
The man, who dares to be a wretch,
Deserves still greater pain.

Joy is our duty, glory, health;
The sunshine of the soul;
Our best encomium on the power
Who sweetly plans the whole:

Joy is our Eden still possess'd:
Begone, ignoble grief!
'Tis joy makes gods, and men exalts,
Their nature, our relief;

Relief, for man to that must stoop,
And his due distance know;

Transport 's the language of the skies,
  Content the style below.

Content is joy, and joy in pain
  Is joy and virtue too;
Thus, whilst good present we possess,
  More precious we pursue:

Of joy the more we have in hand,
  The more have we to come;
Joy, like our money, interest bears,
  Which daily swells the sum.

"But how to smile; to stem the tide
  Of nature in our veins;
Is it not hard to weep in joy?
  What then to smile in pains?"

Victorious joy! which breaks the clouds,
  And struggles through a storm;
Proclaims the mind as great, as good
  And bids it doubly charm:

If doubly charming in our sex,
  A sex, by nature, bold;
What then in yours? 'tis diamond there
  Triumphant o'er our gold.

And should not this complaint repress?
  And check the rising sigh?

Yet farther opiate to your pain
I labour to supply.

Since spirits greatly damp'd distort
Ideas of delight,
Look through the medium of a friend,
To set your notions right:

As tears the sight, grief dims the soul;
Its object dark appears;
True friendship, like a rising sun,
The soul's horizon clears.

A friend 's an optic to the mind
With sorrow clouded o'er;
And gives it strength of sight to see
Redress unseen before.

Reason is somewhat rough in man;
Extremely smooth and fair,
When she, to grace her manly strength,
Assumes a female air:

A friend* you have, and I the same,
Whose prudent, soft address
Will bring to life those healing thoughts
Which died in your distress;

That friend, the spirit of my theme
Extracting for your ease,

* Mrs. Montague.

Will leave to me the dreg, in thoughts
Too common; such as these:

Let those lament to whom full bowls
Of sparkling joys are given;
That triple bane inebriates life,
Imbitters death, and hazards heaven:

Woe to the soul at perfect ease!
'Tis brewing perfect pains;
Lull'd reason sleeps, the pulse is king;
Despotic body reigns;

Have you* ne'er pitied joy's gay scenes,
And deem'd their glory dark?
Alas! poor envy! she 's stone-blind,
And quite mistakes her mark:

Her mark lies hid in sorrow's shades,
But sorrow well subdu'd;
And in proud fortune's frown defied
By meek, unborrow'd good.

By resignation; all in that
A double friend may find,
A wing to heaven, and, while on earth,
The pillow of mankind:

On pillows void of down, for rest
Our restless hopes we place;

* Mrs. Montague.

When hopes of heaven lie warm at heart,
 Our hearts repose in peace :

The peace, which resignation yields,
 Who feel alone can guess ;
'Tis disbeliev'd by murmuring minds,
 They must conclude it less :

The loss, or gain, of that alone
 Have we to hope or fear ;
That fate controls, and can invert
 The seasons of the year :

O ! the dark days, the year around,
 Of an impatient mind !
Thro' clouds, and storms, a summer breaks,
 To shine on the resign'd :

While man by that of every grace,
 And virtue, is possess'd ;
Foul vice her pandæmonium builds
 In the rebellious breast ;

By resignation we defeat
 The worst that can annoy ;
And suffer, with far more repose,
 Than worldlings can enjoy.

From small experience this I speak ;
 O ! grant to those I love

Experience fuller far, ye powers,
  Who form our fates above!

My love were due, if not to those
  Who, leaving grandeur, came
To shine on age in mean recess,
  And light me to my theme!

A theme themselves! A theme, how rare!
  The charms, which they display,
To triumph over captive heads,
  Are set in bright array:

With his own arms proud man's o'ercome,
  His boasted laurels die:
Learning and genius, wiser grown,
  To female bosoms fly.

This revolution, fix'd by fate,
  In fable was foretold;
The dark prediction puzzled wits,
  Nor could the learn'd unfold:

But as those ladies' * works I read,
  They darted such a ray,
The latent sense burst out at once,
  And shone in open day:

So burst, full ripe, distended fruits,
  When strongly strikes the sun;

* Mrs. Montague. Mrs Carter.

And from the purple grape unpress'd
  Spontaneous nectars run.

Pallas, ('tis said,) when Jove grew dull,
  Forsook his drowsy brain;
And sprightly leap'd into the throne
  Of wisdom's brighter reign;

Her helmet took; that is, shot rays
  Of formidable wit;
And lance, — or, genius most acute,
  Which lines immortal writ;

And gorgon shield, — or, power to fright
  Man's folly, dreadful shone,
And many a blockhead (easy change!)
  Turn'd, instantly, to stone.

Our authors male, as, then, did Jove,
  Now scratch a damag'd head,
And call for what once quarter'd there,
  But find the goddess fled.

The fruit of knowledge, golden fruit!
  That once forbidden tree,
Hedg'd-in by surly man, is now
  To Britain's daughters free:

In Eve (we know) of fruit so fair
  The noble thirst began;

And they, like her, have caus'd a fall,
  A fall of fame in man:

And since of genius in our sex,
  O Addison! with thee
The sun is set; how I rejoice
  This sister lamp to see!

It sheds, like Cynthia, silver beams
  On man's nocturnal state;
His lessen'd light, and languid powers,
  I show, whilst I relate.

PART II.

But what in either sex, beyond
  All parts, our glory crowns?
"In ruffling seasons to be calm,
  And smile, when fortune frowns."

Heaven's choice is safer than our own;
  Of ages past inquire,
What the most formidable fate?
  "To have our own desire."

If, in your wrath, the worst of foes
  You wish extremely ill;

Expose him to the thunder's stroke,
   Or that of his own will.

What numbers, rushing down the steep
   Of inclination strong,
Have perish'd in their ardent wish!
   Wish ardent, ever wrong!

'Tis resignation's full reverse,
   Most wrong, as it implies
Error most fatal in our choice,
   Detachment from the skies.

By closing with the skies, we make
   Omnipotence our own;
That done, how formidable ill's
   Whole army is o'erthrown!

No longer impotent, and frail,
   Ourselves above we rise:
We scarce believe ourselves below!
   We trespass on the skies!

The Lord, the soul, and source of all,
   Whilst man enjoys his ease,
Is executing human will,
   In earth, and air, and seas;

Beyond us, what can angels boast?
   Archangels what require?

Whate'er below, above, is done,
  Is done as —— we desire.

What glory this for man so mean,
  Whose life is but a span!
This is meridian majesty!
  This, the sublime of man!

Beyond the boast of pagan song
  My sacred subject shines!
And for a foil the lustre takes
  Of Rome's exalted lines.

"All, that the sun surveys, subdued,
  But Cato's mighty mind."
How grand! most true; yet far beneath
  The soul of the resign'd:

To more than kingdoms, more than worlds,
  To passion that gives law;
Its matchless empire could have kept
  Great Cato's pride in awe;

That fatal pride, whose cruel point
  Transfix'd his noble breast;
Far nobler! if his fate sustain'd
  And left to heaven the rest;

Then he the palm had borne away,
  At distance Cæsar thrown;

Put him off cheaply with the world,
  And made the skies his own.

What cannot resignation do?
  It wonders can perform;
That powerful charm, "Thy will be done,"
  Can lay the loudest storm.

Come, resignation! then, from fields,
  Where, mounted on the wing,
A wing of flame, blest martyrs' souls
  Ascended to their king.

Who is it calls thee? one whose need
  Transcends the common size;
Who stands in front against a foe
  To which no equal rise:

In front he stands, the brink he treads
  Of an eternal state;
How dreadful his appointed post!
  How strongly arm'd by fate:

His threatening foe! what shadows deep
  O'erwhelm his gloomy brow!
His dart tremendous!——at fourscore
  My sole asylum, thou!

Haste, then, O resignation! haste,
  'Tis thine to reconcile

My foe, and me; at thy approach
  My foe begins to smile:

O! for that summit of my wish,
  Whilst here I draw my breath,
That promise of eternal life,
  A glorious smile in death:

What sight, heaven's azure arch beneath,
  Has most of heaven to boast?
The man resign'd; at once serene,
  And giving up the ghost.

At death's arrival they shall smile,
  Who, not in life o'er gay,
Serious and frequent thought send out
  To meet him on his way:

My gay coevals! (such there are)
  If happiness is dear;
Approaching death's alarming day
  Discreetly let us fear:

The fear of death is truly wise,
  Till wisdom can rise higher;
And, arm'd with pious fortitude,
  Death dreaded once, desire:

Grand climacteric vanities
  The vainest will despise;

Shock'd, when beneath the snow of age
  Man immaturely dies:

But am not I myself the man?
  No need abroad to roam
In quest of faults to be chastis'd;
  What cause to blush at home?

In life's decline, when men relapse
  Into the sports of youth,
The sécond child out-fools the first,
  And tempts the lash of truth;

Shall a mere truant from the grave
  With rival boys engage?
His trembling voice attempt to sing,
  And ape the poet's rage?

Here, madam! let me visit one,
  My fault who, partly, shares,
And tell myself, by telling him,
  What more becomes our years;

And if your breast with prudent zeal
  For resignation glows,
You will not disapprove a just
  Resentment at its foes.

In youth, Voltaire! our foibles plead
  For some indulgence due;

When heads are white, their thoughts and aims
  Should change their colour too :

How are you cheated by your wit !
  Old age is bound to pay,
By nature's law, a mind discreet,
  For joys it takes away ;

A mighty change is wrought by years,
  Reversing human lot ;
In age 'tis honour to lie hid,
  'Tis praise to be forgot ;

The wise, as flowers, which spread at noon,
  And all their charms expose,
When evening damps and shades descend,
  Their evolutions close.

What though your muse has nobly soar'd,
  Is that our truth sublime ?
Ours, hoary friend ! is to prefer
  Eternity to time :

Why close a life so justly fam'd
  With such bold trash as this ? *
This for renown ? yes, such as makes
  Obscurity a bliss :

Your trash, with mine, at open war,
  Is obstinately bent, †

* Candide. † Second Part.

Like wits below, to sow your tares
  Of gloom and discontent:

With so much sunshine at command,
  Why light with darkness mix?
Why dash with pain our pleasure?
  Your Helicon with Styx?

Your works in our divided minds
  Repugnant passions raise,
Confound us with a double stroke,
  We shudder whilst we praise;

A curious web, as finely wrought
  As genius can inspire,
From a black bag of poison spun,
  With horror we admire.

Mean as it is, if this is read
  With a disdainful air,
I can't forgive so great a foe
  To my dear friend Voltaire:

Early I knew him, early prais'd,
  And long to praise him late;
His genius greatly I admire,
  Nor would deplore his fate;

A fate how much to be deplor'd!
  At which our nature starts;

Forbear to fall on your own sword.
  To perish by your parts:

"But great your name" — To feed on air,
  Were then immortals born?
Nothing is great, of which more great,
  More glorious is the scorn.

Can fame your carcass from the worm
  Which gnaws us in the grave,
Or soul from that which never dies,
  Applauding Europe save?

But fame you lose; good sense alone
  Your idol, praise, can claim;
When wild wit murders happiness,
  It puts to death our fame!

Nor boast your genius, talents bright;
  E'en dunces will despise,
If in your western beams is miss'd
  A genius for the skies;

Your taste too fails; what most excels
  True taste must relish most!
And what, to rival palms above,
  Can proudest laurels boast?

Sound heads salvation's helmet seek,*
  Resplendent are its rays,

* Ephes. vi. 17.

Let that suffice ; it needs no plume,
  Of sublunary praise.

May this enable couch'd Voltaire
  To see that — " All is right," *
His eye, by flash of wit struck blind,
  Restoring to its sight ;

If so, all 's well : who much have err'd,
  That much have been forgiven ;
I speak with joy, with joy he 'll hear,
  " Voltaires are, now, in heaven."

Nay, such philanthropy divine,
  So boundless in degree,
Its marvellous of love extends
  (Stoops most profound !) to me :

Let others cruel stars arraign,
  Or dwell on their distress ;
But let my page, for mercies pour'd,
  A grateful heart express :

Walking, the present God was seen,
  Of old, in Eden fair ;
The God as present, by plain steps
  Of providential care,

I behold passing through my life ;
  His awful voice I hear ;

* Which his romance ridicules.

And, conscious of my nakedness,
  Would hide myself for fear:

But where the trees, or where the clouds,
  Can cover from his sight?
Naked the centre to that eye,
  To which the sun is night.

As yonder glittering lamps on high
  Through night illumin'd roll;
My thoughts of him, by whom they shine,
  Chase darkness from my soul;

My soul, which reads his hand as clear
  In my minute affairs,
As in his ample manuscript
  Of sun, and moon, and stars;

And knows him not more bent aright
  To wield that vast machine,
Than to correct one erring thought
  In my small world within;

A world, that shall survive the fall
  Of all his wonders here;
Survive, when suns ten thousand drop,
  And leave a darken'd sphere.

Yon matter gross, how bright it shines!
  For time how great his care!

Sure spirit and eternity
  Far richer glories share;

Let those our hearts impress, on those
  Our contemplation dwell;
On those my thoughts how justly thrown,
  By what I now shall tell:

When backward with attentive mind
  Life's labyrinth I trace,
I find him far myself beyond
  Propitious to my peace:

Through all the crooked paths I trod,
  My folly he pursued;
My heart astray to quick return
  Importunately woo'd;

Due resignation home to press
  On my capricious will,
How many rescues did I meet,
  Beneath the mask of ill!

How many foes in ambush laid
  Beneath my soul's desire!
The deepest penitents are made
  By what we most admire.

Have I not sometimes (real good
  So little mortals know!)

Mounting the summit of my wish,
 Profoundly plung'd in woe?

I rarely plann'd, but cause I found
 My plan's defeat to bless:
Oft I lamented an event;
 It turn'd to my success.

By sharpen'd appetite to give
 To good intense delight,
Through dark and deep perplexities
 He led me to the right.

And is not this the gloomy path,
 Which you are treading now?
The path most gloomy leads to light,
 When our proud passions bow:

When labouring under fancied ill,
 My spirits to sustain,
He kindly cur'd with sovereign draughts
 Of unimagin'd pain.

Pain'd sense from fancied tyranny
 Alone can set us free;
A thousand miseries we feel,
 Till sunk in misery.

Cloy'd with a glut of all we wish,
 Our wish we relish less;

Success, a sort of suicide,
Is ruin'd by success:

Sometimes he led me near to death,
And, pointing to the grave,
Bid terror whisper kind advice;
And taught the tomb to save:

To raise my thoughts beyond where worlds
As spangles o'er us shine,
One day he gave, and bid the next
My soul's delight resign.

We to ourselves, but through the means
Of mirrors, are unknown;
In this my fate can you descry
No features of your own?

And if you can, let that excuse
These self-recording lines;
A record, modesty forbids,
Or to small bound confines:

In grief why deep ingulf'd? You see
You suffer nothing rare;
Uncommon grief for common fate!
That wisdom cannot bear.

When streams flow backward to their source,
And humbled flames descend,

And mountains wing'd shall fly aloft,
  Then human sorrows end;

But human prudence too must cease,
  When sorrows domineer,
When fortitude has lost its fire,
  And freezes into fear:

The pang most poignant of my life
  Now heightens my delight;
I see a fair creation rise
  From chaos, and old night:

From what seem'd horror, and despair,
  The richest harvest rose;
And gave me in the nod divine
  An absolute repose.

Of all the plunders of mankind,
  More gross, or frequent, none,
Than in their grief and joy misplac'd,
  Eternally are shown.

But whither points all this parade?
  It says, that near you lies
A book, perhaps yet unperus'd,
  Which you should greatly prize:

Of self-perusal, science rare!
  Few know the mighty gain;

Learn'd prelates, self-unread, may read
 Their Bibles o'er in vain:

Self-knowledge, which from heaven itself
 (So sages tell us) came,
What is it, but a daughter fair
 Of my maternal theme?

Unletter'd and untravel'd men
 An oracle might find,
Would they consult their own contents,
 The Delphos of the mind.

Enter your bosom; there you 'll meet
 A revelation new,
A revelation personal;
 Which none can read but you.

There will you clearly read reveal'd
 In your enlighten'd thought,
By mercies manifold, through life,
 To fresh remembrance brought,

A mighty Being! and in him
 A complicated friend,
A father, brother, spouse; no dread
 Of death, divorce, or end:

Who such a matchless friend embrace,
 And lodge him in their heart,

Full well, from agonies exempt,
With other friends may part:

As when o'erloaded branches bear
Large clusters big with wine,
We scarce regret one falling leaf
From the luxuriant vine.

My short advice to you may sound
Obscure or somewhat odd,
Though 'tis the best that man can give, —
"E'en be content with God."

Through love he gave you the deceas'd,
Through greater took him hence;
This reason fully could evince,
Though murmur'd at by sense.

This friend, far past the kindest kind,
Is past the greatest great;
His greatness let me touch in points
Not foreign to your state;

His eye, this instant, reads your heart;
A truth less obvious hear;
This instant its most secret thoughts
Are sounding in his ear:

Dispute you this? O! stand in awe,
And cease your sorrow; know,

That tears now trickling down, he saw
  Ten thousand years ago;

And twice ten thousand hence, if you
  Your temper reconcile
To reason's bound, will he behold
  Your prudence with a smile;

A smile, which through eternity
  Diffuses so bright rays,
The dimmest deifies e'en guilt,
  If guilt, at last, obeys:

Your guilt (for guilt it is to mourn
  When such a sovereign reigns),
Your guilt diminish; peace pursue;
  How glorious peace in pains!

Here, then, your sorrows cease; if not,
  Think how unhappy they,
Who guilt increase by streaming tears,
  Which guilt should wash away;

Of tears that gush profuse restrain;
  Whence burst those dismal sighs?
They from the throbbing breast of one
  (Strange truth!) most happy rise;

Not angels (hear it, and exult!)
  Enjoy a larger share

Than is indulg'd to you, and yours,
  Of God's impartial care;

Anxious for each, as if on each
  His care for all was thrown;
For all his care as absolute,
  As all had been but one.

And is he then so near! so kind!—
  How little then, and great,
That riddle, man! O! let me gaze
  At wonders in his fate;

His fate, who yesterday did crawl
  A worm from darkness deep,
And shall, with brother worms, beneath
  A turf, to-morrow sleep;

How mean!—And yet, if well obey'd
  His mighty Master's call,
The whole creation for mean man
  Is deem'd a boon too small:

Too small the whole creation deem'd
  For emmets in the dust!
Account amazing! yet most true;
  My song is bold, yet just:

Man born for infinite, in whom
  Nor period can destroy

The power, in exquisite extremes,
  To suffer, or enjoy;

Give him earth's empire (if no more)
  He 's beggar'd, and undone!
Imprison'd in unbounded space!
  Benighted by the sun!

For what the sun's meridian blaze
  To the most feeble ray
Which glimmers from the distant dawn
  Of uncreated day?

'T is not the poet's rapture feign'd
  Swells here the vain to please;
The mind most sober kindles most
  At truths sublime as these;

They warm e'en me. — I dare not say,
  Divine ambition strove
Not to bless only, but confound,
  Nay, fright us with its love;

And yet so frightful what, or kind,
  As that the rending rock,
The darken'd sun, and rising dead,
  So formidable spoke?

And are we darker than that sun?
  Than rocks more hard, and blind?

We are; — if not to such a God
  In agonies resigned.

Yes, e'en in agonies forbear
  To doubt almighty love;
Whate'er endears eternity,
  Is mercy from above;

What most imbitters time, that most
  Eternity endears,
And thus, by plunging in distress,
  Exalts us to the spheres;

Joy's fountain head! where bliss o'er bliss,
  O'er wonders wonders rise,
And an Omnipotence prepares
  Its banquet for the wise:

Ambrosial banquet! rich in wines
  Nectareous to the soul!
What transports sparkle from the stream,
  As angels fill the bowl!

Fountain profuse of every bliss!
  Good-will immense prevails;
Man's line can't fathom its profound
  An angel's plummet fails.

Thy love and might, by what they know,
  Who judge, nor dream of more;

They ask a drop, how deep the sea!
  One sand, how wide the shore!

Of thy exuberant good-will,
  Offended Deity!
The thousandth part who comprehends,
  A deity is he.

How yonder ample azure field
  With radiant worlds is sown!
How tubes astonish us with those
  More deep in ether thrown!

And those beyond of brighter worlds
  Why not a million more?—
In lieu of answer, let us all
  Fall prostrate, and adore.

Since thou art infinite in power,
  Nor thy indulgence less;
Since man, quite impotent and blind,
  Oft drops into distress;

Say, what is resignation? 'T is
  Man's weakness understood;
And wisdom grasping, with a hand
  Far stronger, every good.

Let rash repiners stand appall'd,
  In thee who dare not trust;

Whose abject souls, like demons dark,
  Are murmuring in the dust;

For man to murmur, or repine
  At what by thee is done,
No less absurd, than to complain
  Of darkness in the sun.

Who would not, with a heart at ease,
  Bright eye, unclouded brow,
Wisdom and goodness at the helm,
  The roughest ocean plough?

What, though I 'm swallow'd in the deep?
  Though mountains o'er me roar?
Jehovah reigns! as Jonah safe,
  I 'm landed, and adore:

Thy will is welcome, let it wear
  Its most tremendous form;
Roar, waves; rage, winds! I know that thou
  Canst save me by a storm.

From the immortal spirits born,
  To thee, their fountain, flow,
If wise; as curl'd around to theirs
  Meandering streams below:

Not less compell'd by reason's call,
  To thee our souls aspire,

Than to thy skies, by nature's law,
  High mounts material fire;

To thee aspiring they exult,
  I feel my spirits rise,
I feel myself thy son, and pant
  For patrimonial skies;

Since ardent thirst of future good,
  And generous sense of past,
To thee man's prudence strongly ties,
  And binds affection fast;

Since great thy love, and great our want,
  And men the wisest blind,
And bliss our aim; pronounce us all
  Distracted, or resigned;

Resign'd through duty, interest, shame;
  Deep shame! dare I complain,
When (wondrous truth!) in heaven itself
  Joy ow'd its birth to pain?

And pain for me! for me was drain'd
  Gall's overflowing bowl;
And shall one drop to murmur bold
  Provoke my guilty soul?

If pardon'd this, what cause, what crime
  Can indignation raise?

The sun was lighted up to shine,
And man was born to praise;

And when to praise the man shall cease,
Or sun to strike the view;
A cloud dishonors both; but man's
The blacker of the two:

For oh! ingratitude how black!
With most profound amaze
At love, which man belov'd o'erlooks,
Astonish'd angels gaze.

Praise cheers, and warms, like generous wine;
Praise, more divine than prayer;
Prayer points our ready path to heaven;
Praise is already there.

Let plausive resignation rise,
And banish all complaint;
All virtues thronging into one,
It finishes the saint;

Makes the man bless'd, as man can be;
Life's labours renders light;
Darts beams through fate's incumbent gloom,
And lights our sun by night;

'T is nature's brightest ornament,
The richest gift of grace,

Rival of angels, and supreme
  Proprietor of peace;

Nay, peace beyond, no small degree
  Of rapture 't will impart;
Know, madam! when your heart 's in heaven,
  "All heaven is in your heart."

But who to heaven their hearts can raise?
  Denied divine support,
All virtue dies; support divine
  The wise with ardour court:

When prayer partakes the seraph's fire,
  'T is mounted on his wing,
Bursts thro' heaven's crystal gates, and
  Sure audience of its king:

The labouring soul from sore distress
  That bless'd expedient frees;
I see you far advanc'd in peace;
  I see you on your knees:

How on that posture has the beam
  Divine for ever shone!
An humble heart, God's other seat! *
  The rival of his throne:

And stoops Omnipotence so low!
  And condescends to dwell,

* Isaiah lvii. 15.

Eternity's inhabitant,
  Well pleas'd, in such a cell?

Such honour how shall we repay?
  How treat our guest divine?
The sacrifice supreme be slain!
  Let self-will die: resign.

Thus far, at large, on our disease;
  Now let the cause be shown,
Whence rises, and will ever rise,
  The dismal human groan:

What our sole fountain of distress?
  Strong passion for this scene;
That trifles make important, things
  Of mighty moment mean:

When earth's dark maxims poison shed
  On our polluted souls,
Our hearts and interests fly as far
  Asunder, as the poles.

Like princes in a cottage nurs'd,
  Unknown their royal race,
With abject aims, and sordid joys,
  Our grandeur we disgrace;

O! for an Archimedes new,
  Of moral powers possess'd,

The world to move, and quite expel
  That traitor from the breast.

No small advantage may be reap'd
  From thought whence we descend;
From weighing well, and prizing weigh'd
  Our origin, and end:

From far above the glorious sun
  To this dim scene we came:
And may, if wise, for ever bask
  In great Jehovah's beam:

Let that bright beam on reason rous'd
  In awful lustre rise,
Earth's giant ills are dwarf'd at once,
  And all disquiet dies.

Earth's glories too their splendour lose,
  Those phantoms charm no more;
Empire 's a feather for a fool,
  And Indian mines are poor:

Then levell'd quite, whilst yet alive,
  The monarch and his slave;
Not wait enlighten'd minds to learn
  That lesson from the grave:

A George the Third would then be low
  As Lewis in renown,

Could he not boast of glory more
  Than sparkles from a crown.

When human glory rises high
  As human glory can;
When, though the king is truly great,
  Still greater is the man;

The man is dead, where virtue fails;
  And though the monarch proud
In grandeur shines, his gorgeous robe
  Is but a gaudy shroud.

Wisdom! where art thou? None on earth,
  Though grasping wealth, fame, power,
But what, O death! through thy approach,
  Is wiser every hour;

Approach how swift, how unconfin'd!
  Worms feast on viands rare,
Those little epicures have kings
  To grace their bill of fare:

From kings what resignation due
  To that almighty will,
Which thrones bestows, and, when they fail,
  Can throne them higher still!

Who truly great? The good and brave,
  The masters of a mind

The will divine to do resolv'd,
To suffer it resign'd.

Madam! if that may give it weight,
The trifle you receive
Is dated from a solemn scene,
The border of the grave;

Where strongly strikes the trembling soul
Eternity's dread power,
As bursting on it through the thin
Partition of an hour;

Hear this, Voltaire! but this, from me,
Runs hazard of your frown;
However, spare it; ere you die,
Such thoughts will be your own.

In mercy to yourself forbear
My notions to chastise,
Lest unawares the gay Voltaire
Should blame Voltaire the wise:

Fame's trumpet rattling in your ear,
Now, makes us disagree;
When a far louder trumpet sounds,
Voltaire will close with me:

How shocking is that modesty,
Which keeps some honest men

From urging what their hearts suggest,
When brav'd by folly's pen.

Assaulting truths, of which in all
Is sown the sacred seed!
Our constitution 's orthodox,
And closes with our creed:

What then are they, whose proud conceits
Superior wisdom boast?
Wretches, who fight their own belief,
And labour to be lost!

Though vice by no superior joys
Her heroes keeps in pay;
Through pure disinterested love
Of ruin they obey!

Strict their devotion to the wrong,
Though tempted by no prize;
Hard their commandments, and their creed
A magazine of lies

From fancy's forge: gay fancy smiles
At reason plain, and cool;
Fancy, whose curious trade it is
To make the finest fool.

Voltaire! long life 's the greatest curse
That mortals can receive,

When they imagine the chief end
  Of living is to live;

Quite thoughtless of their day of death,
  That birthday of their sorrow!
Knowing, it may be distant far,
  Nor crush them till — to-morrow.

These are cold, northern thoughts, conceiv'd
  Beneath an humble cot;
Not mine, your genius, or your state,
  No castle is my lot: *

But soon, quite level shall we lie;
  And, what pride most bemoans,
Our parts, in rank so distant now,
  As level as our bones;

Hear you that sound? Alarming sound!
  Prepare to meet your fate!
One, who writes finis to our works,
  Is knocking at the gate;

Far other works will soon be weigh'd;
  Far other judges sit;
Far other crowns be lost or won,
  Than fire ambitious wit:

Their wit far brightest will be prov'd,
  Who sunk it in good sense;

* Letter to Lord Lyttelton.

And veneration most profound
   Of dread omnipotence.

'Tis that alone unlocks the gate
   Of blest eternity;
O! mayst thou never, never lose
   That more than golden key! *

Whate'er may seem too rough excuse,
   Your good I have at heart:
Since from my soul I wish you well;
   As yet we must not part:

Shall you, and I, in love with life,
   Life's future schemes contrive,
The world in wonder not unjust,
   That we are still alive?

What have we left? How mean in man
   A shadow's shade to crave!
When life, so vain! is vainer still,
   'Tis time to take your leave:

Happier, than happiest life, is death,
   Who, falling in the field
Of conflict with his rebel will,
   Writes vici, on his shield;

So falling man, immortal heir
   Of an eternal prize;

* Alluding to Prussia.

Undaunted at the gloomy grave,
Descends into the skies.

O! how disorder'd our machine,
When contradictions mix!
When nature strikes no less than twelve,
And folly points at six!

To mend the moments of your heart,
How great is my delight
Gently to wind your morals up,
And set your hand aright!

That hand, which spread your wisdom wide
To poison distant lands:
Repent, recant; the tainted age
Your antidote demands;

To Satan dreadfully resign'd,
Whole herds rush down the steep
Of folly, by lewd wits possess'd,
And perish in the deep.

Men's praise your vanity pursues;
'Tis well, pursue it still;
But let it be of men deceas'd,
And you'll resign the will;

And how superior they to those
At whose applause you aim;
How very far superior they
In number, and in name!

POSTSCRIPT.

Thus have I written, when to write
  No mortal should presume;
Or only write, what none can blame,
  Hic jacet — for his tomb:

The public frowns, and censures loud
  My puerile employ;
Though just the censure, if you smile,
  The scandal I enjoy;

But sing no more — no more I sing
  Or reassume the lyre,
Unless vouchsaf'd an humble part
  Where Raphael leads the choir:

What myriads swell the concert loud!
  Their golden harps resound
High as the footstool of the throne,
  And deep as hell profound:

Hell (horrid contrast!) chord and song
  Of raptur'd angels drowns
In self-will's peal of blasphemies,
  And hideous burst of groans;

But drowns them not to me; I hear
  Harmonious thunders roll
(In language low of men to speak)
  From echoing pole to pole!

Whilst this grand chorus shakes the skies —
  "Above, beneath the sun,
Through boundless age, by men, by gods,
  Jehovah's will be done!"

'Tis done in heaven; whence headlong hurl'd
  Self-will with Satan fell;
And must from earth be banish'd too,
  Or earth 's another hell;

Madam! self-will inflicts your pains:
  Self-will 's the deadly foe
Which deepens all the dismal shades,
  And points the shafts of woe:

Your debt to nature fully paid,
  Now virtue claims her due:
But virtue's cause I need not plead,
  'Tis safe; I write to you:

You know, that virtue's basis lies
  In ever judging right;
And wiping error's clouds away,
  Which dim the mental sight:

Why mourn the dead? you wrong the grave,
From storm that safe resort;
We still are tossing out at sea,
Our admiral in port.

Was death denied, this world, a scene
How dismal and forlorn!
To death we owe, that 'tis to man
A blessing to be born;

When every other blessing fails,
Or sapp'd by slow decay,
Or, storm'd by sudden blasts of fate,
Is swiftly whirl'd away;

How happy! that no storm, or time,
Of death can rob the just!
None pluck from their unaching heads
Soft pillows in the dust!

Well pleas'd to bear heaven's darkest frown,
Your utmost power employ;
'Tis noble chemistry to turn
Necessity to joy.

Whate'er the colour of my fate,
My fate shall be my choice:
Determin'd am I, whilst I breathe,
To praise and to rejoice;

What ample cause! triumphant hope!
O rich eternity!
I start not at a world in flames,
Charm'd with one glimpse of thee:

And thou! its great inhabitant!
How glorious dost thou shine!
And dart through sorrow, danger, death,
A beam of joy divine!

The void of joy (with some concern
The truth severe I tell)
Is an impenitent in guilt,
A fool or infidel!

Weigh this, ye pupils of Voltaire!
From joyless murmur free;
Or, let us know, which character
Shall crown you of the three.

Resign, resign: this lesson none
Too deeply can instill;
A crown has been resign'd by more,
Than have resign'd the will;

Though will resign'd the meanest makes
Superior in renown,
And richer in celestial eyes,
Than he who wears a crown;

Hence, in the bosom cold of age,
  It kindled a strange aim
To shine in song; and bid me boast
  The grandeur of my theme:

But oh! how far presumption falls
  Its lofty theme below!
Our thoughts in life's December freeze,
  And numbers cease to flow.

First! greatest! best! grant what I wrote
  For others, ne'er may rise
To brand the writer! thou alone
  Canst make our wisdom wise;

And how unwise! how deep in guilt!
  How infamous the fault!
"A teacher thron'd in pomp of words,
  Indeed, beneath the taught!"

Means most infallible to make
  The world an infidel;
And, with instructions most divine,
  To pave a path to hell;

O! for a clean and ardent heart,
  O! for a soul on fire,
Thy praise, begun on earth, to sound
  Where angels string the lyre;

How cold is man! to him how hard
(Hard, what most easy seems)
"To set a just esteem on that,
Which yet he — most esteems!"

What shall we say, when boundless bliss
Is offer'd to mankind,
And to that offer when a race
Of rationals is blind?

Of human nature ne'er too high
Are our ideas wrought;
Of human merit ne'er too low
Depress'd the daring thought.

ON THE LATE QUEEN'S DEATH,

AND HIS MAJESTY'S ACCESSION TO THE THRONE

INSCRIBED TO JOSEPH ADDISON, ESQ. SECRETARY TO THEIR EXCELLENCIES THE LORDS JUSTICES.

Gaudia curis. — HOR.

SIR, I have long, and with impatience, sought
To ease the fulness of my grateful thought,
My fame at once, and duty to pursue,
And please the public, by respect to you.
Though you, long since beyond Britannia known,
Have spread your country's glory with your own;
To me you never did more lovely shine,
Than when so late the kindled wrath divine
Quench'd our ambition, in great Anna's fate,
And darken'd all the pomp of human state.
Though you are rich in fame, and fame decay,
Though rais'd in life, and greatness fade away,
Your lustre brightens: virtue cuts the gloom
With purer rays, and sparkles near a tomb.
Know, sir, the great esteem and honour due,
I chose that moment to profess to you,
When sadness reign'd, when fortune, so severe,
Had warm'd our bosoms to be most sincere.
And when no motives could have force to raise
A serious value, and provoke my praise,
But such as rise above, and far transcend,

Whatever glories with this world shall end,
Then shining forth, when deepest shades shall blot
The sun's bright orb, and Cato be forgot.
I sing—but ah! my theme I need not tell,
See every eye with conscious sorrow swell:
Who now to verse would raise his humble voice,
Can only show his duty, not his choice.
How great the weight of grief our hearts sustain!
We languish, and to speak is to complain.
  Let us look back, (for who too oft can view
That most illustrious scene, for ever new!)
See all the seasons shine on Anna's throne,
And pay a constant tribute, not their own.
Her summer's heats nor fruits alone bestow,
They reap the harvest, and subdue the foe;
And when black storms confess the distant sun,
Her winters wear the wreaths her summers won.
Revolving pleasures in their turns appear,
And triumphs are the product of the year.
To crown the whole, great joys in greater cease,
And glorious victory is lost in peace.
  Whence this profusion on our favour'd isle?
Did partial fortune on our virtue smile?
Or did the sceptre, in great Anna's hand,
Stretch forth this rich indulgence o'er our land?
Ungrateful Britain! quit thy groundless claim,
Thy queen and thy good fortune are the same.
  Hear, with alarms our trumpets fill the sky;
'Tis Anna reigns! the Gallic squadrons fly.
We spread our canvass to the southern shore;

'Tis Anna reigns! the south resigns her store.
Her virtue smooths the tumult of the main,
And swells the field with mountains of the slain
Argyll and Churchill but the glory share,
While millions lie subdu'd by Anna's prayer.
 How great her zeal! how fervent her desire!
How did her soul in holy warmth expire!
Constant devotion did her time divide,
Not set returns of pleasure or of pride.
Not want of rest, or the sun's parting ray,
But finish'd duty, limited the day.
How sweet succeeding sleep! what lovely themes
Smil'd in her thoughts, and soften'd all her dreams!
Her royal couch descending angels spread,
And join'd their wings a shelter o'er her head.
 Though Europe's wealth and glory claim'd a part,
Religion's cause reign'd mistress of her heart:
She saw, and griev'd to see, the mean estate
Of those who round the hallow'd altar wait;
She shed her bounty, piously profuse,
And thought it more her own in sacred use.
 Thus on his furrow see the tiller stand,
And fill with genial seed his lavish hand;
He trusts the kindness of the fruitful plain,
And providently scatters all his grain.
 What strikes my sight? does proud Augusta rise
New to behold, and awfully surprise!
Her lofty brow more numerous turrets crown,
And sacred domes on palaces look down:
A noble pride of piety is shown,

And temples cast a lustre on the throne.
How would this work another's glory raise!
But Anna's greatness robs her of the praise.
Drown'd in a brighter blaze it disappears,
Who dried the widow's and the orphan's tears?
Who stoop'd from high to succour the distrest
And reconcile the wounded heart to rest?
Great in her goodness, well could we perceive,
Whoever sought, it was a queen that gave.
Misfortune lost her name, her guiltless frown
But made another debtor to the crown;
And each unfriendly stroke from fate we bore,
Became our title to the regal store.
  Thus injur'd trees adopt a foreign shoot,
And their wounds blossom with a fairer fruit.
  Ye numbers, who on your misfortunes thriv'd,
When first the dreadful blast of fame arriv'd,
Say what a shock, what agonies you felt,
How did your souls with tender anguish melt!
That grief which living Anna's love suppress'd,
Shook like a tempest every grateful breast,
A second fate our sinking fortunes tried!
A second time our tender parents died!
  Heroes returning from the field we crown,
And deify the haughty victor's frown.
His splendid wealth too rashly we admire,
Catch the disease, and burn with equal fire:
Wisely to spend, is the great art of gain;
And one reliev'd transcends a million slain.
When time shall ask, where once Ramillia lay,

Or Danube flow'd that swept whole troops away,
One drop of water, that refresh'd the dry,
Shall rise a fountain of eternal joy.
But ah! to that unknown and distant date
Is virtue's great reward push'd off by fate;
Here random shafts in every breast are found,
Virtue and merit but provoke the wound.
August in native worth and regal state,
Anna sate arbitress of Europe's fate;
To distant realms did every accent fly,
And nations watch'd each motion of her eye.
Silent, nor longer awful to be seen,
How small a spot contains the mighty queen!
No throng of suppliant princes mark the place,
Where Britain's greatness is compos'd in peace:
The broken earth is scarce discern'd to rise,
And a stone tells us where the monarch lies.
Thus end maturest honours of the crown!
This is the last conclusion of renown!
So when with idle skill the wanton boy
Breathes through his tube; he sees, with eager joy,
The trembling bubble, in its rising small;
And by degrees expands the glittering ball.
But when, to full perfection blown, it flies
High in the air, and shines in various dyes,
The little monarch, with a falling tear,
Sees his world burst at once, and disappear,
'Tis not in sorrow to reverse our doom,
No groans unlock th' inexorable tomb!
Why then this fond indulgence of our woe!

What fruit can rise, or what advantage flow!
Yes, this advantage; from our deep distress
We learn how much in George the gods can bless
Had a less glorious princess left the throne,
But half the hero had at first been shown:
An Anna falling all the king employs,
To vindicate from guilt our rising joys:
Our joys arise and innocently shine,
Auspicious monarch! what a praise is thine!
  Welcome, great stranger, to Britannia's throne!
Nor let thy country think thee all her own.
Of thy delay how oft did we complain!
Our hopes reach'd out, and met thee on the main.
With prayer we smooth the billows for thy fleet;
With ardent wishes fill thy swelling sheet;
And when thy foot took place on Albion's shore,
We bending bless'd the gods, and ask'd no more.
What hand but thine should conquer and compose,
Join those whom interest joins, and chase our foes?
Repel the daring youth's presumptuous aim,
And by his rival's greatness give him fame?
Now in some foreign court he may sit down,
And quit without a blush the British crown.
Secure his honour, though he lose his store,
And take a lucky moment to be poor.
  Nor think, great sir, now first, at this late hour,
In Britain's favour, you exert your power;
To us, far back in time, I joy to trace
The numerous tokens of your princely grace.
Whether you chose to thunder on the Rhine,

Inspire grave councils, or in courts to shine;
In the more scenes your genius was display'd,
The greater debt was on Britannia laid:
They all conspir'd this mighty man to raise,
And your new subjects proudly share the praise.
All share; but may not we have leave to boast
That we contemplate, and enjoy it most?
This ancient nurse of arts, indulged by fate
On gentle Isis' bank, a calm retreat;
For many rolling ages justly fam'd,
Has through the world her loyalty proclaim'd;
And often pour'd (too well the truth is known!)
Her blood and treasure to support the throne!
For England's church her latest accents strain'd;
And freedom with his dying hand retain'd.
No wonder then her various ranks agree
In all the fervencies of zeal for thee.
What though thy birth a distant kingdom boast,
And seas divide thee from the British coast?
The crown 's impatient to enclose thy head:
Why stay thy feet? the cloth of gold is spread.
Our strict obedience through the world shall tell
That king 's a Briton, who can govern well!

THE INSTALMENT.

TO THE RIGHT HON. SIR ROBERT WALPOLE, KNIGHT OF THE MOST NOBLE ORDER OF THE GARTER.

Quæsitam meritis. — Hor.

With invocations some their breasts inflame;
I need no muse, a Walpole is my theme.
Ye mighty dead, ye garter'd sons of praise!
Our morning stars! our boast in former days!
Which hovering o'er, your purple wings display,
Lur'd by the pomp of this distinguish'd day,
Stoop, and attend: by one, the knee be bound;
One, throw the mantle's crimson folds around;
By that, the sword on his proud thigh be plac'd;
This, clasp the diamond girdle round his waist;
His breast, with rays, let just Godolphin spread;
Wise Burleigh plant the plumage on his head;
And Edward own, since first he fix'd the race,
None press'd fair glory with a swifter pace.
When fate would call some mighty genius forth
To wake a drooping age to godlike worth,
Or aid some favourite king's illustrious toil,
It bids his blood with generous ardour boil;
His blood, from virtue's celebrated source,
Pour'd down the steep of time, a lengthen'd course;
That men prepar'd may just attention pay,
Warn'd by the dawn to mark the glorious day,
When all the scatter'd merits of his line
Collected to a point, intensely shine.

See, Britain, see thy Walpole shine from far,
His azure ribbon, and his radiant star;
A star that, with auspicious beams, shall guide
Thy vessel safe, through fortune's roughest tide.
If peace still smiles, by this shall commerce steer
A finish'd course, in triumph round the sphere;
And, gathering tribute from each distant shore,
In Britain's lap the world's abundance pour.
If war 's ordain'd, this star shall dart its beams
Through that black cloud which, rising from the Thames,
With thunder, form'd of Brunswick's wrath, is sent
To claim the seas, and awe the continent.
This shall direct it where the bolt to throw,
A star for us, a comet to the foe.
At this the muse shall kindle, and aspire:
My breast, O Walpole, glows with grateful fire.
The streams of royal bounty, turn'd by thee,
Refresh the dry domains of poesy.
My fortune shows, when arts are Walpole's care,
What slender worth forbids us to despair:
Be this thy partial smile from censure free;
'Twas meant for merit, though it fell on me.
Since Brunswick's smile has authoris'd my muse,
Chaste be her conduct, and sublime her views.
False praises are the whoredoms of the pen,
Which prostitute fair fame to worthless men:
This profanation of celestial fire
Makes fools despise, what wise men should admire.
Let those I praise to distant times be known,

Not by their author's merit, but their own.
If others think the task is hard, to weed
From verse rank flattery's vivacious seed,
And rooted deep; one means must set them free,
Patron! and patriot! let them sing of thee.
While vulgar trees ignobler honours wear,
Nor those retain, when winter chills the year;
The generous orange, favourite of the sun,
With vigorous charms can through the seasons run;
Defies the storm with her tenacious green;
And flowers and fruits in rival pomp are seen:
Where blossoms fall, still fairer blossoms spring;
And midst their sweets the feather'd poets sing.
On Walpole, thus, may pleas'd Britannia view
At once her ornament and profit too;
The fruit of service, and the bloom of fame,
Matur'd and gilded by the royal beam.
He, when the nipping blasts of envy rise
Its guilt can pity, and its rage despise;
Lets fall no honours, but, securely great,
Unfaded holds the colour of his fate:
No winter knows, though ruffling factions press;
By wisdom deeply rooted in success;
One glory shed, a brighter is display'd; *
And the charm'd muses shelter in his shade.
O how I long, enkindled by the theme,
In deep eternity to launch thy name!
Thy name in view, no rights of verse I plead,
But what chaste truth indites, old time shall read.

* Knight of the Bath, and then of the Garter.

" Behold! a man of ancient faith and blood,
Which, soon, beat high for arts, and public good;
Whose glory great, but natural appears,
The genuine growth of services and years;
No sudden exhalation drawn on high,
And fondly gilt by partial majesty:
One bearing greatest toils with greatest ease,
One born to serve us, and yet born to please:
Whom, while our rights in equal scales he lays,
The prince may trust, and yet the people praise;
His genius ardent, yet his judgment clear,
His tongue is flowing, and his heart sincere,
His counsel guides, his temper cheers our isle,
And, smiling, gives three kingdoms cause to smile."
Joy then to Britain, blest with such a son,
To Walpole joy, by whom the prize is won;
Who nobly conscious meets the smiles of fate;
True greatness lies in daring to be great.
Let dastard souls, or affectation, run
To shades, nor wear bright honours fairly won;
Such men prefer, misled by false applause,
The pride of modesty to virtue's cause.
Honours, which make the face of virtue fair,
'Tis great to merit, and 'tis wise to wear;
'Tis holding up the prize to public view,
Confirms grown virtue, and inflames the new;
Heightens the lustre of our age and clime,
And sheds rich seeds of worth for future time.
Proud chiefs alone, in fields of slaughter fam'd,
Of old, this azure bloom of glory claim'd,

As when stern Ajax pour'd a purple flood,
The violet rose, fair daughter of his blood.
Now rival wisdom dares the wreath divide,
And both Minervas rise in equal pride;
Proclaiming loud, a monarch fills the throne,
Who shines illustrious not in wars alone.
  Let fame look lovely in Britannia's eyes;
They coldly court desert, who fame despise.
For what 's ambition, but fair virtue's sail?
And what applause, but her propitious gale?
When swell'd with that, she fleets before the wind
To glorious aims, as to the port design'd;
When chain'd, without it, to the labouring oar,
She toils! she pants! nor gains the flying shore,
From her sublime pursuits, or turn'd aside
By blasts of envy, or by fortune's tide:
For one that has succeeded ten are lost,
Of equal talents, ere they make the coast.
  Then let renown to worth divine incite,
With all her beams, but throw those beams aright.
Then merit droops, and genius downward tends,
When godlike glory, like our land, descends.
Custom the garter long confin'd to few,
And gave to birth, exalted virtue's due:
Walpole has thrown the proud enclosure down;
And high desert embraces fair renown.
Though rival'd, let the peerage smiling see
(Smiling, in justice to their own degree)
This proud reward by majesty bestow'd

On worth like that whence first the peerage flow'd.
From frowns of fate Britannia 's bliss'd to guard,
Let subjects merit, and let kings reward.
Gods are most gods by giving to excel,
And kings most like them, by rewarding well.
 Though strong the twanging nerve, and drawn aright,
Short is the winged arrow's upward flight;
But if an eagle it transfix on high,
Lodg'd in the wound, it soars into the sky.
 Thus while I sing thee with unequal lays,
And wound perhaps that worth I mean to praise;
Yet I transcend myself, I rise in fame,
Not lifted by my genius, but my theme.
 No more: for in this dread suspense of fate,
Now kingdoms fluctuate, and in dark debate
Weigh peace and war, now Europe's eyes are bent
On mighty Brunswick, for the great event,
Brunswick of kings the terror or defence!
Who dares detain thee at a world's expense?

AN EPISTLE

TO THE RIGHT HON. GEORGE LORD LANSDOWNE.

1712.

Parnassia laurus
Parva sub ingenti matris se subjicit umbra. — VIRG.

WHEN Rome, my lord, in her full glory shone,
And great Augustus rul'd the globe alone,
While suppliant kings in all their pomp and state
Swarm'd in his courts, and throng'd his palace gate;
Horace did oft the mighty man detain,
And sooth'd his breast with no ignoble strain;
Now soar'd aloft, now struck an humbler string;
And taught the Roman genius how to sing.
  Pardon, if I his freedom dare pursue,
Who know no want of Cæsar, finding you;
The muse's friend is pleas'd the muse should press
Through circling crowds, and labor for access,
That partial to his darling he may prove,
And shining throngs for her reproach remove,
To all the world industrious to proclaim
His love of arts, and boast the glorious flame.
  Long has the western world reclin'd her head,
Pour'd forth her sorrow, and bewail'd her dead;
Fell discord through her borders fiercely rang'd,
And shook her nations, and her monarchs chang'd;
By land and sea, its utmost rage employ'd;
Nor heaven repair'd so fast as men destroy'd.

In vain kind summers plentuous fields bestow'd,
In vain the vintage liberally flow'd;
Alarms from loaden boards all pleasures chas'd,
And robb'd the rich Burgundian grape of taste;
The smiles of Nature could no blessing bring,
The fruitful autumn, or the flowery spring;
Time was distinguish'd by the sword and spear,
Not by the various aspects of the year;
The trumpet's sound proclaim'd a milder sky,
And bloodshed told us when the sun was nigh.
But now (so soon is Britain's blessing seen,
When such as you are near her glorious queen!)
Now peace, though long repuls'd, arrives at last,
And bids us smile on all our labours past;
Bids every nation cease her wonted moan,
And every monarch call his crown his own:
To valour gentler virtues now succeed;
No longer is the great man born to bleed;
Renown'd in councils, brave Argyle shall tell,
Wisdom and prowess in one breast may dwell:
Through milder tracts he soars to deathless fame,
And without trembling we resound his name.
No more the rising harvest whets the sword,
No longer waves uncertain of its lord;
Who cast the seed, the golden sheaf shall claim,
Nor chance of battle change the master's name.
Each stream unstain'd with blood more smoothly flows;
The brighter sun a fuller day bestows;

All nature seems to wear a cheerful face,
And thank great Anna for returning peace.
The patient thus, when on his bed of pain,
No longer he invokes the gods in vain,
But rises to new life; in every field
He finds Elysium, rivers nectar yield;
Nothing so cheap and vulgar but can please,
And borrow beauties from his late disease.
Nor is it peace alone, but such a peace,
As more than bids the rage of battle cease.
Death may determine war, and rest succeed,
'Cause nought survives on which our rage may feed:
In faithful friends we lose our glorious foes,
And strifes of love exalt our sweet repose.
See graceful Bolingbroke, your friend, advance,
Nor miss his Lansdowne in the court of France;
So well receiv'd, so welcome, so at home,
(Blest change of fate,) in Bourbon's stately dome;
The monarch pleas'd, descending from his throne,
Will not that Anna call him all her own;
He claims a part, and looking round to find
Something might speak the fulness of his mind,
A diamond shines, which oft had touch'd him near,
Renew'd his grief, and robb'd him of a tear;
Now first with joy beheld, well plac'd on one,
Who makes him less regret his darling son;
So dear is Anna's minister, so great,
Your glorious friend in his own private state.
To make our nations longer two, in vain
Does nature interpose the raging main:

The Gallic shore to distant Britain grows,
For Lewis Thames, the Seine for Anna flows:
From conflicts pass'd each other's worth we find,
And thence in stricter friendship now are join'd;
Each wound receiv'd, now pleads the cause of love,
And former injuries endearments prove.
What Briton but must prize th' illustrious sword,
That cause of fear to Churchill could afford?
Who sworn to Bourbon's sceptre, but must frame
Vast thoughts of him, that could brave Tallard tame?
Thus generous hatred in affection ends,
And war, which rais'd the foes, completes the friends.
A thousand happy consequences flow
(The dazzling prospect makes my bosom glow);
Commerce shall lift her swelling sails, and roll
Her wealthy fleets secure from pole to pole;
The British merchant, who with care and pain
For many moons sees only skies and main;
When now in view of his loved native shore,
The perils of the dreadful ocean o'er,
Cause to regret his wealth no more shall find,
Nor curse the mercy of the sea and wind;
By hardest fate condemn'd to serve a foe,
And give him strength to strike a deeper blow.
Sweet Philomela providently flies
To distant woods and streams, for such supplies,
To feed her young, and make them try the wing,
And with their tender notes attempt to sing:
Meanwhile, the fowler spreads his secret snare,
And renders vain the tuneful mother's care.

Britannia's bold adventurer of late
The foaming ocean plow'd with equal fate.
  Goodness is greatness in its utmost height,
And power a curse, if not a friend to right:
To conquer is to make dissension cease,
That man may serve the King of kings in peace.
Religion now shall all her rays dispense,
And shine abroad in perfect excellence;
Else we may dread some greater curse at hand,
To scourge a thoughtless and ungrateful land:
Now war is weary, and retir'd to rest;
The meagre famine, and the spotted pest,
Deputed in her stead, may blast the day,
And sweep the relics of the sword away.
  When peaceful Numa fill'd the Roman throne,
Jove in the fulness of his glory shone;
Wise Solomon, a stranger to the sword,
Was born to raise a temple to the Lord.
Anne too shall build, and every sacred pile
Speak peace eternal to Britannia's isle.
Those mighty souls, whom military care
Diverted from their only great affair,
Shall bend their full united force, to bless
Th' Almighty Author of their late success.
And what is all the world subdued to this?
The grave sets bounds to sublunary bliss;
But there are conquests to great Anna known,
Above the splendour of an earthly throne;
Conquests! whose triumph is too great, within
The scanty bounds of matter to begin;

Too glorious to shine forth, till it has run
Beyond this darkness of the stars and sun,
And shall whole ages past be still, still but begun.
Heroic shades! whom war has swept away,
Look down, and smile on this auspicious day:
Now boast your deaths; to those your glory tell,
Who or at Agincourt or Cressy fell;
Then deep into eternity retire,
Of greater things than peace or war inquire;
Fully content, and unconcern'd, to know
What farther passes in the world below.
The bravest of mankind shall now have leave
To die but once, nor piece-meal seek the grave:
On gain or pleasure bent, we shall not meet
Sad melancholy numbers in each street
(Owners of bones dispers'd on Flandria's plain,
Or wasting in the bottom of the main);
To turn us back from joy, in tender fear,
Lest it an insult of their woes appear,
And make us grudge ourselves that wealth, their blood
Perhaps preserv'd, who starve, or beg for food.
Devotion shall run pure, and disengage
From that strange fate of mixing peace with rage.
On heaven without a sin we now may call,
And guiltless to our Maker prostrate fall;
Be Christians while we pray, nor in one breath
Ask mercy for ourselves, for others death.
But O! I view with transport arts restor'd,
Which double use to Britain shall afford;

Secure her glory purchas'd in the field,
And yet for future peace sweet motives yield :
While we contemplate on the painted wall,
The pressing Briton, and the flying Gaul,
In such bright images, such living grace,
As leave great Raphael but the second place ;
Our cheeks shall glow, our heaving bosoms rise,
And martial ardours sparkle in our eyes ;
Much we shall triumph in our battles past,
And yet consent those battles prove our last ;
Lest, while in arms for brighter fame we strive,
We lose the means to keep that fame alive.
  In silent groves the birds delight to sing,
Or near the margin of a secret spring :
Now all is calm, sweet music shall improve,
Nor kindle rage, but be the nurse of love.
  But what 's the warbling voice, the trembling string,
Or breathing canvass, when the muses sing ?
The muse, my lord, your care above the rest,
With rising joy dilates my partial breast ;
The thunder of the battle ceas'd to roar,
Ere Greece her godlike poets taught to soar ;
Rome's dreadful foe, great Hannibal, was dead,
And all her warlike neighbours round her bled ;
For Janus shut, her Iö Pæans rung,
Before an Ovid or a Virgil sung.
  A thousand various forms the muse may wear,
(A thousand various forms become the fair ;)
But shines in none with more majestic mien,

Than when in state she draws the purple scene;
Calls forth her monarchs, bids her heroes rage,
And mourning beauty melt the crowded stage;
Charms back past ages, gives to Britain's use
The noblest virtues time did e'er produce;
Leaves fam'd historians' boasted art behind;
They keep the soul alone, and that 's confin'd,
Sought out with pains, and but by proxy speaks
The hero's presence deep impression makes;
The scenes his soul and body reunite,
Furnish a voice, produce him to the sight;
Make our contemporary him that stood
High in renown, perhaps before the flood;
Make Nestor to this age advice afford,
And Hector for our service draw his sword.
 More glory to an author what can bring,
Whence nobler service to his country spring,
Than from those labours, which, in man's despight,
Possess him with a passion for the right?
With honest magic make the knave inclin'd
To pay devotion to the virtuous mind;
Through all her toils and dangers bid him rove,
And with her wants and anguish fall in love?
 Who hears the godlike Montezuma groan,
And does not wish the glorious pain his own?
Lend but your understanding, and their skill
Can domineer at pleasure o'er your will:
Nor is the short-liv'd conquest quickly past;
Shame, if not choice, will hold the convert fast.
 How often have I seen the generous bowl

With pleasing force unlock a secret soul,
And steal a truth, which every sober hour
(The prose of life) had kept within her power!
The grape victorious often has prevail'd,
When gold and beauty, racks and tortures, fail'd:
Yet when the spirit's tumult was allay'd,
She mourn'd, perhaps, the sentiment betray'd;
But mourn'd too late, no longer could deny,
And on her own confession charge the lie.
  Thus they, whom neither the prevailing love
Of goodness here, or mercy from above,
Or fear of future pains, or human laws
Could render advocates in virtue's cause,
Caught by the scene, have unawares resign'd
Their wonted disposition of the mind:
By slow degrees prevails the pleasing tale,
As circling glasses on our senses steal;
Till thoroughly by the muses' banquet warm'd,
The passions tossing, all the soul alarm'd,
They turn mere zealots flush'd with glorious rage,
Rise in their seats, and scarce forbear the stage,
Assistance to wrong'd innocence to bring,
Or turn the poniard on some tyrant king.
How can they cool to villains? how subside
To dregs of vice, from such a godlike pride?
To spoiling orphans how to day return,
Who wept last night to see Monimia mourn?
In this gay school of virtue, whom so fit
To govern, and control the world of wit,
As Talbot, Lansdowne's friend, has Britain known?

Him polish'd Italy has call'd her own;
He in the lap of elegance was bred,
And trac'd the muses to their fountain head:
But much we hope, he will enjoy at home
What 's nearer ancient than the modern Rome.
Nor fear I mention of the court of France,
When I the British genius would advance;
There too has Shrewsbury improv'd his taste;
Yet still we dare invite him to our feast:
For Corneille's sake I shall my thoughts suppress
Of Oroonoko, and presume him less:
What though we wrong him? Isabella's woe
Waters those bays that shall for ever grow.
 Our foes confess, nor we the praise refuse,
The drama glories in the British muse.
The French are delicate, and nicely lead
Of close intrigue the labyrinthian thread;
Our genius more affects the grand, than fine,
Our strength can make the great plain action shine:
They raise a great curiosity indeed,
From his dark maze to see the hero freed;
We rouse th' affections, and that hero show
Gasping beneath some formidable blow:
They sigh; we weep: the Gallic doubt and care
We heighten into terror and despair;
Strike home, the strongest passions boldly touch,
Nor fear our audience should be pleas'd too much.
What 's great in nature we can greatly draw,
Nor thank for beauties the dramatic law.
The fate of Cæsar is a tale too plain

The fickle Gallic taste to entertain;
Their art would have perplex'd, and interwove
The golden arras with gay flowers of love:
We know heaven made him a far greater man
Than any Cæsar, in a human plan,
And such we draw him, nor are too refin'd,
To stand affected with what heaven design'd.
To claim attention, and the heart invade,
Shakespeare but wrote the play th' Almighty made.
Our neighbour's stage-art too bare-fac'd betrays,
'Tis great Corneille at every scene we praise;
On nature's surer aid Britannia calls,
None think of Shakespeare till the curtain falls;
Then with a sigh returns our audience home,
From Venice, Egypt, Persia, Greece, or Rome.
 France yields not to the glory of our lines,
But manly conduct of our strong designs;
That oft they think more justly we must own,
Not ancient Greece a truer sense has shown:
Greece thought but justly, they think justly too;
We sometimes err by striving more to do.
So well are Racine's meanest persons taught,
But change a sentiment, you make a fault;
Nor dare we charge them with the want of flame:
When we boast more, we own ourselves to blame.
 And yet in Shakespeare something still I find,
That makes me less esteem all human kind;
He made one nature, and another found,
Both in his page with master strokes abound:
His witches, fairies, and enchanted isle.

Bid us no longer at our nurses smile;
Of lost historians we almost complain,
Nor think it the creation of his brain.
Who lives, when his Othello 's in a trance?
With his great Talbot * too he conquer'd France.
  Long we may hope brave Talbot's blood will run
In great descendants, Shakespeare has but one;
And him, my lord, permit me not to name,
But in kind silence spare his rival's shame: —
Yet I in vain that author would suppress,
What can't be greater, cannot be made less:
Each reader will defeat my fruitless aim,
And to himself great Agamemnon name.
  Should Shakespeare rise unbless'd with Talbot's smile,
E'en Shakespeare's self would curse this barren isle:
But if that reigning star propitious shine,
And kindly mix his gentle rays with thine;
E'en I, by far the meanest of your age,
Shall not repent my passion for the stage.
  Thus did the will almighty disallow,
No human force could pluck the golden bough,
Which left the tree with ease at Jove's command,
And spar'd the labour of the weakest hand.
  Auspicious fate! that gives me leave to write
To you, the muses' glory and delight;
Who know to read, nor false encomiums raise,

* An ancestor of the Duke of Shrewsbury, who conquered France, drawn by Shakespeare. — YOUNG.

And mortify an author with your praise:
Praise wounds a noble mind, when 'tis not due,
But censure's self will please, my lord, from you;
Faults are our pride and gain, when you descend
To point them out, and teach us how to mend.
What though the great man set his coffers wide,
That cannot gratify the poet's pride;
Whose inspiration, if 'tis truly good,
Is best rewarded, when best understood.
The muses write for glory, not for gold,
'Tis far beneath their nature to be sold:
The greatest gain is scorn'd, but as it serves
To speak a sense of what the muse deserves;
The muse which from her Lansdowne fears no wrong,
Best judge, as well as subject, of her song.
Should this great theme allure me further still,
And I presume to use your patience ill,
The world would plead my cause, and none but you
Will take disgust at what I now pursue:
Since what is mean my muse can't raise, I 'll choose
A theme that 's able to exalt my muse.
For who, not void of thought, can Granville name,
Without a spark of his immortal flame?
Whether we seek the patriot, or the friend,
Let Bolingbroke, let Anna recommend;
Whether we choose to love or to admire,
You melt the tender, and th' ambitious fire.
Such native graces without thought abound,

And such familiar glories spread around,
As more incline the stander by to raise
His value for himself, than you to praise.
Thus you befriend the most heroic way,
Bless all, on none an obligation lay;
So turn'd by nature's hand for all that 's well,
'Tis scarce a virtue when you most excel.
Tho' sweet your presence, graceful is your mien,
You to be happy want not to be seen;
Though priz'd in public, you can smile alone,
Nor court an approbation but your own:
In throngs, not conscious of those eyes that gaze
In wonder fix'd, though resolute to please;
You, were all blind, would still deserve applause;
The world 's your glory's witness, not its cause;
That lies beyond the limits of the day,
Angels behold it, and their God obey.
You take delight in others' excellence;
A gift, which nature rarely does dispense:
Of all that breathe 'tis you, perhaps, alone
Would be well pleas'd to see yourself outdone.
You wish not those, who show your name respect,
So little worth, as might excuse neglect;
Nor are in pain lest merit you should know;
Nor shun the well deserver as a foe;
A troublesome acquaintance, that will claim
To be well us'd, or dye your cheek with shame.
You wish your country's good; that told so well
Your powers are known, th' event I need not tell.
When Nestor spoke, none ask'd if he prevail'd;

That god of sweet persuasion never fail'd:
And such great fame had Hector's valour wrought,
Who meant he conquer'd, only said he fought.
When you, my lord, to sylvan scenes retreat,
No crowds around for pleasure, or for state,
You are not cast upon a stranger land,
And wander pensive o'er the barren strand;
Nor are you by receiv'd example taught,
In toys to shun the discipline of thought;
But unconfin'd by bounds of time and place,
You choose companions from all human race;
Converse with those the deluge swept away,
Or those whose midnight is Britannia's day.
Books not so much inform, as give consent
To those ideas your own thoughts present;
Your only gain from turning volumes o'er,
Is finding cause to like yourself the more:
In Grecian sages you are only taught
With more respect to value your own thought:
Great Tully grew immortal, while he drew
Those precepts we behold alive in you:
Your life is so adjusted to their schools,
It makes that history they meant for rules.
What joy, what pleasing transport, must arise
Within your breast, and lift you to the skies,
When, in each learned page that you unfold,
You find some part of your own conduct told!
So pleas'd, and so surpris'd, Æneas stood,
And such triumphant raptures fir'd his blood,
When far from Trojan shores the hero spied

His story shining forth in all its pride;
Admir'd himself, and saw his actions stand
The praise and wonder of a foreign land.
He knows not half his being, who 's confin'd
In converse, and reflection on mankind:
Your soul, which understands her charter well,
Disdains imprison'd by those skies to dwell;
Ranges eternity without the leave
Of death, nor waits the passage of the grave.
When pains eternal, and eternal bliss,
When these high cares your weary thoughts dismiss,
In heavenly numbers you your soul unbend,
And for your ease to deathless fame descend.
Ye kings! would ye true greatness understand,
Read Seneca grown rich in Granville's hand.*
Behold the glories of your life complete!
Still at a flow, and permanently great;
New moments shed new pleasures as they fly,
And yet your greatest is, that you must die.
Thus Anna saw, and rais'd you to the seat
Of honour, and confess'd her servant great;
Confess'd, not made him such; for faithful fame
Her trumpet swell'd long since with Granville's name;
Though you in modesty the title wear,
Your name shall be the title of your heir;
Farther than ermine, make his glory known,
And cast in shades the favour of a throne.

* See his lordship's tragedy entitled "Heroic Love."
YOUNG.

From thrones the beam of high distinction springs;
The soul's endowments from the King of kings,
Lo! one great day calls forth ten mighty peers!
Produce ten Granvilles in five thousand years;
Anna, be thou content to fix the fate
Of various kingdoms, and control the great;
But O! to bid thy Granville brighter shine!
To him that great prerogative resign,
Who the sun's height can raise at pleasure higher,
His lamp illumine, set his flames on fire.
  Yet still one bliss, one glory, I forbear,
A darling friend whom near your heart you wear;
That lovely youth, my lord, whom you must blame,
That I grow thus familiar with your name.
  He 's friendly, open, in his conduct nice,
Nor serve these virtues to atone for vice:
Vice has he none, or such as none wish less,
But friends indeed, good-nature in excess.
You cannot boast the merit of a choice,
In making him your own, 'twas nature's voice,
Which call'd too loud by man to be withstood,
Pleading a tie far nearer than of blood;
Similitude of manners, such a mind
As makes you less the wonder of mankind.
Such ease his common converse recommends,
As he ne'er felt a passion, but his friend's;
Yet fix'd his principles, beyond the force
Of all beneath the sun, to bend his course.*

* His lordship's nephew, who took orders. — YOUNG.

Thus the tall cedar, beautiful and fair,
Flatters the motions of the wanton air;
Salutes each passing breeze with head reclin'd:
The pliant branches dance in every wind:
But fix'd the stem her upright state maintains,
And all the fury of the north disdains.
How are you bless'd in such a matchless friend!
Alas! with me the joys of friendship end;
O Harrison! I must, I will complain;
Tears soothe the soul's distress, tho' shed in vain;
Didst thou return, and bless thy native shore
With welcome peace, and is my friend no more?—
Thy task was early done, and I must own
Death kind to thee, but ah! to thee alone.
But 'tis in me a vanity to mourn,
The sorrows of the great thy tomb adorn;
Strafford and Bolingbroke the loss perceive,
They grieve, and make thee envied in thy grave.
With aching heart, and a foreboding mind,
I night to day in painful journey join'd,
When first inform'd of his approaching fate;
But reach'd the partner of my soul too late:
'Twas past, his cheek was cold; that tuneful tongue,
Which Isis charm'd with its melodious song,
Now languish'd, wanted strength to speak his pain,
Scarce rais'd a feeble groan, and sunk again:
Each art of life, in which he bore a part,
Shot like an arrow through my bleeding heart.
To what serv'd all his promis'd wealth and power,
But more to load that most unhappy hour?

Yet still prevail'd the greatness of his mind;
That, not in health, or life itself confin'd,
Felt through his mortal pangs Britannia's peace,
Mounted to joy, and smil'd in death's embrace.
His spirit now just ready to resign,
No longer now his own, no longer mine,
He grasps my hand, his swimming eyeballs roll,
My hand he grasps, and enters in my soul:
Then with a groan—Support me, O! beware
Of holding worth, however great, too dear! *
Pardon, my lord, the privilege of grief,
That in untimely freedom seeks relief;
To better fate your love I recommend,
O! may you never lose so dear a friend!
May nothing interrupt your happy hours;
Enjoy the blessings peace on Europe showers:
Nor yet disdain those blessings to adorn;
To make the muse immortal, you was born.
Sing; and in latest time, when story 's dark,
This period your surviving fame shall mark;
Save from the gulf of years this glorious age,
And thus illustrate their historian's page.
The crown of Spain in doubtful balance hung,
And Anna Britain sway'd, when Granville sung:
That noted year Europa sheath'd her sword,
When this great man was first saluted lord.

* The author here bewails that most ingenious gentleman, Mr. William Harrison, fellow of New-College, Oxon.—YOUNG.

[See a more particular account of him in the Supplement to Swift.]

TWO EPISTLES TO MR. POPE,

CONCERNING THE AUTHORS OF THE AGE. 1730.

EPISTLE I.

WHILST you at Twickenham plan the future wood,
Or turn the volumes of the wise and good,
Our senate meets; at parties, parties bawl,
And pamphlets stun the streets, and load the stall;
So rushing tides bring things obscene to light,
Foul wrecks emerge, and dead dogs swim in sight;
The civil torrent foams, the tumult reigns,
And Codrus' prose works up, and Lico's strains.
Lo! what from cellars rise, what rush from high,
Where speculation roosted near the sky;
Letters, essays, sock, buskin, satire, song,
And all the garret thunders on the throng!
O Pope! I burst; nor can, nor will, refrain;
I 'll write; let others, in their turn, complain:
Truce, truce, ye Vandals! my tormented ear
Less dreads a pillory than a pamphleteer;
I 've heard myself to death; and, plagu'd each hour,
Shan't I return the vengeance in my power?
For who can write the true absurd like me?——
Thy pardon, Codrus! who, I mean, but thee?
Pope! if like mine, or Codrus', were thy style,
The blood of vipers had not stain'd thy file;

Merit less solid, less despite had bred;
They had not bit, and then they had not bled.
Fame is a public mistress, none enjoys,
But, more or less, his rival's peace destroys;
With fame, in just proportion, envy grows;
The man that makes a character, makes foes:
Slight, peevish insects round a genius rise,
As a bright day awakes the world of flies;
With hearty malice, but with feeble wing,
(To show they live) they flutter, and they sting:
But as by depredations wasps proclaim
The fairest fruit, so these the fairest fame.
  Shall we not censure all the motley train,
Whether with ale irriguous, or champaign?
Whether they tread the vale of prose, or climb,
And whet their appetites on cliffs of rhyme;
The college sloven, or embroider'd spark;
The purple prelate, or the parish clerk;
The quiet quidnunc, or demanding prig;
The plaintiff tory, or defendant whig;
Rich, poor, male, female, young, old, gay, or sad;
Whether extremely witty, or quite mad;
Profoundly dull, or shallowly polite;
Men that read well, or men that only write;
Whether peers, porters, tailors, tune the reeds,
And measuring words to measuring shapes succeeds;
For bankrupts write, when ruin'd shops are shut,
As maggots crawl from out a perish'd nut.
His hammer this, and that his trowel quits,

And, wanting sense for tradesmen, serve for wits.
By thriving men subsists each other trade;
Of every broken craft a writer 's made:
Thus his material, paper, takes its birth
From tatter'd rags of all the stuff on earth.
Hail, fruitful isle! to thee alone belong
Millions of wits, and brokers in old song:
Thee well a land of liberty we name,
Where all are free to scandal and to shame;
Thy sons, by print, may set their hearts at ease,
And be mankind's contempt, whene'er they please;
Like trodden filth, their vile and abject sense
Is unperceiv'd, but when it gives offence:
Their heavy prose our injur'd reason tires;
Their verse immoral kindles loose desires:
Our age they puzzle, and corrupt our prime,
Our sport and pity, punishment and crime.
What glorious motives urge our authors on,
Thus to undo, and thus to be undone?
One loses his estate, and down he sits,
To show (in vain!) he still retains his wits:
Another marries, and his dear proves keen;
He writes as an hypnotic for the spleen:
Some write, confin'd by physic; some, by debt;
Some, for 'tis Sunday; some, because 'tis wet;
Through private pique some do the public right,
And love their king and country out of spite:
Another writes because his father writ,
And proves himself a bastard by his wit.
Has Lico learning, humour, thought profound?

Neither: why write then? He wants twenty pound:
His belly, not his brains, this impulse give;
He 'll grow immortal; for he cannot live:
He rubs his awful front, and takes his ream,
With no provision made, but of his theme;
Perhaps a title has his fancy smit,
Or a quaint motto, which he thinks has wit:
He writes, in inspiration puts his trust,
Tho' wrong his thoughts, the gods will make them just;
Genius directly from the gods descends,
And who by labour would distrust his friends?
Thus having reason'd with consummate skill,
In immortality he dips his quill:
And, since blank paper is denied the press,
He mingles the whole alphabet by guess:
In various sets, which various words compose,
Of which, he hopes, mankind the meaning knows.
So sounds spontaneous from the sibyl broke,
Dark to herself the wonders which she spoke;
The priests found out the meaning, if they could;
And nations star'd at what none understood.
Clodio dress'd, danc'd, drank, visited, (the whole
And great concern of an immortal soul!)
Oft have I said, "Awake! exist! and strive
For birth! nor think to loiter is to live!"
As oft I overheard the demon say,
Who daily met the loit'rer in his way,
"I 'll meet thee, youth, at White's:" the youth replies,

"I 'll meet thee there," and falls his sacrifice;
His fortune squander'd, leaves his virtue bare
To ev'ry bribe, and blind to ev'ry snare:
Clodio for bread his indolence must quit,
Or turn a soldier, or commence a wit.
Such heroes have we! all, but life, they stake;
How must Spain tremble, and the German shake!
Such writers have we! all, but sense, they print;
Ev'n George's praise is dated from the mint.
In arms contemptible, in arts profane,
Such swords, such pens, disgrace a monarch's reign.
Reform your lives before you thus aspire,
And steal (for you can steal) celestial fire.
O the just contrast! O the beauteous strife!
'Twixt their cool writings, and pindaric life:
They write with phlegm, but then they live with fire;
They cheat the lender, and their works the buyer.
I reverence misfortune, not deride;
I pity poverty, but laugh at pride:
For who so sad, but must some mirth confess
At gay Castruchio's miscellaneous dress?
Though there 's but one of the dull works he wrote,
There 's ten editions of his old lac'd coat.
These, nature's commoners, who want a home,
Claim the wide world for their majestic dome;
They make a private study of the street;
And, looking full on every man they meet,
Run souse against his chaps; who stands amaz'd
To find they did not see, but only gaz'd.

"I 'll meet thee there," and falls his sacrifice;
His fortune squander'd, leaves his virtue bare
To ev'ry bribe, and blind to ev'ry snare:
Clodio for bread his indolence must quit,
Or turn a soldier, or commence a wit.
Such heroes have we! all, but life, they stake;
How must Spain tremble, and the German shake!
Such writers have we! all, but sense, they print;
Ev'n George's praise is dated from the mint.
In arms contemptible, in arts profane,
Such swords, such pens, disgrace a monarch's reign.
Reform your lives before you thus aspire,
And steal (for you can steal) celestial fire.
O the just contrast! O the beauteous strife!
'Twixt their cool writings, and pindaric life:
They write with phlegm, but then they live with fire;
They cheat the lender, and their works the buyer.
I reverence misfortune, not deride;
I pity poverty, but laugh at pride:
For who so sad, but must some mirth confess
At gay Castruchio's miscellaneous dress?
Though there 's but one of the dull works he wrote,
There 's ten editions of his old lac'd coat.
These, nature's commoners, who want a home,
Claim the wide world for their majestic dome;
They make a private study of the street;
And, looking full on every man they meet,
Run souse against his chaps; who stands amaz'd
To find they did not see, but only gaz'd.

He finds that without sleeping he could dream:
So sparks, they say, take goddesses to bed,
And find next day the devil in their stead.
In vain advertisements the town o'erspread;
They 're epitaphs, and say the work is dead.
Who press for fame, but small recruits will raise;
'Tis volunteers alone can give the bays.
A famous author visits a great man,
Of his immortal work displays the plan,
And says, "Sir, I 'm your friend; all fears dismiss;
Your glory, and my own, shall live by this;
Your power is fixt, your fame thro' time convey'd,
And Britain Europe's queen — if I am paid."
A statesman has his answer in a trice:
"Sir, such a genius is beyond all price;
What man can pay for this?" — Away he turns;
His work is folded, and his bosom burns:
His patron he will patronize no more;
But rushes like a tempest out of door.
Lost is the patriot, and extinct his name!
Out comes the piece, another, and the same;
For A, his magic pen evokes an O,
And turns the tide of Europe on the foe:
He rams his quill with scandal, and with scoff;
But 'tis so very foul, it wont go off:
Dreadful his thunders, while unprinted, roar;
But when once publish'd, they are heard no more.
Thus distant bugbears fright, but, nearer draw,
The block 's a block, and turns to mirth your awe.
Can those oblige, whose heads and hearts are such?

No; every party 's tainted by their touch.
Infected persons fly each public place;
And none, or enemies alone, embrace:
To the foul fiend their every passion 's sold:
They love, and hate, extempore, for gold:
What image of their fury can we form?
Dulness and rage, a puddle in a storm.
Rest they in peace? If you are pleas'd to buy,
To swell your sails, like Lapland winds, they fly:
Write they with rage? The tempest quickly flags;
A state Ulysses tames 'em with his bags;
Let him be what he will, Turk, Pagan, Jew:
For Christian ministers of state are few.
Behind the curtain lurks the fountain head,
That pours his politics through pipes of lead,
Which far and near ejaculate, and spout
O'er tea and coffee, poison to the rout:
But when they have bespatter'd all they may,
The statesman throws his filthy squirts away!
With golden forceps, these, another takes,
And state elixirs of the vipers makes.
The richest statesman wants wherewith to pay
A servile sycophant, if well they weigh
How much it costs the wretch to be so base;
Nor can the greatest powers enough disgrace,
Enough chastise, such prostitute applause,
If well they weigh how much it stains their cause.
But are our writers ever in the wrong?
Does virtue ne'er seduce the venal tongue?
Yes; if well brib'd, for virtue's self they fight;

Still in the wrong, tho' champions for the right:
Whoe'er their crimes for interest only quit,
Sin on in virtue, and good deeds commit.
   Nought but inconstancy Britannia meets,
And broken faith in their abandon'd sheets;
From the same hand how various is the page!
What civil war their brother pamphlets wage!
Tracts battle tracts, self-contradictions glare;
Say, is this lunacy? — I wish it were.
If such our writers, startled at the sight,
Felons may bless their stars they cannot write!
   How justly Proteus' transmigrations fit
The monstrous changes of a modern wit!
Now, such a gentle stream of eloquence
As seldom rises to the verge of sense;
Now, by mad rage, transform'd into a flame,
Which yet fit engines, well applied, can tame;
Now, on immodest trash, the swine obscene,
Invites the town to sup at Drury Lane;
A dreadful lion, now he roars at power,
Which sends him to his brothers at the Tower;
He 's now a serpent, and his double tongue
Salutes, nay licks, the feet of those he stung;
What knot can bind him, his evasion such?
One knot he well deserves, which might do much.
   The flood, flame, swine, the lion, and the snake,
Those fivefold monsters, modern authors make:
The snake reigns most; snakes, Pliny says, are bred
When the brain 's perish'd in a human head.

Ye grov'ling, trodden, whipt, stript, turncoat things,
Made up of venom, volumes, stains, and stings!
Thrown from the tree of knowledge, like you, curst
To scribble in the dust, was snake the first.
What if the figure should in fact prove true!
It did in Elkenah, why not in you?
Poor Elkenah, all other changes past,
For bread in Smithfield dragons hist at last,
Spit streams of fire to make the butchers gape,
And found his manners suited to his shape:
Such is the fate of talents misapplied;
So liv'd your prototype; and so he died.
Th' abandon'd manners of our writing train
May tempt mankind to think religion vain;
But in their fate, their habit, and their mien,
That gods there are is eminently seen:
Heaven stands absolv'd by vengeance on their pen,
And marks the murderers of fame from men:
Through meagre jaws they draw their venal breath,
As ghastly as their brothers in Macbeth:
Their feet through faithless leather meet the dirt,
And oftener chang'd their principles than shirt.
The transient vestments of these frugal men,
Hastens to paper for our mirth again:
Too soon (O merry melancholy fate!)
They beg in rhyme, and warble through a grate:
The man lampoon'd forgets it at the sight;
The friend through pity gives, the foe through spite;
And though full conscious of his injur'd purse,
Lintot relents, nor Curll can wish them worse.

So fare the men, who writers dare commence
Without their patent, probity, and sense.
From these, their politics our quidnuncs seek,
And Saturday 's the learning of the week:
These labouring wits, like paviours, mend our ways,
With heavy, huge, repeated, flat essays;
Ram their coarse nonsense down, though ne'er so dull;
And hem at every thump upon your skull:
These staunch bred writing hounds begin the cry,
And honest folly echoes to the lie.
O how I laugh, when I a blockhead see,
Thanking a villain for his probity;
Who stretches out a most respectful ear,
With snares for woodcocks in his holy leer:
It tickles thro' my soul to hear the cock's
Sincere encomium on his friend the fox,
Sole patron of his liberties and rights!
While graceless Reynard listens — till he bites.
As when the trumpet sounds, th' o'erloaded state
Discharges all her poor and profligate;
Crimes of all kinds dishonour'd weapons wield,
And prisons pour their filth into the field;
Thus nature's refuse, and the dregs of men,
Compose the black militia of the pen.

EPISTLE II. FROM OXFORD.

All write at London; shall the rage abate
Here, where it most should shine, the muses' seat?
Where, mortal or immortal, as they please,
The learn'd may choose eternity, or ease?
Has not a *royal patron wisely strove
To woo the muse in her Athenian grove?
Added new strings to her harmonious shell,
And given new tongues to those who spoke so well?
Let these instruct, with truth's illustrious ray,
Awake the world, and scare our owls away.
  Meanwhile, O friend! indulge me, if I give
Some needful precepts how to write, and live!
Serious should be an author's final views;
Who write for pure amusement, ne'er amuse.
  An author! 'tis a venerable name!
How few deserve it, and what numbers claim!
Unblest with sense above their peers refin'd,
Who shall stand up, dictators to mankind?
Nay, who dare shine, if not in virtue's cause?
That sole proprietor of just applause.
  Ye restless men, who pant for letter'd praise,
With whom would you consult to gain the bays?—
With those great authors whose fam'd works you read?

* His late majesty's benefaction for modern languages.

'Tis well: go, then, consult the laurell'd shade.
What answer will the laurell'd shade return?
Hear it, and tremble! he commands you burn
The noblest works his envied genius writ,
That boast of nought more excellent than wit.
If this be true, as 'tis a truth most dread,
Woe to the page which has not that to plead!
Fontaine and Chaucer, dying, wish'd unwrote,
The sprightliest efforts of their wanton thought:
Sidney and Waller, brightest sons of fame,
Condemn the charm of ages to the flame:
And in one point is all true wisdom cast,
To think that early we must think at last.
  Immortal wits, ev'n dead, break nature's laws,
Injurious still to virtue's sacred cause;
And their guilt growing, as their bodies rot,
(Revers'd ambition!) pant to be forgot.
  Thus ends your courted fame: does lucre then,
The sacred thirst of gold, betray your pen?
In prose 'tis blameable, in verse 'tis worse,
Provokes the muse, extorts Apollo's curse:
His sacred influence never should be sold:
'Tis arrant simony to sing for gold:
'Tis immortality should fire your mind;
Scorn a less paymaster than all mankind.
  If bribes you seek, know this, ye writing tribe!
Who writes for virtue has the largest bribe:
All 's on the party of the virtuous man;
The good will surely serve him, if they can;
The bad, when interest, or ambition guide,

And 'tis at once their interest and their pride:
But should both fail to take him to their care,
He boasts a greater friend, and both may spare.
  Letters to man uncommon light dispense;
And what is virtue, but superior sense?
In parts and learning you who place your pride,
Your faults are crimes, your crimes are double dyed.
What is a scandal of the first renown,
But letter'd knaves, and atheists in a gown?
  'Tis harder far to please than give offence;
The least misconduct damns the brightest sense;
Each shallow pate, that cannot read your name,
Can read your life, and will be proud to blame.
Flagitious manners make impressions deep
On those, that o'er a page of Milton sleep:
Nor in their dulness think to save your shame,
True, these are fools; but wise men say the same.
  Wits are a despicable race of men,
If they confine their talents to the pen;
When the man shocks us, while the writer shines,
Our scorn in life, our envy in his lines.
Yet, proud of parts, with prudence some dispense,
And play the fool, because they 're men of sense.
What instances bleed recent in each thought,
Of men to ruin by their genius brought!
Against their wills what numbers ruin shun,
Purely through want of wit to be undone!
Nature has shown, by making it so rare,
That wit 's a jewel which we need not wear.

Of plain sound sense life's current coin is made;
With that we drive the most substantial trade.
 Prudence protects and guides us; wit betrays;
A splendid source of ill ten thousand ways;
A certain snare to miseries immense;
A gay prerogative from common sense;
Unless strong judgment that wild thing can tame,
And break to paths of virtue and of fame.
 But grant your judgment equal to the best,
Sense fills your head, and genius fires your breast;
Yet still forbear: your wit (consider well)
'Tis great to show, but greater to conceal;
As it is great to seize the golden prize
Of place or power; but greater to despise.
 If still you languish for an author's name,
Think private merit less than public fame,
And fancy not to write is not to live;
Deserve, and take, the great prerogative.
But ponder what it is; how dear 'twill cost,
To write one page which you may justly boast.
 Sense may be good, yet not deserve the press;
Who write, an awful character profess;
The world as pupil of their wisdom claim,
And for their stipend an immortal fame:
Nothing but what is solid or refin'd,
Should dare ask public audience of mankind.
 Severely weigh your learning, and your wit:
Keep down your pride by what is nobly writ:
No writer, fam'd in your own way, pass o'er;
Much trust example, but reflection more:

More had the ancients writ, they more had taught;
Which shows some work is left for modern thought.
This weigh'd, perfection know; and known, adore;
Toil, burn for that; but do not aim at more;
Above, beneath it, the just limits fix;
And zealously prefer four lines to six.
Write, and re-write, blot out, and write again,
And for its swiftness ne'er applaud your pen.
Leave to the jockeys that Newmarket praise,
Slow runs the Pegasus that wins the bays.
Much time for immortality to pay,
Is just and wise; for less is thrown away.
Time only can mature the labouring brain;
Time is the father, and the midwife pain:
The same good sense that makes a man excel,
Still makes him doubt he ne'er has written well.
Downright impossibilities they seek;
What man can be immortal in a week?
Excuse no fault; though beautiful, 'twill harm;
One fault shocks more than twenty beauties charm.
Our age demands correctness; Addison
And you this commendable hurt have done.
Now writers find, as once Achilles found,
The whole is mortal, if a part 's unsound,
He that strikes out, and strikes not out the best,
Pours lustre in, and dignifies the rest:
Give e'er so little, if what 's right be there,
We praise for what you burn, and what you spare:

The part you burn, smells sweet before the shrine,
And is as incense to the part divine.
  Nor frequent write, though you can do it well;
Men may too oft, though not too much, excel.
A few good works gain fame; more sink their
        price;
Mankind are fickle, and hate paying twice:
They granted you writ well, what can they more,
Unless you let them praise for giving o'er?
  Do boldly what you do, and let your page
Smile, if it smiles, and if it rages, rage.
So faintly Lucius censures and commends,
That Lucius has no foes, except his friends.
  Let satire less engage you than applause;
It shows a gen'rous mind to wink at flaws:
Is genius yours? be yours a glorious end,
Be your king's, country's, truth's, religion's friend;
The public glory by your own beget;
Run nations, run posterity, in debt.
And since the fam'd alone make others live,
First have that glory you presume to give.
  If satire charms, strike faults, but spare the man
'Tis dull to be as witty as you can.
Satire recoils whenever charg'd too high;
Round your own fame the fatal splinters fly.
As the soft plume gives swiftness to the dart,
Good breeding sends the satire to the heart.
  Painters and surgeons may the structure scan;
Genius and morals be with you the man:
Defaults in those alone should give offence!

Who strikes the person, pleads his innocence.
My narrow minded satire can't extend
To Codrus' form; I 'm not so much his friend:
Himself should publish that (the world agree)
Before his works, or in the pillory.
Let him be black, fair, tall, short, thin, or fat,
Dirty or clean, I find no theme in that.
Is that call'd humour? It has this pretence,
'Tis neither virtue, breeding, wit, or sense.
Unless you boast the genius of a Swift,
Beware of humour, the dull rogue's last shift.
Can others write like you? Your task give o'er,
'Tis printing what was publish'd long before.
If nought peculiar through your labours run,
They 're duplicates, and twenty are but one.
Think frequently, think close, read nature, turn
Men's manners o'er, and half your volumes burn;
To nurse with quick reflection be your strife,
Thoughts born from present objects, warm from life:
When most unsought, such inspirations rise,
Slighted by fools, and cherish'd by the wise:
Expect peculiar fame from these alone;
These make an author, these are all your own.
Life, like their Bibles, coolly men turn o'er;
Hence unexperienc'd children of threescore.
True, all men think of course, as all men dream;
And if they slightly think, 'tis much the same.
Letters admit not of a half renown;

They give you nothing, or they give a crown.
No work e'er gain'd true fame, or ever can,
But what did honour to the name of man.
Weighty the subject, cogent the discourse,
Clear be the style, the very sound of force;
Easy the conduct, simple the design,
Striking the moral, and the soul divine:
Let nature art, and judgment wit, exceed;
O'er learning reason reign; o'er that, your creed:
Thus virtue's seeds, at once, and laurel's, grow;
Do thus, and rise a Pope, or a Despreau:
And when your genius exquisitely shines,
Live up to the full lustre of your lines:
Parts but expose those men who virtue quit;
A fallen angel is a fallen wit;
And they plead Lucifer's detested cause,
Who for bare talents challenge our applause.
Would you restore just honours to the pen?
From able writers rise to worthy men.
"Who 's this with nonsense, nonsense would restrain?
Who 's this (they cry) so vainly schools the vain?
Who damns our trash, with so much trash replete?
As, three ells round, huge Cheyne rails at meat?"
Shall I with Bavius then my voice exalt,
And challenge all mankind to find one fault?
With huge examens overwhelm my page,
And darken reason with dogmatic rage?
As if, one tedious volume writ in rhyme,
In prose a duller could excuse the crime:

Sure, next to writing, the most idle thing
Is gravely to harangue on what we sing.
At that tribunal stands the writing tribe,
Which nothing can intimidate or bribe:
Time is the judge; time has nor friend nor foe;
False fame must wither, and the true will grow.
Arm'd with this truth, all critics I defy;
For if I fall, by my own pen I die;
While snarlers strive with proud but fruitless pain
To wound immortals, or to slay the slain.
Sore prest with danger, and in awful dread
Of twenty pamphlets levell'd at my head,
Thus have I forg'd a buckler in my brain,
Of recent form, to serve me this campaign:
And safely hope to quit the dreadful field
Delug'd with ink, and sleep behind my shield;
Unless dire Codrus rouses to the fray
In all his might, and damns me — for a day.
As turns a flock of geese, and, on the green,
Poke out their foolish necks in awkward spleen,
(Ridiculous in rage!) to hiss, not bite,
So war their quills, when sons of dulness write.

AN EPISTLE

TO THE RIGHT HONOURABLE SIR ROBERT WALPOLE.

BY MR. DODDINGTON, AFTERWARDS LORD MELCOMBE.

— Quæ censet amiculus, ut si
Cæcus iter monstrare velit — HOR.

THOUGH strength of genius, by experience taught,
Gives thee to sound the depths of human thought,
To trace the various workings of the mind,
And rule the secret springs, that rule mankind;
(Rare gift!) yet, Walpole, wilt thou condescend
To listen, if thy unexperienc'd friend
Can aught of use impart, though void of skill,
And win attention by sincere good-will;
For friendship, sometimes, want of parts supplies,
The heart may furnish what the head denies.
As when the rapid Rhone, o'er swelling tides,
To grace old ocean's court, in triumph rides,
Tho' rich his source, he drains a thousand springs,
Nor scorns the tribute each small rivulet brings.
So thou shalt, hence, absorb each feeble ray,
Each dawn of meaning, in thy brighter day;
Shalt like, or, where thou canst not like, excuse,
Since no mean interest shall profane the muse,
No malice, wrapt in truth's disguise, offend,
Nor flattery taint the freedom of the friend.

When first a generous mind surveys the great,
And views the crowds that on their fortune wait;
Pleas'd with the show (though little understood)
He only seeks the power, to do the good;
Thinks, till he tries, 'tis godlike to dispose,
And gratitude still springs, where bounty sows;
That every grant sincere affection wins,
And where our wants have end, our love begins:
But those who long the paths of state have trod,
Learn from the clamours of the murmuring crowd,
Which cıamm'd, yet craving still, their gates besiege,
'Tis easier far to give, than to oblige.
This of thy conduct seems the nicest part,
The chief perfection of the statesman's art,
To give to fair assent a fairer face,
Or soften a refusal into grace:
But few there are that can be truly kind,
Or know to fix their favours on the mind;
Hence, some, whene'er they would oblige, offend,
And, while they make the fortune, lose the friend;
Still give, unthank'd; still squander, not bestow;
For great men want not, what to give, but how.
The race of men that follow courts, 'tis true,
Think all they get, and more than all, their due;
Still ask, but ne'er consult their own deserts,
And measure by their interest, not their parts:
From this mistake so many men we see
But ill become the thing they wish'd to be;
Hence discontent, and fresh demands arise,

More power, more favour in the great man's eyes;
All feel a want, though none the cause suspects,
But hate their patron, for their own defects;
Such none can please, but who reforms their hearts,
And, when he gives them places, gives them parts.
As these o'erprize their worth, so sure the great
May sell their favour at too dear a rate;
When merit pines, while clamour is preferr'd,
And long attachment waits among the herd;
When no distinction, where distinction 's due,
Marks from the many the superior few;
When strong cabal constrains them to be just,
And makes them give at last — because they must;
What hopes that men of real worth should prize,
What neither friendship gives, nor merit buys?
The man who justly o'er the whole presides,
His well-weigh'd choice with wise affection guides;
Knows when to stop with grace, and when advance,
Nor gives through importunity or chance;
But thinks how little gratitude is ow'd,
When favours are extorted, not bestow'd.
When, safe on shore ourselves, we see the crowd
Surround the great, importunate, and loud;
Through such a tumult, 'tis no easy task
To drive the man of real worth to ask:
Surrounded thus, and giddy with the show,
'Tis hard for great men rightly to bestow;
From hence so few are skill'd, in either case,
To ask with dignity, or give with grace.

Sometimes the great, seduc'd by love of parts,
Consult our genius, and neglect our hearts;
Pleas'd with the glittering sparks that genius flings,
They lift us, towering on their eagle's wings,
Mark out the flights by which themselves begun,
And teach our dazzled eyes to bear the sun;
Till we forget the hand that made us great,
And grow to envy, not to emulate:
To emulate, a generous warmth implies,
To reach the virtues, that make great men rise;
But envy wears a mean malignant face,
And aims not at their virtues — but their place.
Such to oblige, how vain is the pretence!
When every favour is a fresh offence,
By which superior power is still implied,
And, while it helps their fortune, hurts their pride.
Slight is the hate, neglect or hardships breed;
But those who hate from envy, hate indeed.
"Since so perplex'd the choice, whom shall we trust?"
Methinks I hear thee cry — The brave and just;
The man by no mean fears or hopes controll'd,
Who serves thee from affection, not for gold.
We love the honest, and esteem the brave,
Despise the coxcomb, but detest the knave;
No show of parts the truly wise seduce,
To think that knaves can be of real use.
The man, who contradicts the public voice,
And strives to dignify a worthless choice,
Attempts a task that on that choice reflects,

And lends us light to point out new defects.
One worthless man, that gains what he pretends,
Disgusts a thousand unpretending friends:
And since no art can make a counterpass,
Or add the weight of gold to mimic brass,
When princes to bad ore their image join,
They more debase the stamp, than raise the coin.
  Be thine the care, true merit to reward
And gain the good — nor will that task be hard;
Souls form'd alike so quick by nature blend,
An honest man is more than half thy friend.
  Him, no mean views, or haste to rise, shall sway,
Thy choice to sully, or thy trust betray:
Ambition, here, shall at due distance stand
Nor is wit dangerous in an honest hand:
Besides, if failings at the bottom lie,
We view those failings with a lover's eye;
Though small his genius, let him do his best,
Our wishes and belief supply the rest.
  Let others barter servile faith for gold,
His friendship is not to be bought or sold:
Fierce opposition he, unmov'd, shall face,
Modest in favour, daring in disgrace,
To share thy adverse fate alone, pretend;
In power, a servant; out of power, a friend.
Here pour thy favours in an ample flood,
Indulge thy boundless thirst of doing good:
Nor think that good to him alone confin'd;
Such to oblige, is to oblige mankind.

If thus thy mighty master's steps thou trace,
The brave to cherish, and the good to grace;
Long shalt thou stand from rage and faction free,
And teach us long to love the king, through thee:
Or fall a victim dangerous to the foe,
And make him tremble when he strikes the blow;
While honour, gratitude, affection join
To deck thy close, and brighten thy decline;
(Illustrious doom!) the great, when this displac'd,
With friendship guarded, and with virtue grac'd,
In awful ruin, like Rome's senate, fall,
The prey and worship of the wondering Gaul.
No doubt, to genius some reward is due,
(Excluding that, were satirizing you;)
But yet, believe thy undesigning friend,
When truth and genius for thy choice contend,
Tho' both have weight when in the balance cast,
Let probity be first, and parts the last.
On these foundations if thou dar'st be great,
And check the growth of folly and deceit;
When party rage shall droop thro' length of days,
And calumny be ripen'd into praise,
Then future times shall to thy worth allow
That fame, which envy would call flattery now.
Thus far my zeal, though for the task unfit,
Has pointed out the rocks where others split;
By that inspir'd, though stranger to the Nine,
And negligent of any fame — but thine,
I take the friendly, but superfluous part;
You act from nature what I teach from art.

THE OLD MAN'S RELAPSE.

VERSES OCCASIONED BY THE FOREGOING EPISTLE.

Sopitos suscita ignes.—VIRG.

FROM man's too curious and impatient sight,
The future, Heaven involves in thickest night.
Credit gray hairs: though freedom much we boast,
Some least perform, what they determine most.
What sudden changes our resolves betray!
To-morrow is the satire on to-day,
And shows its weakness. Whom shall men believe,
When constantly themselves, themselves deceive?

Long had I bid my once-loved muse adieu;
You warm old age; my passion burns anew.
How sweet your verse! how great your force of mind!
What power of words! what skill in dark mankind!
Polite the conduct; generous the design;
And beauty files, and strength sustains, each line.
Thus Mars and Venus are, once more, beset;
Your wit has caught them in its golden net.

But what strikes home with most exalted grace
Is, haughty genius taught to know its place;
And, where worth shines, its humbled crest to bend,

With zeal devoted to that godlike end.
When we discern so rich a vein of sense,
Through the smooth flow of purest eloquence;
'Tis like the limpid streams of Tagus roll'd
O'er boundless wealth, o'er shining beds of gold.

But whence so finish'd, so refin'd a piece?
The tongue denies it to old Rome and Greece;
The genius bids the moderns doubt their claim,
And slowly take possession of the fame.
But I nor know, nor care, by whom 'twas writ,
Enough for me that 'tis from human wit;
That soothes my pride: all glory in the pen
Which has done honour to the race of men.

But this have others done; a like applause
An ancient and a modern Horace draws.*
But they to glory by degrees arose,
Meridian lustre you at once disclose.
'Tis continence of mind, unknown before,
To write so well, and yet to write no more.
More bright renown can human nature claim,
Than to deserve, and fly immortal fame?

Next to the godlike praise of writing well,
Is on that praise with just delight to dwell.
O, for some God my drooping soul to raise!
That I might imitate, as well as praise;
For all commend: e'en foes your fame confess;

* Boileau.

Nor would Augustus' age have priz'd it less;
An age, which had not held its pride so long,
But for the want of so complete a song.

A golden period shall from you commence:
Peace shall be sign'd 'twixt wit and manly sense;
Whether your genius or your rank they view,
The muses find their Halifax in you.
Like him succeed! nor think my zeal is shown
For you; 'tis Britain's interest, not your own;
For lofty stations are but golden snares,
Which tempt the great to fall in love with cares.

I would proceed, but age has chill'd my vein,
'Twas a short fever, and I 'm cool again.
Though life I hate, methinks I could renew
Its tasteless, painful course, to sing of you.
When such the subject, who shall curb his flight?
When such your genius, who shall dare to write?
In pure respect, I give my rhyming o'er,
And, to commend you most, commend no more.

Adieu, whoe'er thou art! on death's pale coast
Erelong I 'll talk thee o'er with Dryden's ghost;
The bard will smile. A last, a long farewell!
Henceforth I hide me in my dusky cell;
There wait the friendly stroke that sets me free,
And think of immortality and thee —
My strains are number'd by the tuneful Nine;
Each maid presents her thanks, and all present
thee mine.

VERSES

SENT BY LORD MELCOMBE TO DR. YOUNG, NOT LONG BEFORE HIS LORDSHIP'S DEATH.*

KIND companion of my youth,
Lov'd for genius, worth, and truth!
Take what friendship can impart,
Tribute of a feeling heart;
Take the muse's latest spark,†
Ere we drop into the dark.
He, who parts and virtue gave,
Bad thee look beyond the grave
Genius soars, and virtue guides;
Above, the love of God presides.
There 's a gulf 'twixt us and God;
Let the gloomy path be trod:
Why stand shivering on the shore?
Why not boldly venture o'er?
Where unerring virtue guides,
Let us have the winds and tides:
Safe, through seas of doubts and fears,
Rides the bark which virtue steers.

* A Poetical Epistle from the late Lord Melcombe to the Earl of Bute, with corrections by the author of the Night Thoughts, was published in 4to, 1776.

† See Mr. Cust's Life of Young.

THE END.

www.ingramcontent.com/pod-product-compliance
Lightning Source LLC
LaVergne TN
LVHW010137110826
845151LV00002B/371

* 9 7 8 1 4 2 5 5 3 9 4 3 6 *